ALL THE Aires MOUNTAINS

We are very grateful that users of our guides inform us about changes of details and recommend new entries. Please make the effort to send your comments and help us make the next edition even better. An online submission form and printable submissions form are available at www.alltheaires.co.uk/submissions.htm
Many thanks to the following Aire Heads, who provided information and pictures of the Aires they visited: Peter Gordon, Darren Fasey, S Pirnie, Kev Hardwick, www.motorhomeandaway.co.uk, Ruth Grant, Sally Bethell, Charlie and Angie Anderson, Colin Read, Pat and Philip Wilde, Rita Remminghoff, Jan Dennett, Sandy Hazzard, Rodney Martin, Ken and Jean Fowler, Phil and Julie Hutchins, Sue and Trev Smith, Judy Crane, Harry Risdale, Penny and David Hurst, Malcolm and Janet Webb, Susan Bratt, James and Judith White, Carol Weaver, Rodney Martin

About the Inspectors:
Experienced skiers and fulltime motorhomers, Andy and Sue Glasgow travelled throughout Europe in the 2008/9 and 2009/10 ski seasons enduring some of the worst weather, and the best skiing, in years. They gathered the wealth of essential information provided in this Guide. Keith and Sue Lawrence, also fulltime motorhomers, provided the walking information for the French Pyrenees.

Andy and Sue Glasgow would like to thank: Dunky, Darach, Nethernut, Kevin Maskery and family, Val and Howie, and everyone we've met in the snow.

First published in Great Britain by Vicarious Books Ltd, 2010.

This edition published September 2010.

Front cover image: Col de Vars en-route to St Crepin.

ISBN: 978-0-9552808-8-7

Vicarious Books Ltd, 62 Tontine Street, Folkestone, Kent, CT20 1JP. Tel: 0131 2083333
www.VicariousBooks.co.uk

Editors: Meli George and Chris Doree.

Design and Artwork by: Chris Gladman Design 07745 856652.

Printed in the UK.

The mountains of Europe offer something for everyone. These picturesque alpine villages provide skiing, sledging, biking, walking, or just relaxing in a hot outdoor pool. Whilst driving in the high passes you will see dramatic scenery around every bend but if you seek an easier ride then tunnels are there for your convenience.

Many people find France to be the most convenient ski destination as it is close to the UK, has reliable snowfall and resorts with good facilities. Crossing the Alps gets you to Italy's sunny and well-groomed pistes. Alternatively, you could take an easy, toll free drive down Germany's autobahns to Bavaria's little known and motorhome friendly resorts.

Switzerland is surprisingly accessible for winter touring. An excellent system of motorways and tunnels can have you "parked up and kettle on", under the Matterhorn, Eiger or Jungfrau, within a day of entering the country. Austria has few Aires but good winter campsites, usually located in picturesque villages with ski lifts down into the village centre and a lively nightlife scene. For something more exotic try the pistes of Spain, many have top clss lifts developed for a winter olympics bid.

Europe has something to suit every desire. With a little preparation and planning, you can join the hundreds of continental motorhomers who take to the slopes each winter making the most of the sun and snow. Many people follow the snow, chasing blue skies and deep fresh powder. In summer the mountains come alive with walkers, climbers and numerous other sports enthusiasts.

Camping in the mountains is easy and this guide lists 81 comfortable campsites specially equipped for summer and winter visitors. Motorhomes have the option to park overnight in special areas outside of campsites. In this guide the 191 motorhome entries are referred to as stellplatze in Germany, Austria and Switzerland and referred to as Aires in France, Spain and Italy. Each entry in this guide identifies the types of camping units it takes.

SKI AREAS SHOWN IN GUIDE

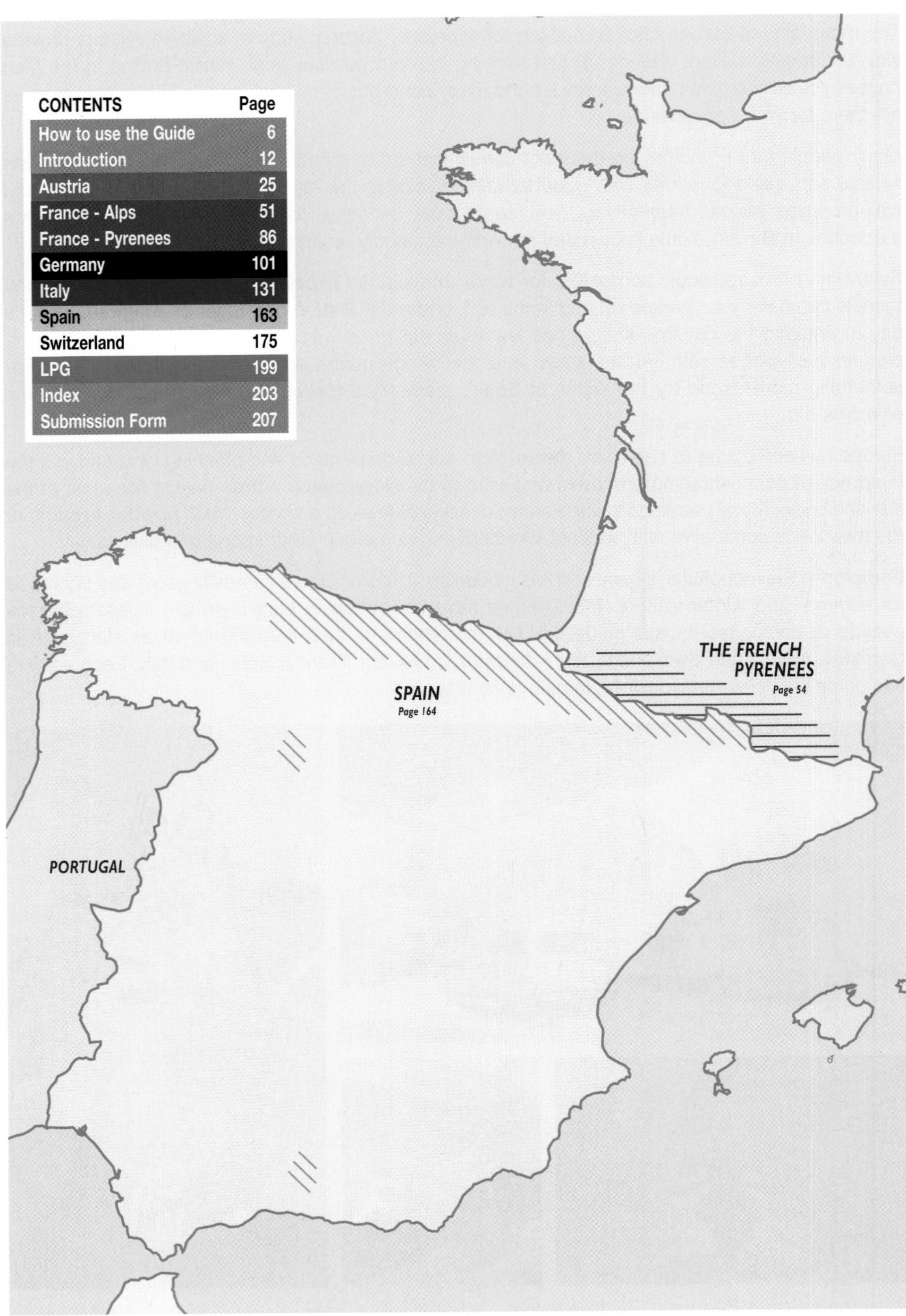

SKI AREAS SHOWN IN GUIDE

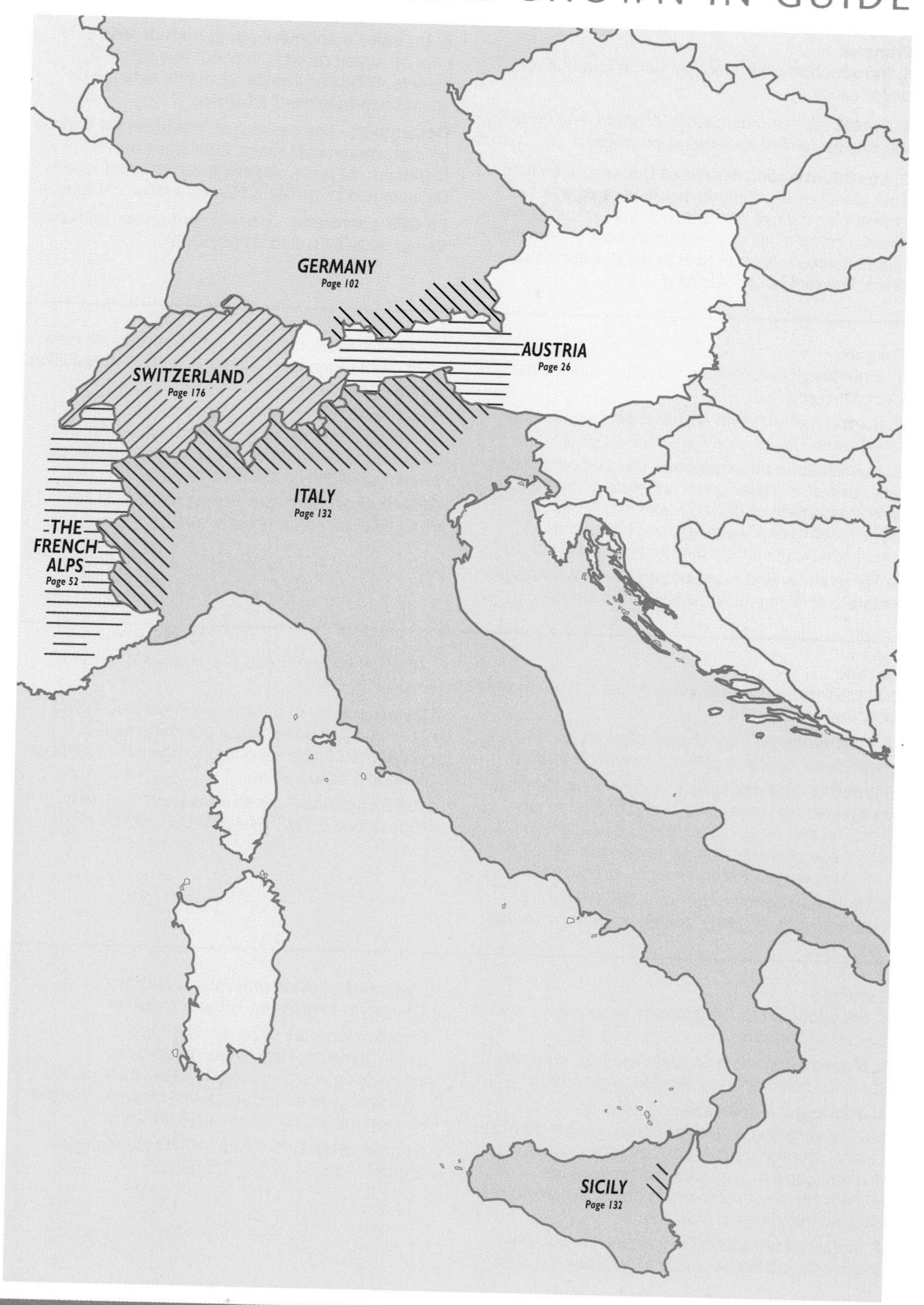

HOW TO USE THIS GUIDE

Français
1. Introduction L'introduction fournit tout que vous devez savoir.

2. Cartes Au début de chaque chapitre, une carte identifie seulement les listes appropriées.

3. Les informations détaillées Des emplacements sont identifiés et énumérés par le nom de ville. Utilisant les mêmes nombres que sur les cartes en chaque chapitre les emplacements sont commencer numériquement énuméré par le nombre le plus peu élevé, finissant sur le plus haut.

4. Un index a énuméré par le nom de ville et le nom de terrain de camping peut être trouvé à l'arrière. N'oubliez pas de soumettre la forme de soumission également à l'arrière.

Description - une description impartiale est donnée au sujet de l'emplacement. Les forces ou les faiblesses et l'appel de l'emplacement sont fournis. Davantage d'information utile est également fournie.

Le GPS coordonne - ceux-ci sont présentés dans le format de N35°31.926 W005°59.920.

Deutsch
1. Einleitung Die Einleitung vermittelt allgemeine Informationen.

2. Karten Karten helfen auch bei der Orientierung jeweils zum Beginn eine Kapitels.

3. Ausführliche Informationen Die Campingplätze werden durch Städtenamen gekennzeichnet und sind mit denselben Zahlen wie in den Karten zu Beginn der Kapitel versehen, beginnend mit der niedrigsten und endend mit der höchsten Zahl.

4. Verzeichnis und Fragebogen Ein Verzeichnis der Städte und Campingplätze finden Sie auf der Rückseite dieses Führers. Und vergessen Sie bitte nicht den Fragebogen auf der Rückseite auszufüllen und abzuschicken.

Beschreibung - Der Campingplätz wird unvoreingenommen bewertet und mit seinen Stärken und Schwächen dargestellt. Dazu gibt es weitere nützliche Informationen.

GPS-Koordinaten - Sie werden im N35°31.926 W005°59.920-Format beschrieben.

Italiano
1. Introduzione L'introduzione fornisce tutto che dobbiate sapere.

2. Programmi All'inizio di ogni capitolo, un programma identifica soltanto gli elenchi relativi.

3. Informazioni dettagliate I luoghi sono identificati ed elencati dal nome della città. Utilizzando gli stessi numeri di sui programmi in ogni capitolo i luoghi sono numericamente cominciare elencato con il numero più basso, rifinente sull'più alto.

4. Un indice elencato dal nome della città può essere trovato alla parte posteriore. Non dimentichi di presentare la forma di presentazione anche alla parte posteriore.

Descrizione - una descrizione imparziale è data circa il luogo. Le resistenze o le debolezze e l'appello del luogo sono forniti. Ulteriori informazioni utili inoltre sono fornite.

Il GPS coordina - questi sono presentati nella disposizione di N35°31.926 W005°59.920.

Español
1. Introducción La introducción proporciona todo lo que usted necesita.

2. Mapas Al principio de cada capítulo, un mapa identifica solamente los listados relevantes.

3. Información detallada Los sitios son identificados y enumerados por el nombre de cada ciudad. Usando los mismos números que los mapas de cada capítulo. Los sitios son ordenados numéricamente, comenzando desde el número más bajo, acabando en el más alto.

4. Indice y Formulario Un índice ordenado por nombre de ciudad se puede encontrar en la parte posterior. No olvide presentar el impreso de la inscripción también en la parte posterior.

Descripción - los sitios son descritos imparcialmente. También se proporciona información acerca de los detalles positivos, negativos y de lo que se podría mejorar. Además se proporciona útil información adicional.

Coordenadas GPS - éstas son presentadas en formato: N35°31.926 W005°59.920.

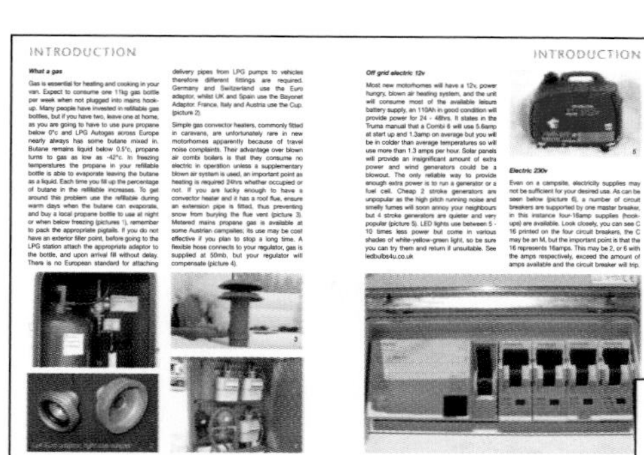

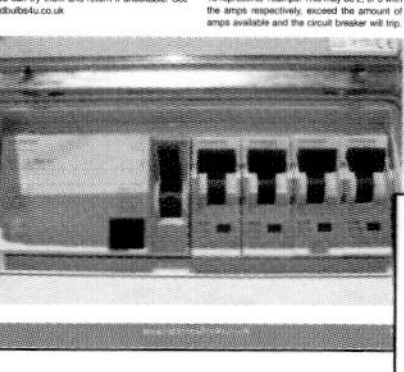

1. Introduction
The introduction provides everything you need to know.

2. Maps
At the beginning of each chapter, a map identifies only the relevant listings.

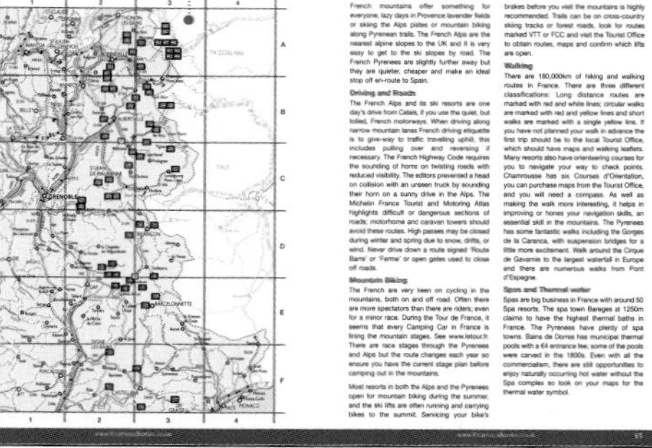

3. Detailed Information
Sites are identified and listed by town name. Using the same numbers as on the maps in each chapter the sites are listed numerically starting with the lowest number, finishing on the highest.

Description – An unbiased description is given about the site. The strengths or weaknesses and appeal of the site are provided. Further useful information is also given.

GPS Co-ordinates – These are presented in the N35°31.926' W005°59.920' format.

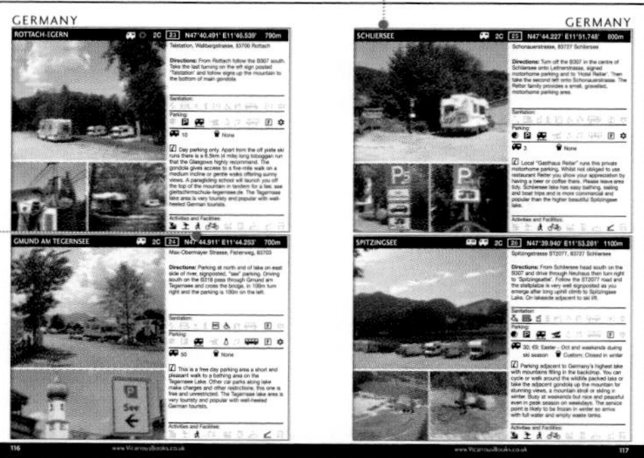

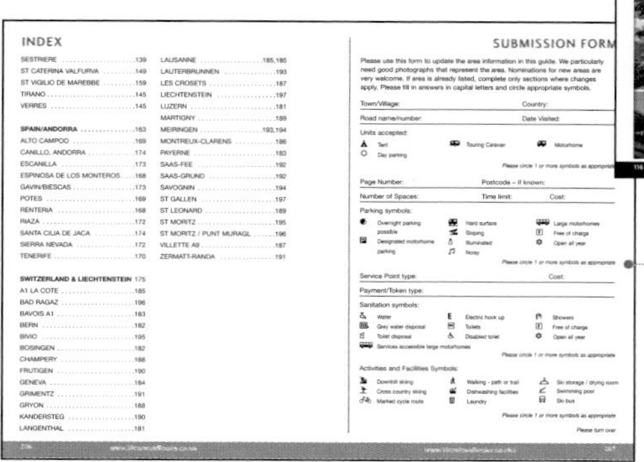

4. Index and Submission Forms
An index listed by town name can be found at the rear. Don't forget to submit the submission form also at the rear.

HOW TO USE THIS GUIDE

Français

1 Nom de ville
2 Unités admises
3 Référence de grille
4 Nombre de carte
5 Le GPS coordonne
6 Altitude
7 Nom de terrain de camping, adresse et site web
8 Directions
9 Équipements
10 Dispositifs
11 Nombre de lancements
12 Prix
13 Détails et frais pour le service
14 Description
15 Agréments locaux
16 Photographies d'emplacement

Deutsch

1 Stadtname
2 Masseinheiten
3 Gitterkoordinaten
4 Karten-Zahl
5 GPS-Koordinaten
6 Altitude
7 Campingplatzname, Adresse und Website
8 Richtungen
9 Einrichtungen
10 Eigenschaften
11 Zahl der Parzellen
12 Preis
13 Details und Gebühren für Service
14 Beschreibung
15 Lokale Annehmlichkeiten
16 Campingplätz-Photos

Italiano

1 Nome della città
2 Le unità hanno accettato
3 Riferimento di griglia
4 Numero del programma
5 Il GPS coordina
6 Altitude
7 Nome del Campsite, indirizzo e web site
8 Sensi
9 Facilità
10 Caratteristiche
11 Numero dei passi
12 Prezzo
13 Particolari e spese per servizio
14 Descrizione
15 Amenità locali
16 Fotografie del luogo

Español

1 Nombre de la ciudad
2 Las unidades aceptaron
3 Referencia de rejilla
4 Número del mapa
5 El GPS coordina
6 Altitude
7 Nombre del sitio para acampar, dirección y web site
8 Direcciones
9 Instalaciones
10 Características
11 Número de echadas
12 Precio
13 Detalles y cargas para el servicio
14 Descripción
15 Amenidades locales
16 Fotografías del sitio

Explanation of an entry (also see key to symbols on pages 10 and 11)

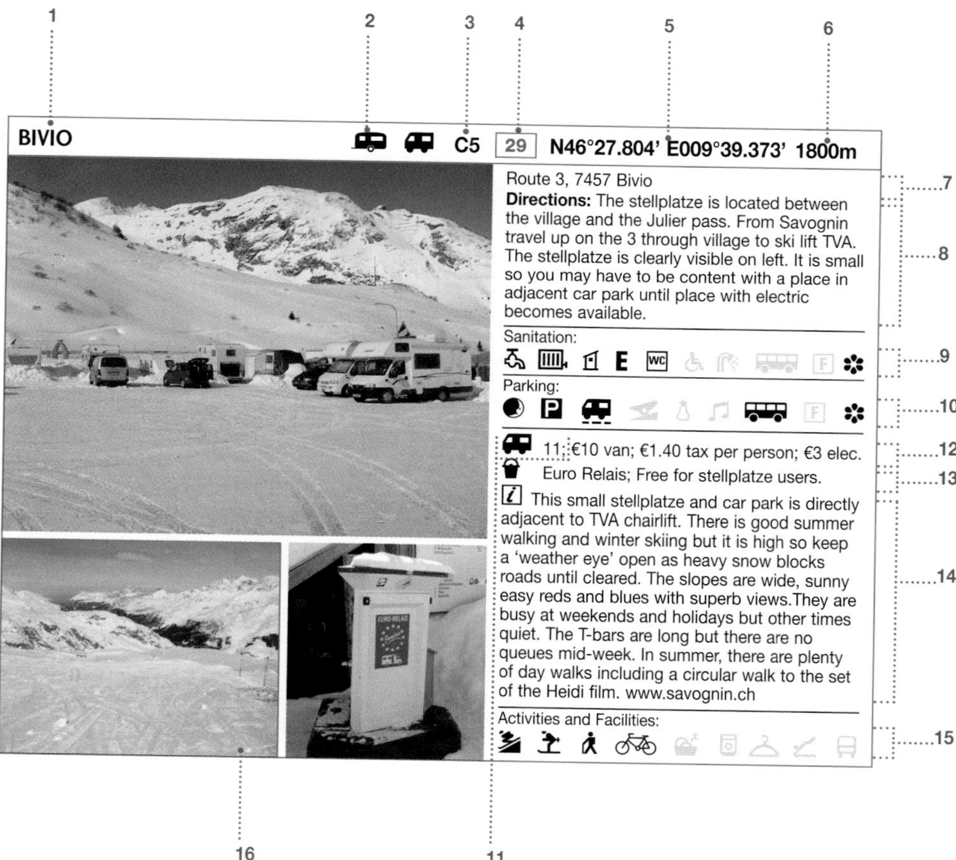

English

1 Town name
2 Units accepted
3 Grid reference
4 Map number
5 GPS co-ordinates
6 Altitude
7 Campsite name, address and website
8 Directions
9 Facilities
10 Features
11 Number of pitches
12 Price; based on 2 people and one van
13 Details and charges for service
14 Description
15 Local amenities
16 Site photographs

HOW TO USE THIS GUIDE

	KEY TO SYMBOLS	CLEF AUX SYMBOLS	SCHLÜSSEL ZU DEN SYMBOLEN	CHIAVE AI SIMBOLI	LLAVE A LOS SÍMBOLOS
	English	**Français**	**Deutsch**	**Italiano**	**Español**
	Tent	Tente	Zelt	Tenda	Tienda
	Touring caravan	Tourisme de la caravane	Wohnwagen	Visita del caravan	Viajar la caravana
	Motorhome	Camping Car	Reisemobil	Camper	Autocaravana
	Day parking	Stationnement de jour	Tagesparken	Parcheggio di giorno	Estacionamiento del día
	Water	L'eau	Wasser	Acqua	Agua
	Grey water disposal	Disposition grise de l'eau	Grauhasser-Entsorgung Wasserbeseitigung	Eliminazione grigia dell'acqua	Disposición gris del agua
	Toilet disposal	Disposition de toilette	Entsorgung	Eliminazione della toletta	Disposición del tocador
E	Electric hook-up	Connexion électrique	Elektrischer Haken oben	Collegamento elettrico	Gancho eléctrico para arriba
WC	Toilets	Toilettes	Toiletten	Tolette	Tocadores
	Disabled toilet	Toilette handicapée	Behindertengerichte Toilette	Toletta disabile	Tocador lisiado
	Showers	Douches	Duschen	Acquazzoni	Duchas
	Motorhome 8m+	Camping Car 8m+	Reisemobil 8m+	Camper 8m+	Autocaravana 8m+
F	Free of charge	Gratuitement	Kostenlos	Gratis	Gratuitamente
	Open all year	Ouvrez toute l'année	Ganzjährig geoffnet	Apra tutto l'anno	Abra todo el año
	Overnight parking possible	Stationnement durant la nuit	Nachtparken	Parcheggio di notte	Estacionamiento de noche
P	Designated motorhome parking	Stationnement indiqué de camping car	Gekennzeichnetes wohnmobile parken	Parcheggio indicato del camper	Estacionamiento señalado del auto caravan
	Hard standing pitches	Lancements durs de position	Fester Untergrund	Passi duri di condizione	Echadas duras de l a situación

English	Français	Deutsch	Italiano	Español
Sloping	Surface en pente	Schräge Oberfläche	Superficie pendente	Superficie que se inclina
Illuminated	Illuminé	Beleuchtet	Illuminato	Iluminado
Noisy	Bruyant	Raut	Rumoroso	Ruidoso
Downhill skiing	Ski incline	Abfahrtskilauf	Corsa con gli sci in discesa	Esqui en declive
Cross country skiing	Ski de pays en travers	Querland ski fahren	Corsa con gli sci del paese trasversale	Esqui del pais cruzada
Walking - path or trail	Chemin de marche/traînée	Gehender Weg / Spur	Percorso ambulante/traccia	Caminata
Marked cycle route	Itinéraire marqué de cycle	Markierter Zyklusweg	Itinerario contrassegnato del ciclo	Ruta del ciclo
Dishwashing facilities	Équipements de vaisselle	Spülmaschine	Facilità di lavatura dei piatti	Instalaciones del lavaplatos
Laundry	Blanchisserie	Wäscherei	Lavanderia	Lavadero
Ski storage / drying room	Stockage de ski / piece de Séchage	Skispeicher / Trockenraum	Immagazzinaggio del pattino / stanza di Secchezza	Almacenaje del esqui / sitio de sequia
Swimming	Natation	Schwimmen	Nuoto	Natación
Ski bus	Ski bus	Skibus	Bus del pattino	Autobus del esqui

Note: Facilities only available when symbol highlighted.	*Note : Équipements seulement disponibles quand le symbole a accentué.*	*Anmerkung: Ausstattung nur dan vorhanden. Wenn das symbol hervorgehoben ist.*	*Nota: Facilità soltanto disponibili quando il simbolo ha evidenziato.*	*Nota: Instalaciones solamente disponibles cuando el símbolo destacó.*

Anyone visiting the mountains with a motorhome, caravan or tent is going to find this guide invaluable whether visiting in summer or winter. Both the popular and undiscovered resorts are covered, and they are just as exhilarating in the summer for walking and mountain biking as they are in winter for skiing and boarding. No matter when you go, a little preparation will enhance your trip.

Preparing your Vehicle

Ensuring your vehicle is in good working order is essential before embarking on a trip up the mountains. If you are in any doubt about the condition of your vehicle get it serviced or checked by a mechanic. To help you prepare consider the following points.

Tyres, the most important element of preparation

Ensuring your vehicle has the correct tyres is the most important element of preparation if you want the best chance of staying on the road in icy conditions. The editors looked at a cross-section of UK motorhomes' and campervans' tyres whilst preparing this guide, and discovered that 95% are not fitted with winter tyres. Tyres with an M&S (mud and snow), snowflake, or snow capped mountains image are winter rated tyres. Both the editors and the Glasgows agree that Michelin M+S camper tyres perform extremely well in winter mountain conditions. The Vanco tyres fitted to new Ducatos over the past few years are generally good but do not display any M+S identification. Tyres older than 5 - 7 years are probably nearing the end of their life regardless of how good the tread is. The 1501 printed on the sidewall of the tyre in the picture above identifies the manufacture date to be week 15 year 2001.

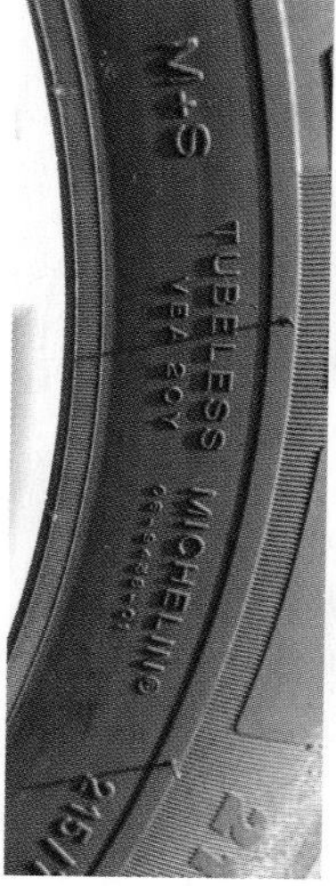

Rules regarding winter tyres vary from country to country. In Austria, from November to April, winter rated tyres or tyres marked M+S with a minimum tread depth of 4mm must be fitted. Snow chains are compulsory where indicated by signs. Germany advises visitors to fit winter tyres or purchase snow chains. On-the-spot fines are issued to ill-prepared drivers that become stuck or impede the flow of traffic, so snow chains must be fitted when there is a covering of snow or ice. In France snow chains must be fitted on snow covered roads when indicated by signs. In general, every country will expect winter visitors to be equipped to drive safely in snow, failure to do so could result in a fine.

4x4 is nice but not necessary

A

B

C

D

Snow chains

Snow chains fitted to the vehicle's driving wheels makes driving possible even in the iciest of conditions and it is advisory to carry them in Andorra, Austria, France, Germany, Italy, and Switzerland. It is important to follow the Highway Code for each country and always follow chain manufacturer's instructions. Snow chains should only be fitted when the roads are completely covered in snow and ice.

E

Fitting snow chains for the first time is equivalent in difficulty to learning to ride a bike, so practice fitting and refitting them in warm dry conditions, until you can fit them without thinking about it. Wear tough but thin work gloves, fitting chains is fiddly and thick leather gloves are useless. To assist in clearing snow around tyres it is worth carrying a stiff brush, a folding shovel, and a kneeling mat. Once fitted, drive 4 - 5 metres and then re-tighten the chains, periodically stop and check chains whilst driving. Should you ever hear a repetitive cloncking noise whilst driving with chains, stop immediately as a broken section of chain may be flailing around the inside of your wheel arch. Repair links are often supplied with chain sets for a temporary fix, and a bungee will replace the elastic should it be necessary and can help to tighten the chains evenly. To prevent your chains from breaking: keep your speed down (in Germany the max speed is 30mph), avoid harsh acceleration / braking, spinning wheels, driving on tarmac. Also take care mounting levelling blocks and do not drive over the connectors when removing chains. Untangled chains stored between sheets of newspaper will be ready for next time.

When making parking choices consider your exit, and avoid parking down a slope. If snow is forecast, fit your chains before going to bed or out for the day.

Winter diesel

In very cold conditions diesel solidifies into a waxy gel if antifreeze is not included. Depending when and where you buy diesel you may also need to buy and add special antifreeze to your fuel tank. From early November, all fuel stations in Austria change over to winter diesel rated to -20°c. If you buy fuel in southern Spain or Sicily, then climb to the top of the respective mountains, park overnight and wake up to -10°c or below, you won't be going anywhere until the diesel warms up. Diesel pumps at mountain fuel stations usually identify that the fuel is treated as shown below.

Wet diesel

When outside temperatures fall and rise quickly, particularly overnight, atmospheric moisture condenses into water droplets on the inside of the fuel tank, above the fuel level. Truckers and farmers habitually fuel up their tanks at the end of the day to prevent this happening. Water is heavier than diesel and readily separates if mixed together. Fuel filters catch water and slowly fill from the bottom up over time; this water can freeze thus preventing the engine from starting or running. In freezing conditions regularly drain off the fuel filter. Simply unscrew the drain tap located at the bottom of the filter a couple of turns until diesel replaces water. You will need a receptacle to catch the water/diesel.

Engine coolant antifreeze and other cold precautions

The only way you can be sure that there is enough antifreeze in your engine coolant system is to measure it with a hygrometer, these cost as little as £5. The glycol ethanol level needs to be between 40 - 50% to withstand potential temperatures as low as -25°c. Also, ensure your screen wash is concentrated enough to cope with the cold. Check your vehicle handbook to confirm whether low viscosity, cold temperature oil is required for your engine. Your engine battery must be in good condition, if in doubt take it to a garage to be tested.

Engine condition

Before embarking on a trip to the mountains it is important to ensure your vehicle is in good running order. Tired older vehicles may struggle with the gradients, lower oxygen levels at altitudes, and the cold. The vehicle's brakes should be checked to ensure they are in good condition before you undertake miles of steep descents.

Life in the freezer, preparing your utilities

Most modern motorhomes will be perfectly suitable for taking on a skiing holiday; although they are not known to be good skiers, they will provide warm and comfortable accommodation. The three utilities: gas, electric and water need managing to ensure a comfortable trip. Make sure that your caravan/motorhome has recently had an annual habitation service and that the gas systems were serviced, not just visually inspected. Also, ensure that your carbon monoxide detector and fire alarm are working.

What a gas

Gas is essential for heating and cooking in your van. Expect to consume one 11kg gas bottle per week when not plugged into mains hook-up. Many people have invested in refillable gas bottles, but if you have two, leave one at home, as you are going to have to use pure propane below 0°c and LPG Autogas across Europe nearly always has some butane mixed in. Butane remains liquid below 0.5°c, propane turns to gas as low as -42°c. In freezing temperatures the propane in your refillable bottle is able to evaporate leaving the butane as a liquid. Each time you fill up the percentage of butane in the refillable increases. To get around this problem use the refillable during warm days when the butane can evaporate, and buy a local propane bottle to use at night or when below freezing (pictures 1), remember to pack the appropriate pigtails. If you do not have an exterior filler point, before going to the LPG station attach the appropriate adaptor to the bottle, and upon arrival fill without delay. There is no European standard for attaching delivery pipes from LPG pumps to vehicles therefore different fittings are required. Germany and Switzerland use the Euro adaptor, whilst UK and Spain use the Bayonet Adaptor. France, Italy and Austria use the Cup. (picture 2).

Simple gas convector heaters, commonly fitted in caravans, are unfortunately rare in new motorhomes apparently because of travel noise complaints. Their advantage over blown air combi boilers is that they consume no electric in operation unless a supplementary blown air system is used, an important point as heating is required 24hrs whether occupied or not. If you are lucky enough to have a convector heater and it has a roof flue, ensure an extension pipe is fitted, thus preventing snow from burying the flue vent (picture 3). Metered mains propane gas is available at some Austrian campsites; its use may be cost effective if you plan to stop a long time. A flexible hose connects to your regulator, gas is supplied at 50mb, but your regulator will compensate (picture 4).

1

Left Euro adaptor, right cup adaptor 2

3

4

Off grid electric 12v

Most new motorhomes will have a 12v, power hungry, blown air heating system, and the unit will consume most of the available leisure battery supply, an 110Ah in good condition will provide power for 24 - 48hrs. It states in the Truma manual that a Combi 6 will use 5.6amp at start up and 1.3amp on average but you will be in colder than average temperatures so will use more than 1.3 amps per hour. Solar panels will provide an insignificant amount of extra power and wind generators could be a blowout. The only reliable way to provide enough extra power is to run a generator or a fuel cell. Cheap 2 stroke generators are unpopular as the high pitch running noise and smelly fumes will soon annoy your neighbours but 4 stroke generators are quieter and very popular (picture 5). LED lights use between 5 - 10 times less power but come in various shades of white-yellow-green light, so be sure you can try them and return if unsuitable. See ledbulbs4u.co.uk

5

Electric 230v

Even on a campsite, electricity supplies may not be sufficient for your desired use. As can be seen below (picture 6), a number of circuit breakers are supported by one master breaker, in this instance four-16amp supplies (hook-ups) are available. Look closely, you can see C 16 printed on the four circuit breakers, the C may be an M, but the important point is that the 16 represents 16amps. This may be 2, or 6 with the amps respectively, exceed the amount of amps available and the circuit breaker will trip.

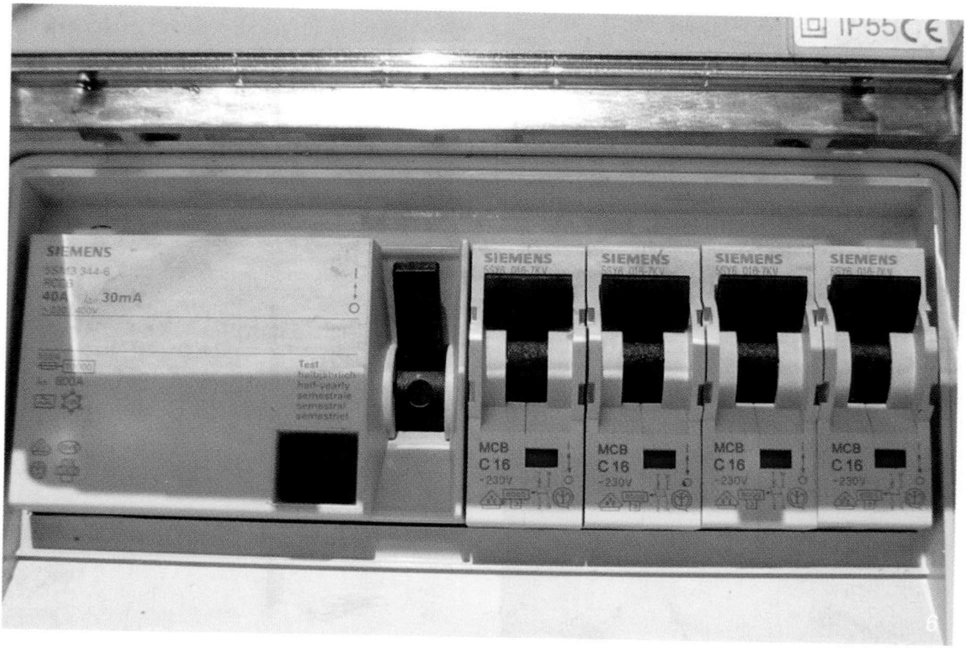

The master breaker would trip if someone received an electric shock or a faulty device was used, often a kettle, or heater.

A 2kw (2000w) heater or kettle uses 9amps. Power consumption is easy to calculate, using the following formula, watts divided by volts equals amps, so a 2000w appliance is calculated 2000w/220v = 9amps. A 16amp supply provides 3520w, the calculation is; volts times by amps equals watts, so 220v x 16amps = 3520w. The picture of the heater control knob with the three settings power consumption shows the Glasgows' foolproof way of preventing the circuit breaker tripping (picture 7).

To prevent your water system and liquid goods from freezing you have to run heating constantly, possibly on the lowest setting during the day whilst out. If you run a blown air system with ducts running through lockers, these should prevent any problems. Simple convector heaters, gas or electric, will not prevent pipes from freezing located in the depths of lockers. The Glasgows find their water pump and drop valve suffer first, but keeping cupboard and internal locker doors open helps. Electric fan heaters can blow warm air into cold/damp spots, defrost frozen windscreens and other frozen areas like engines for example. Parking with the sun on the side of the van containing pipes is a great help.

Water and servicing

Top tip; visit a service area before ascending the mountains. It is common for water to be off or frozen at motorhome Aires. Do not turn off water taps found running as the warmth in the water stops them freezing. Always fill up in the afternoon as taps are often frozen in the morning (picture 8). Water and waste stored in under slung tanks is prone to freezing, insulation helps but the only way to ensure the water stays liquid is to fit a heater element. Many campers also opt to carry drinking water in plastic containers inside the van. Ensure you have somewhere to secure them in transit and they do not leak. This may be your only supply if your fresh water tank is underslung and freezes.

Most modern vans have a built in frost safety valve near to the water heater. This valve opens automatically when the temperature gets close to freezing point and allows the water stored in the boiler to drain; if a pressure sensing water pump is on then all the water in the system will drain. Truma set their frost valves at 7°c, this safety feature is very useful if you have laid up your van for winter, but not so useful if you are using it in cold conditions. The valve is unlikely to trip when the boiler is in use. Be aware that when on hook-up and using secondary electric heating the water boiler cupboard will need heating. It states in the Truma manual that you can run the heater before you fill the boiler with water, thus bringing the temperature above 7°c. An optional 0.4amp heating element is available for the frost valve.

Keeping the grey tank tap open and draining water into a container is good practice, but is

7

8

9

10

still prone to freezing. Water expands by nine percent when frozen so do not fill your grey tank and reduce the amount of water entering it. Use as many on site facilities as possible and wash up in a bucket or bowl and dispose of the water at the onsite disposal point. The larger the amount of frozen water in your grey tank, the longer it will take to defrost.

During the summer the grey tank can cause some nasty niffs in the van. Always travel with all the plugs in their holes, as this will reduce this smell.

Preparing the Living Accommodation

What to pack

First, remove all unnecessary items from the van: summer chairs and tables, windbreaks, lanterns, flags, buckets and spades, BBQ, wetsuits, and summer clothes. Then load snow chains, a shovel, gloves, kneeling mat, water storage bottles (filled), hot water bottles, electric heater, hand brush, broom, cardboard/carpet, extra bedding, insulating screens, generator and fuel, tow rope/wire, winter clothes and shoes/boots. Now weigh your van and see if there is any payload left for you, your luggage and food.

Insulating window screens and cab curtains

Insulating screens are essential as the cab glass offers the least insulation of the whole caravan conversion. The cab itself offers the second least insulated area and curtains that isolate the cab area are worth retrofitting (picture 9).

Both the editors and the Glasgows agree that on balance, internal screens are preferable to externally fitted screens, despite offering less insulation. When using motorhome Aires you are not allowed to camp, but park, and you may want to leave quickly for a variety of reasons, so internal screens are favoured (picture 11). External screens will inevitably be wet when you want to pack them away and are bulkier (picture 12 overleaf). Condensation will form on the glass whatever type of screen is used and once defrosted is quickly removed with a squeegee (picture 10). Van Comfort has a good range of screens, see www.vancomfort.co.uk

In really cold weather you may need to insulate every window. All you need is bubble wrap, double-sided sticky tape, scissors and some attachable suction pads. These items are available from most DIY stores in Europe. Simply tape two or more layers of bubble wrap together and cut to the right size for your window.

11

12

Windows with roller blinds will hold the bubble wrap in place, but on cab windows, suction pads will hold the bubble wrap in place. The editors have tested these homemade screens down to -18°c and found they helped considerably.

Flooring

A second layer of carpet on the floor offers extra insulation, takes the wear and tear, and can be discarded at the end of the season. The editors also lay cardboard above their carpet to absorb the inevitable water that comes in each time you enter the van, the cardboard is replaced periodically.

Bedding

The editors use a four-duvet system in winter; it sounds over the top but works well. Typical 5" foam mattresses or cushions do not offer enough comfort or insulation so one covered duvet is used as a mattress topper/sheet and all duvets are laid on the bed. Then depending on how cold it is you can choose to sleep under one, two or three duvets. Place hot water bottles in beds one hour before retiring. Choose bottles with thick fluffy covers, as they stay warm all night. Hooded tops are ideal for sleeping in when it is really cold. Andy and Sue Glasgow love their Luton cab overbed as they find it the warmest place to be (picture 13). The top tip is do not let yourself get cold before going to bed, it takes ages to warm up and it stops you from sleeping.

Storing your equipment

Whatever your chosen mountain pursuit it is likely to involve some wet, muddy clothes and some cumbersome or sharp equipment. Most people opt to dry clothes in the shower cubicle but you need to think about how you are going to hang them up. The Glasgows use the wardrobe above their convector heater. Boxes, lined with newspaper, are ideal for muddy boots. Skis have very sharp edges which easily mark the fixtures and fittings, so you need to consider how you are going to store them. Some people attach their skis to their rear ladder (picture 14), if you leave any of your equipment outside you must make sure it is under lock and key.

Guide books

Obtain guide books to help with your chosen activity before you depart. Winter visitors should have the latest edition of 'Where to Ski and Snowboard' so they can assess the resorts. There are several walking guidebooks by Cicerone, Lonely Planet, and Sunflower

13

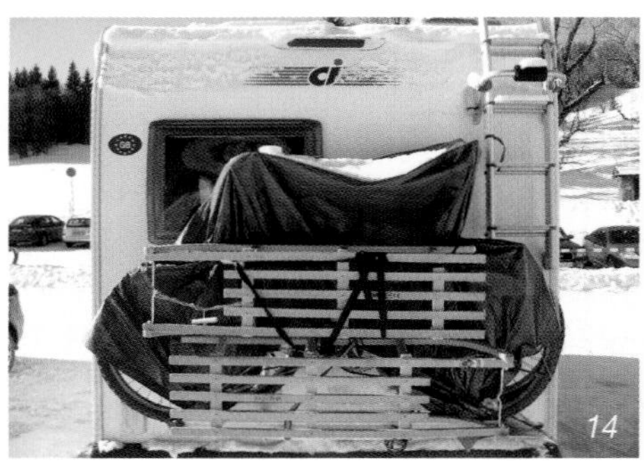

14

Books which cover short and long walks. Tourist guides such as French Alps by Michelin provide information on tourist sites as well as some walks and drives.

Anyone departing on a camping trip should consider investing in an ACSI Camping Card which offers discounts on campsites in the scheme, some of which are located in mountain areas.

Life on the Road

Once you are on the road it is important that you travel safely and carry out regular maintenance to stop issues becoming problems in winter temperatures as low as -18°c. Even summer travellers should consider that temperatures are cooler up mountains.

Condensation and ventilation

Condensation occurs when moisture in the air rises above 60% and there is a surface colder than room temperature for the airborne moisture to condense on. Removing your silver screens in cold conditions demonstrates this instantly. The best way to control condensation is good ventilation but this makes the occupants cold. Motorhomes/caravans are reasonably airtight apart from the intentional and essential vents so do not block them with the exception of fitting the winter fridge covers. Cooking and showering produce high levels of moisture. Gas releases 1 litre of water for every litre burnt, so avoid long cooking sessions. Always cook with lids on pans and keep a top vent open, run extractors if fitted, turn the heating up to compensate as this also helps to expel the steam. Keep up the regime whilst eating and until the washing up is dried up. Shower with the top vent ajar, use blown air heating if available and squeegee the walls dry as soon as possible. Use the bathroom as your airing cupboard for damp clothes and towels and keep the top vent ajar and heating vent open. Fan heaters help to keep the air moving thus preventing some condensation build-up. Cardboard is useful in the doorway as it absorbs most of the inevitable wet and can be disposed of frequently. When driving between sites, run the cab heating fans on full. Should you be lucky enough to get too hot, open a rear window or top vent to create a through draft. Some sort of outside step to raise you off the snow and ice is beneficial, the Glasgows recommend a small pallet (picture 15).

Bed-wetting

Poor bladder control may not be the culprit of bed wetting in very cold conditions. Moisture constantly evaporates from our skin, and beds suffer a build up during prolonged use. When the base of the bed is cold, moisture naturally condenses where the mattress touches it. This is a real problem on beds without slats but a coir underlay mat, www.drymesh.co.uk, helps to keep the air moving (picture 16). Make a conscious effort to air the mattress or cushions daily, simply propping them up should be enough.

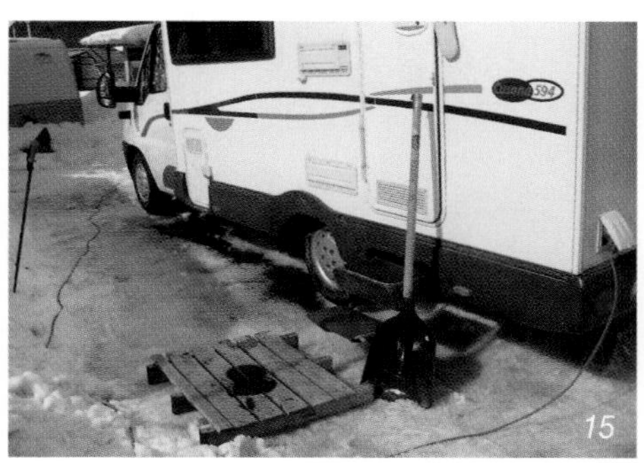

15

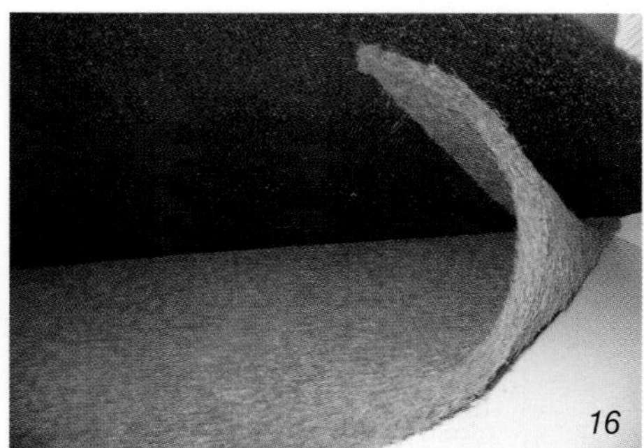

16

Snow on the roof

The title is not intended as a euphemism more a warning. Snow is known as a good insulator but thawing and refreezing could create your very own rooftop glacier, so sweep off fresh snow as soon and as best as you can, pressure washers may help remove ice on roofs (pictures 17 and 18). Take great care on the roof of your motorhome in winter - it's like an ice skating rink. Ensure a build up of snow does not block vents and flues (picture 19). This is a daily task and it is good practice to sweep the area around the van as well to keep it clear, dry and ice free. There is nothing more frustrating than injuring yourself by falling over in the parking area. Digging your van out of the snow sounds fun but there is nothing like a few days of freezing temperatures, high winds and blizzards to shorten the fuse of any camper (picture 20). A shovel will be essential to dig your vehicle out of the snow should you have been lucky enough to get some or accidentally end up in some.

Stocking up/emptying out

Mountain resorts can be isolated with limited supplies. Out of season (spring and autumn) shops may be closed. In winter, service points may be frozen. Before arriving at your chosen resort stop in the lower valleys to stock up with

17

18

19

Winter fridge vents fitted

20

21

22

anything you may need. Fill up the water tank and extra water bottles if you carry them. Empty the toilet and the grey tank. Check your gas levels filling up the LPG tank. Stock up with food but remember that some packet food will expand as you increase altitude so make sure it has enough space and ensure it is double bagged should it leak or burst.

Mountain roads

Mountain roads are often narrow and twisty and it takes both skill and concentration to safely drive them (picture 21). Details of specific road conditions are noted in the introduction for each country. General etiquette dictates that on narrow mountain lanes the driver heading down hill is expected to pull over when traffic is met coming uphill. Driving with dipped headlights on during the day has significantly reduced accidents in those countries that it is obligatory. Sounding the horn on twisting roads with reduced visibility is highly recommended whilst mountain driving. The editors have had first-hand experience of this when the sounding of horns on a sunny afternoon's drive through the Alps prevented a head on collision with a truck! Study maps and plan routes carefully as difficult or dangerous sections of roads are often marked and are best avoided. In winter and spring, high passes may be closed due to snow, drifts or wind. Never drive down a route marked as closed or open closed gates (picture 22).

Driving down a mountain with a fully loaded motorhome takes a lot more skill than in a car especially in snow. You have to descend slowly and utilise your gears, only using the brakes when necessary. Brake fade is the name given to loss of braking due to overheating. When brakes overheat this heat alters the characteristics of the compounds resulting in friction being lost and therefore reduced braking and induced fear. The warning signs are a strong chemical smell similar to burning electrics or metal being cut by an angle grinder. Pulling over and allowing brakes to cool should make them function again but if they have reached the stage of smoke coming from the wheels it may be too late. If you have suffered brake fade and have any doubt on their condition get them checked by a qualified engineer. Avoidance is always the best strategy so descend in the same gear you used to ascend, if third gear is too fast, instead of braking, change down to second gear. Do not rest your foot on the pedal but brake harder periodically. Don't worry about the local traffic, however fast you drive it will not be fast enough for them, so pull over where you can and let them past. Avoid departing from the ski resort exactly as the lifts close, or arriving just before the lifts open as you will be battling locals who won't appreciate you being there.

It is always advisable to drive in the mountains during the day in clear weather. Always check the weather forecasts before departing and call in at local Tourist Offices to check the routes and resorts are open. Avoid, where possible, driving at night, in falling snow, high winds or fog.

Out and about

Before engaging in any mountain pursuits make sure you do your homework first. Ensure you have the correct insurance just in case mountain rescue is required. Ski insurance can be purchased with lift passes for €1/€2, however a good travel insurance is always recommended. Pack clothes for all weather as it can change quickly in the mountains and check weather reports. Do not overestimate your ability and build in extra time as a contingency. Carry as much information as possible to navigate with, have maps and a compass and do not rely solely on pre placed footpath markers. When possible let someone know where you are going and what time you will return.

Weidach

AUSTRIA

Bruck

AUSTRIA

Austria is a landlocked, predominantly alpine country with seven neighbours, clockwise; Czech Republic, Slovakia, Hungary, Slovenia, Italy, Switzerland and Germany. Innsbruck is just 10 hours drive from Calais. Austria is the perfect destination for a mountain holiday with easy driving, good organisation and quality campsites. Ski Amade is one of the world's largest ski resorts but there is more to the mountains than snow. There are good walking and mountain biking trails and plenty of Wellness centres to relax tired muscles in warm thermal waters at the end of an exhilarating day.

Driving and Roads

Despite mountains making up over half of Austria's landmass, it is easy to drive around; there are no high passes to go over and good motorways crisscross the country. However, ensure you have a Vignette (toll sticker) for motorway and expressway driving.

Our researchers reported that at Sölden, north of the Italian border, Vignettes checks took place during weekends. Tourists thinking they would be OK just 'nipping' in for a week's skiing were not so lucky, being required to pay a €120 on the spot fine. Cameras also check for Vignettes.

Vignettes are available at borders and most fuel stations and must be purchased for all motorised vehicles with a maximum laden weight of 3.5t. The sticker costs €7.90 for 10 days and €22.90 for 2 months. Motorcycles are charged at half rate and trailers including caravans are free. Dates are printed around the edge of the stickers and issuing staff will punch them to identify the start date but this does not have to be the date of purchase. The sticker must be adhered to the inside of the windscreen either under the mirror or the top left hand side below any tinting. Get this right first time as self-destruction is built in upon removal. This is a simple system and compared to French tolls very inexpensive.

Vehicles exceeding 3.5t must be fitted (velcroed to the windscreen) with a 'GO-Box'. This box records the distance travelled on taxable roads and you are charged accordingly.

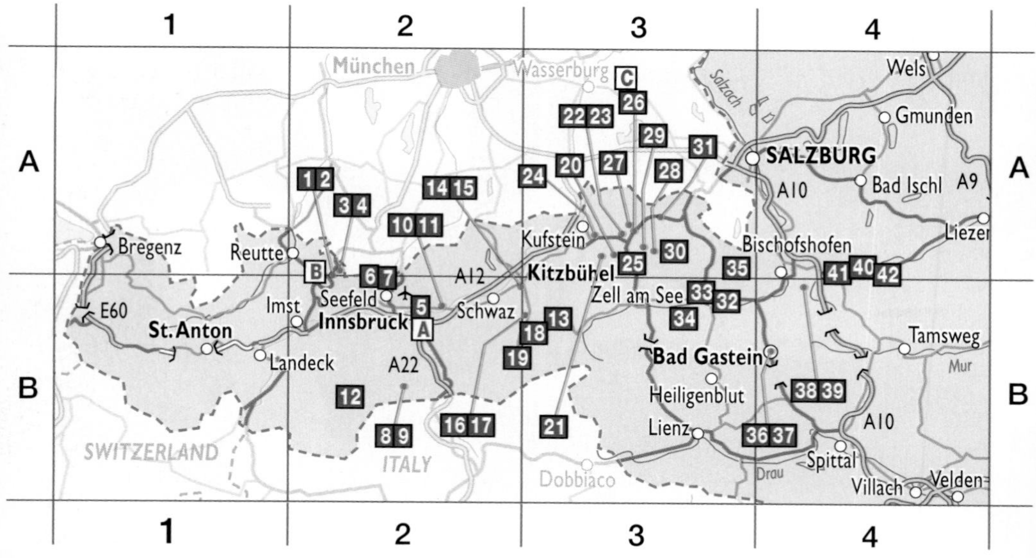

GO-Boxes are programmed for each individual vehicle and the Euro rating of the engine is taken into consideration. Your vehicle documents will be required or you can complete the form in advance at http://www.go-maut.at/go/ Price per km in March 2010 was Category 2 (vehicles with 2 axles): EUR 0.158/km (excl. 20% VAT). Category 3 [vehicles with 3 axles (trailers behind motorhomes are free)]: EUR 0.2212/km (excl. 20% VAT).

Further information about driving in Austria can be found at www.austria.info/uk/how-to-get-there/austria-by-road-1134817.html

Mountain Biking

Do you have all the gear but live in the Fens? Many of the Austrian lifts take mountain bikes up so why not zoom downhill on a real mountain! Consider servicing your brakes before you set off. The 'Bike and Fun Map' details routes and appropriate lifts around Innsbruck, it is available from the Tourist Office or online at www.innsbruck.info Also, visit the Tourist Office in Innsbruck, as there are some organised mountain bike rides. Overview mountain biking maps are viewable at www.bike-pinzgau.at/bikemap/bikemap

Walking

Austria offers great walking for all abilities from hut to hut rucksack routes to simple circular strolls. Innsbruck not only offers walkers great scenery but, on presentation of a Club Innsbruck Card, allows free travel to the nearby villages on the Hiking bus from May to October. Innsbruck Alpine School organises numerous, free, organised hikes with certified mountain guides, advanced booking may be required at the Tourist Office. See further information at www.innsbruck.info. Lifts can make mountain and even glacier access easy.

Take the cable car up the Patscherkofel Mountain and walk the Zirbenweg (Pine Tree Trail), a four mile walk in the midst of a nature reserve. See side holidaymakers can take a break from busy lakeside activities at Zell am See and follow one of the 83 summer hiking routes from the campsite.

The first port of call for all walkers should be the local Tourist Office; often maps and walks will be available. Anyone planning to visit Austria for a prolonged period should invest in joining the Austrian Alpine Club (UK) as benefits include mountain rescue insurance and the club sells detailed walking maps 1:125000 scale www.aacuk.org.uk Walking in Austria by Kev Reynolds published by Cicerone www.cicerone.co.uk details walking in Austria.

Spas & Thermal Water

Austrians are very keen on 'Wellness', their term for spas. These 'Wellness' centres consist of swimming pools and possibly saunas and steam rooms. Treatments such as massage are usually available, additional charges apply. Stopping at a wellness centre is sure to make a holiday relaxing and a great way to relieve sore muscles after a busy day out in the mountains. The campsites at Ehrwald, Fügen, Brixen-im-Thale, Kitzbuhel, and Fieberbrunn all have wellness centres on site. Aschau has one with a Wild West theme. Campsite fees often include access into the spa.

Bad Gastein is famous for its thermal spas but also has two campsites. Warm thermal waters feed several spa centres nearby; they have outside pools and one of the largest is Alpen Therme www.alpentherme.com. Local, warm caves are reputed to have healing properties. Visit www.gastein.com for further information on the area.

Skiing in Austria

Zugspitze Arena: Nestling amongst summer pastures and tucked away behind the mighty Zugspitze is a string of 8 Tyrol villages, each with its own ski area, all connected by ski bus and a cross-country path. The Zugspitze glacier can be reached via the cable car which departs 2km to the west of Ehrwald. Visit www.zugspitzarena.com for tourist information and more information about the two resorts featured in this guide **Biberwier** and **Ehrwald**.

Innsbruck/Stubai valley: Innsbruck is a town surrounded by ski resorts. None are directly accessible from town, but a free ski bus runs during the December - April ski season, just show your guest card or lift pass. People not wanting to stay in Innsbruck may choose to camp in the small ski area of **Weidach/Leutasch**. South of Innsbruck the **Stubai Valley** at the foot of Austria's biggest glacier is your gateway up. **Neustift** is the closest major village to the glacier but **Seefeld in Tirol** and **Hall in Tirol** are en-route. www.stubai.at provides further information.

Zillertal Arena: This ski area combines 10 ski resorts. **Mayrhofen** is popular with experienced snow boarders but overall the Zillertal area is best suited to intermediate skiers. **Zell am Ziller** has the oldest working brewery in the Tirol. **Gerlos** is located in the centre of the ski area, but Konigsletten ski area is recommended as it has a large free day parking for cars and motorhomes. The campsites of Fügen and Aschau are 2km away by ski bus.

Ski Welt Area: The Ski Welt is Austria's largest linked ski area, 8 resorts are connected including **Brixen–im-Thale**, **Westendorf, Itter** and **Söll**. The campsite in **Söll** is 1.5km from the slopes but the ski bus stops outside. Söll village has remodelled since the party 80s and has now become a nice Tyrol village suitable for family holidays but still has bars and lively nightclubs. **Kitzbuhel** ski area is famous for the Hahnenkamm down hill race. The lifts can be reached by ski bus but it may be easier to drive there early and park in the large free car parks. The Ski Welt is an ideal area for those skiers who like to tour, there are lots of nice Tyrolean bars in the mountains some with accordions playing at lunchtime.

Zell am See: Zell am See is a popular summer resort set around a large lake. There are a wealth of cross country paths as well as plenty of activities for non-skiers. The nearby Kaprum glacier has a large car park and is easy to drive to. There are campsites in **Zell am See, Kaprun** and **Bruck**. Visit www.zellamsee-kaprun.com for more resort information.

Ski Amade: Ski Amade has 270 lifts over four peaks making this one of the world's biggest ski areas. Having your own transport is beneficial as many of the lifts are out of town and there are no high passes to cross. Most ski lift stations have large car parks so it is possible to park during the day and drive back to a campsite after skiing. www.skiamade.com In 2013 **Schladming** plays host to the FIS Alpine Ski World Championships. In preparation there is extensive expansion, remodelling and investments on all four mountains. The Schladming Mountain Christmas markets run from the end of November until just before Christmas. **Dachstein** glacier offers year round skiing. **Pichl** and **Radstadt** are around 2km from Schladming by ski bus.

Hochkonig ski area: Stretching from **Maria Alm** to **Muhlbach**, the ski area spreads along a gentle valley taking in several small villages. The skiing is suitable for intermediates and beginners.

Other areas: Smaller Austrian ski areas featured in this guide include: **Kossen** which is not visited by many British skiers, **Hochfilzen, Fieberbrunn, Leogang** which are linked to the Ski Circus ski area www.skicircus.at, **Waidring, Bad Gastein,** and **St Johann im Pongau**.

BIBERWIER

A2 | 1 | N47°22.487' E10°53.500' 1007m

Alpencamp Marienberg, Biberwier, (Zugspitze), Marienbergweg 15, A6633
www.alpencamp-marienberg.at

Directions: Exit the A12 at either Junctions 133-Imst-Au or 113-Mötz onto the B189 toward Nassereith. From Nassereith join the B179 and drive 14km north and turn off the B179, at Weissen See Lake toward Biberwier. Follow road until you reach village, turning right and going back on yourself to the chairlift. The parking is at the chairlift. Claims are made this area can be reached 'toll free' from Germany (15km away) so no need to buy a Vignette until you reach Innsbruck.

Sanitation:

 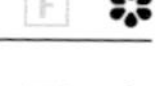

Parking:

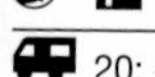 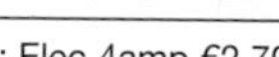

20; €12.60 Custom; Elec 4amp €2.70

Located on village outskirts the motorhome Aire is 50m from the main chairlift or the free ski bus stop. The Zugspitze glacier is reachable from the valley. During the summer, 300km of walking trails, cycle paths and mountain bike routes for all abilities are accessible. The large Heiterwanger Lake has pleasure boats. Local saunas and swimming pools offer discounts with a Guest Card.

Activities and Facilities:

BIBERWIER

A2 | 2 | N47°22.487' E10°53.500' 1007m

Alpencamp Marienberg, Biberwier, (Zugspitze), Marienbergweg 15, A6633
www.alpencamp-marienberg.at

Directions: Exit the A12 at either Junctions 133-Imst-Au or 113-Mötz onto the B189 toward Nassereith. From Nassereith join the B179 and drive 14km north and turn off the B179 at Weissen See Lake towards Biberwier. Follow road until you reach village, turning right and going back on yourself to the chairlift. The campsite is near the chairlift. Claims are made this area can be reached 'toll free' from Germany (15km away) so no need to buy a Vignette until you reach Innsbruck.

Sanitation:

Parking:

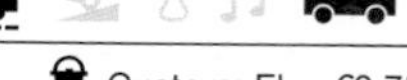

50; €25 Custom; Elec €0.75 kWh

Located 50m from the main chairlift and the free ski bus stop, this campsite is perfectly placed and popular all year. During the summer, 300km of walking trails, cycle paths and mountain bike routes for all abilities are accessible. The large Heiterwanger Lake has pleasure boats. Local saunas and swimming pools offer discounts with a Guest Card.

Activities and Facilities:

EHRWALD

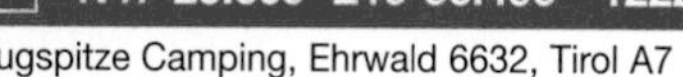
A2 | 3 | N47°25.609' E10°56.496' 1222m

Zugspitze Camping, Ehrwald 6632, Tirol A7
Tel: 56732309
www.zugspitze-resort.at or www.zugspitze.com

Directions: Located at the foot of Zugspitze Mountain by the gondola, it is an easy drive from Germany or via two mountain passes from Innsbruck. From Innsbruck, turn off the B179 onto the B187 past Biberwier towards Lermoos, Ehrwald and Germany. Then turn off to Ehrwald into Garmischer strasse and then take the second left into Zugspitzstrasse. Follow this road out of the village for 2km to the gondola and the parking is on the left.

Sanitation:

Parking:

€15 8pm – 8am

Holiday Clean; €1 for water, Elec €0.80 per kWh (1000w for 1hr)

Located at Zugspitz Gondola, outside of the campsite, this large car park has a service point, toilet, and showers. You can catch a free bus to the village, 2km away, or to other local ski areas. Ehrwald is a nice Austrian style resort with low villages and attractive scenery.

Activities and Facilities:

EHRWALD

A2 | 4 | N47°25.609' E10°56.496' 1222m

Zugspitze Camping, Ehrwald 6632, Tirol A7,
Tel: 56732309 www.zugspitze-resort.at or
www.zugspitze.com

Directions: Located at the foot of Zugspitze Mountain by the gondola, it is an easy drive from Germany or via two mountain passes from Innsbruck. From Innsbruck, turn off the B179 onto the B187 past Biberwier towards Lermoos, Ehrwald and Germany. Then turn off to Ehrwald into Garmischer strasse and then take the second left into Zugspitzstrasse. Follow this road out of the village for 2km to the gondola and the campsite is on the left.

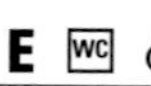 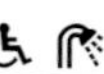 

Sanitation:

Parking:

 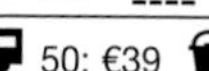 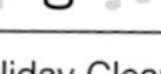    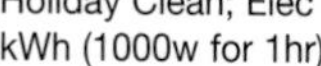

50; €39 Holiday Clean; Elec €0.80 per kWh (1000w for 1hr)

Located under the main gondola this is a prime location and the campsite is trying to become a 'Wellness Centre', so use of swimming pool, sauna, whirlpool and fitness facilities are included in the fees. You can catch a free bus to the village, 2km away, or to other local ski areas. Ehrwald is a nice Austrian style resort with low villages and attractive scenery.

Activities and Facilities:

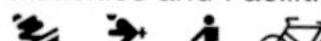

INNSBRUCK

B2 | 5 | N47°14.256' E11°20.560' 800m

Natterer See, Natterer See 1, A-6161
www.natterersee.com

Directions: From Natters, just south of Innsbruck, follow the road named Seestrasse to Natterer See. The campsite is adjacent to the Natterer lake.

Sanitation:

Parking:

100; €30

Custom; Elec 16amp or standard pitch 6amp (5kw max)

A swish resort-cum-campsite set on a lakeside used for swimming and water sports in the summer. There is a free ski bus, 3km, to the expanding ski areas in Axams and Lizum, Olympia Skiwelt, Innsbruck, and the popular snowboarding area of Axamer Lizum. Campsite staff can arrange transport to local ski areas and Innsbruck town with December Christmas markets, but using your own car to tour area would be convenient. The area is popular with summer walkers and ski shoes can be hired for snow walking. Crystal lovers will enjoy the Swarovski Kristallwelten.

Activities and Facilities:

    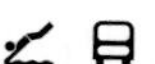 

WEIDACH/LEUTASCH

B2 | 6 | N47°21.854' E11°10.000' 1143m

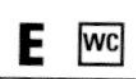  

Camping Kreith, Kreith chairlift, Near Weidach
www.alpenhof-leutasch.at

Directions: Follow the B171/E533 northwest from Innsbruck to Seefeld in Tirol, once you leave the valley the first part is very steep. From Seefeld in Tirol follow signs to Weidach/Leutasch. As you enter Weidach turn left to the ski lifts. The parking is adjacent to Kreith chairlift. Alternatively take the easier route from Germany, drive through Weidach towards Seefeld in Tirol. Turn into the ski lift station as you exit the town.

Sanitation:

Parking:

30; €21 Custom; Elec 3 amp inc; 10amp avail at 50c per kWh (1000w for 1hr)

This private parking area is very welcoming, but English not spoken. Standard campsite facilities include hot showers for €1. The village is 500m away with bars, restaurants and a new swimming pool and sauna complex. The ski area is small, having only one chairlift and two drag (T) lifts and cross-country skiing. The slope side access is ideal for beginners, and there is a kids' ski school adjacent, in summer there is some excellent walking. A 1km forest footpath gets you to an Innsbruck bus stop.

Activities and Facilities:

SEEFELD IN TIROL

B2 | 7 | N47°20.236' E11°10.700' 900m

Seefeld Alpin camp, Leutascher Strasse 810, Seefeld in Tirol
www.camp-alpin.at

Directions: 10km west of Innsbruck exit the A12/E60 junction 87 Zirl Ost, onto B177/E533/Seefelder-Bundesstrasse toward Garmisch/Seefeld. In 4km the road is very steep for 2km. From Seefeld in Tirol follow signs to Wedach/Leutasch. The campsite is on the left 1km northwest of the village.

Sanitation:

Parking:

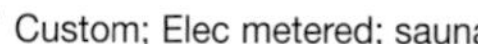

50; €39 Custom; Elec metered; sauna.

Just 100m from the ski area this campsite offers 5* facilities, including a sauna, free WiFi and English is spoken. Seefeld is a typical Austrian resort set amongst trees; it is popular with tourists and has a lively nightlife. This resort has more ski lifts here than nearby Leutasch, with further slopes accessible by ski bus. All the slopes have many drag (T) lifts.

Activities and Facilities:

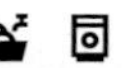

NEUSTIFT/STUBAI

B2 | 8 | N47°04.095' E11°15.168' 1140m

Camping Edelweiss, Familie Pfurtscheller
A-6167, Neustift-Voldernau
www.camping-edelweiss.com

Directions: 8km south of Innsbruck exit the A13/E45 onto the B183 toll free road with 3.5t limit. Travel 11km southwest past Camping Stubai in Neustift and Camping Edelweiss is 6km further on the right adjacent to the main road at a farmstead.

Sanitation:

Parking:

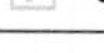

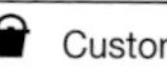
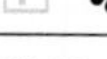

30; €18.50 Custom Elec €2.60

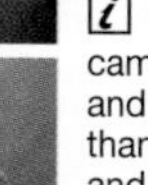

This is a nice, quiet, and economical campsite with all the necessary skiing facilities and a restaurant/bar adjacent but is cheaper than Camping Stubai. The area is picturesque and cross-country ski trails pass the campsite but it is 10km by ski bus to the excellent glacier resort of Stubai. In summer there is glacier skiing, walking, including a waterfall walk and mountain biking.

Activities and Facilities:

NEUSTIFT/STUBAI

B2 9 N47°06.593' E11°18.523' 1000m

Camping Stubai, A6167 Neustift, Tirol
www.campingstubai.at

Directions: 8km south of Innsbruck exit the A13/E45 onto the B183 toll free road with 3.5t limit. Travel 11km southwest to Neustift and Camping Stubai is on the left. Neustift is the last village up the valley before the long private road to the Stubai glacier ski area.

Sanitation:

Parking:

 50; €22 Custom; Elec €2.90

Camping Stubai is in the centre of this lively and often very busy village just 500m from the shops. This campsite is livelier and more expensive than other nearby campsites but you get a lot for your money. There are comprehensive facilities and English is spoken. Take a ski bus to access Stubai slopes. In summer there is glacier skiing, walking, including a waterfall walk and mountain biking.

Activities and Facilities:

HALL IN TIROL

(no twin axels) B2 10 N47°17.082' E11°29.775' 590m

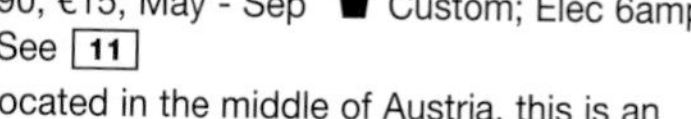

Schwimmbad Wohnmobil Park,
Scheidensteinstrasse 24, Hall in Tirol
www.stw-hall.at

Directions: Travelling east from Innsbruck, turn off the B171 main route at the large traffic lighted crossroads and turn left towards Thaur. At the roundabout, take the third exit then at the end of the road turn left. The campsite is on your right at the sports facilities, 500m from the old town.

Sanitation:

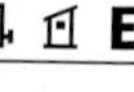

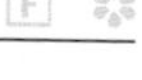

Parking:

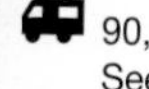 90, €15; May - Sep Custom; Elec 6amp
See 11

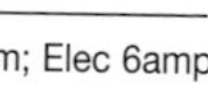
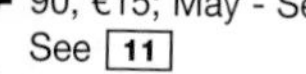

Located in the middle of Austria, this is an excellent stopover. You can walk 500m into the historic town with medieval centre and the bus makes Innsbruck easy to visit. The campsite is popular in summer, site fees also includes entry into the adjacent municipal open-air pool. The campsite has a terrace restaurant with views; children's play area, mountain bike hire and cycle and walking routes are adjacent.

Activities and Facilities:

HALL IN TIROL B2 11 N47°17.082' E11°29.775' 580m

Schwimmbad Wohnmobil Park, Scheidensteinstrasse 24, Hall in Tirol
www.hall.ag

Directions: Travelling east from Innsbruck, turn off the B171 main route at the large traffic lighted cross roads and turn left towards Thaur. At the roundabout, take the third exit then at the end of the road turn left. The parking is on your right at the sports facilities, 500m from the old town.

Sanitation:

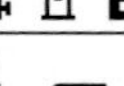  

Parking:

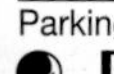    

 8; €7.50; Oct - Apr; No tag Axels.
Holiday Clean; Elec 16amp

Well located when crossing Austria via the Brenner Pass. You can walk 500m into the historic town with medieval centre (very quiet in winter) and the bus makes Innsbruck easy to visit. The service point is always accessible; parking is restricted to 1 night during the summer. The ski slopes, including Patscherkofel and Olex, are 30 minutes drive; all have large, free car parks that are busy at weekends.

Activities and Facilities:

SÖLDEN B2 12 N46°57.474' E11°00.711' 1377m

Camping Sölden, Wohlfahrtstrasse 22, A6450
www.camping-soelden.com

Directions: Exit the A12/E60 at junction 123 onto the B186 and follow this road south 38km to Sölden. In Sölden take the last turning on the left as you exit the village just after you go under a bridge for the cable car station on your left. Follow this road and the campsite is on the right just before the river bridge.

Sanitation:

Parking:

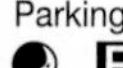  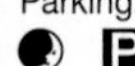    

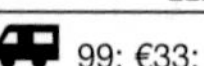 99; €33; Closed May - June
 Custom; Elec €0.70 per kWh

The campsite is located beside a river on the outskirts of Sölden, it is an easy walk to town, which is popular with partying Dutch, UK and German youths. Reception has English speakers and facilities include a sauna, steam room and climbing wall. The main gondola is 100m away providing access to easy skiing. Catch a ski bus to Hochgurgl or Obergurgl, a much higher and posher resort. 300km of marked footpaths are accessible in summer, as well as climbing, mountain biking and rafting.

Activities and Facilities:

GERLOS

   B3 13 N47°13.609' E12°03.312' 1290m

Gerlos Farm campsite, Bauernhof Schonachof, Schonachtal 242

Directions: 35km northeast of Innsbruck exit the A12/E45 junction 39 onto Zillertal Bundesstrasse B169 and follow the road south for 21.6km to Zell am Ziller. Turn off the B169, before the tunnel, onto B165 and drive 18km east toward Mittersill. Drive through Gerlos turning right at Pizzeria Davollo, cross the river then left. Drive 700m, turning first left and the small campsite is at the end of the road.

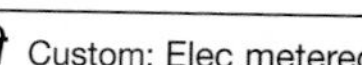

Sanitation:

Parking:

30; €25 Custom; Elec metered

Overlooking the village and slopes this is a good value small campsite. The guesthouse restaurant serves good, traditional cooking. An easy 10min footpath walk gets you to the main gondola in the village that is lively in the evening. At 1290m, Gerlos is higher than other Zilletal villages thus more likely to have snow. The local downhill ski area is easy and extensive with the excellent cross-country ski and summer walking trails.

Activities and Facilities:

FÜGEN (ZILLERTAL)

B2 14 N47°21.532' E11°51.142' 562m

Camping Hell, Fügen Gageriner Strasse 1
www.zillertal-camping.at

Directions: 35km northeast of Innsbruck exit the A12/E45 junction 39 onto Zillertal Bundesstrasse B169 and follow the road south for 6km towards Fügen. This is the first resort in Zillertal valley. The campsite is on the left, adjacent to the main road before you enter Fügen. Enter the campsite from the parallel side road, turn onto the left hand side road either before or after the campsite.

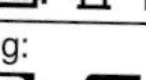
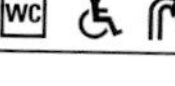

Sanitation:

Parking:

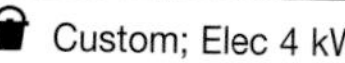

50; €34 Custom; Elec 4 kWh

Despite the name, this is a pleasant campsite in a small rural resort. The campsite has a wellness centre, restaurant, and English is spoken. In summer, there are two outdoor swimming pools, a children's play area and numerous hiking and mountain biking trails. Best off all it provides an excellent opportunity to go to 'Hell' and back, free! Take the free ski bus 2km to the gondola station.

Activities and Facilities:

FÜGEN (ZILLERTAL)

B2 15 N47°21.532' E11°51.142' 562m

Camping Hell, Fügen Gageriner Strasse 1
www.zillertal-camping.at

Directions: 35km northeast of Innsbruck exit the A12/E45 junction 39 onto Zillertal Bundesstrasse B169 and follow the road south for 6km towards Fügen. This is the first resort in Zillertal valley. The campsite is on the left, adjacent to the main road before you enter Fügen. Enter the campsite from the parallel side road, turn onto the left hand side road either before or after the campsite. Parking before reception.

Sanitation:

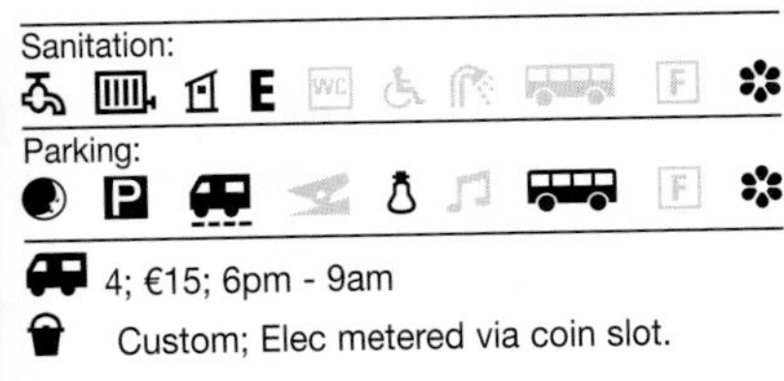

Parking:

4; €15; 6pm - 9am

Custom; Elec metered via coin slot.

This is an overnight stop only, between 6pm and 9am. If you wish to stay in the resort, you will need to book into the campsite.

Activities and Facilities:

ASCHAU (ZILLERTAL)

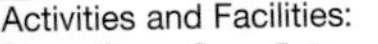

B3 16 N47°15.772' E11°54.036' 546m

Aufenfeld Camp, Aschau, Aufenfeldweg 10
www.camping-zillertal.at

Directions: 35km northeast of Innsbruck exit the A12/E45 junction 39 onto Zillertal Bundesstrasse B169 and follow the road south for 18km past Fügen to Aschau. Drive past the campsite on the left and take the turning to Aschau on the right. At the T-junction turn left, after the bend turn right and the campsite is on the right by itself 2km from village.

Sanitation:

Parking:

100, €36 Custom; Elec €0.60 per kWh (1000w for 1hr)

This large campsite has excellent facilities including restaurants, shop and swimming pools open all year. Ski rental, ski school, and lift passes can be booked at the campsite and English is spoken. The ski slopes are 2km by ski bus. Take your cowboy outfit as this campsite has a Wild West theme with a Wild West camp complete with saloon bar and a Wild West themed wellness centre! Horse riding and hiking trails are popular in summer.

Activities and Facilities:

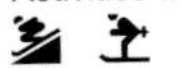   

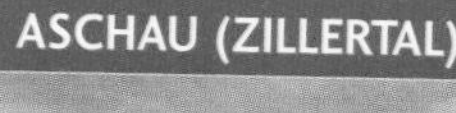

ASCHAU (ZILLERTAL)

 B3 17 N47°15.772' E11°54.036' 546m

Aufenfeld Camp attached Aire, Aschau, Aufenfeldweg 10
www.camping-zillertal.at

Directions: 35km northeast of Innsbruck exit the A12/E45 junction 39 onto Zillertal Bundesstrasse B169 and follow the road south for 18km past Fügen to Aschau. Drive past the campsite on the left and take the turning to Aschau on the right. At the T-junction turn left, after the bend turn right and the campsite is on the right by itself 2km from village.

Sanitation:

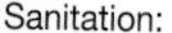 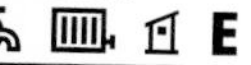 

Parking:

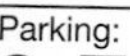  

 20, €10; 7pm - 8am

 Custom; Elec via meter

Overnight parking located outside campsite barrier, from 7pm-8am only. If you wish to stay longer, you must book into the campsite.

Activities and Facilities:

ZELL AM ZILLER (ZILLERTAL)

  B3 18 N47°13.730' E11°53.175' 590m

Camping Dorfhofer, Gerlosstrasse 33, Zell am Ziller
www.campingdorf.at

Directions: 35km northeast of Innsbruck exit the A12/E45 junction 39 onto Zillertal Bundesstrasse B169 and follow the road south for 21.6km to Zell am Ziller. Turn off the B169, before the tunnel, onto the B165 to Zell am Ziller. Turn first right into Gerlosstrasse and the campsite is on the right adjacent to the main road.

Sanitation:

Parking:

100; €30   Custom; Elec via meter

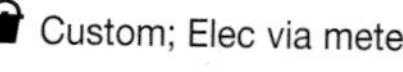

This campsite seems to be a favourite with locals; statics and long termers occupy many pitches. The campsite bar and restaurant can be lively at night during weekends and summer events and English is spoken. There is good walking in the area and a swimming pool in summer. Ski bus stops outside the campsite taking you 2km to the slopes.

Activities and Facilities:

MAYRHOFEN

  B2 | 19 | N47°10.581' E11°52.187' 600m

Mayrhofen, Laubichl 125, Mayrhofen
www.mayrhofen.at

Directions: 35km northeast of Innsbruck exit the A12/E45 junction 39 onto Zillertal Bundesstrasse B169 and follow the road south for 29km. Turn left off the B169 just before Mayrhofen to the Hamlet of Laubichl. In 200m at crossroads turn right towards Mayrhofen and the campsite is on the left just past a large sawmill/timber yard.

Sanitation:

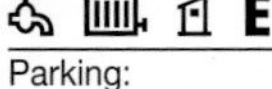

Parking:

 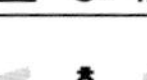 

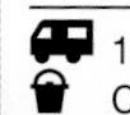 100; €26; Closed November

Custom; 16amp elec metered

This large campsite is 600m away from the town and nightlife. The resort attracts many Brits so English is widely spoken. The resort and campsite can be crowded. Pitches can be boggy but hard standing is available. Eggalm, Rastkogel and Horberg are 2km away by ski bus and a cross-country trail passes the campsite. In summer there are trips up to Hintertux Glacier. Nearby there is a strange Milk Museum and a local steam train 'Zillerbahn'.

Activities and Facilities:

   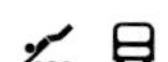

BRIXEN-IM-THALE

  A3 | 20 | N47°26.757' E12°15.441' 700m

Camping Welt, Badhausweg 9, Brixen-im-Thale
www.camping-brixen.at

Directions: Exit the A12/E45 junction 17 Wörgl Ost towards Lofer/Sankt Johann in Tirol. In 6km take the ramp and at the roundabout take the first exit onto B170/Brixental strasse. The campsite is adjacent to the B170 in 15km on outskirts, south of village.

Sanitation:

Parking:

 60; €35  Custom; Elec €0.80 

This campsite is morphing into a pricey 'Wellness Centre' with chalets, a bar, and restaurants. Popular with Dutch caravanners and a reservation is needed at popular times. The village centre is quiet and pleasant. A 2km ski bus ride takes you to new lifts providing convenient access to the large 'Ski Welt' area of interconnected lifts.

Activities and Facilities:

WESTENDORF — A3 | 21 | N47°25.969' E12°12.131' 800m

Panorama Camping, B170, Westendorf
www.panoramacamping.at

Directions: Exit the A12/E45 junction 17 Wörgl Ost toward Lofer/Sankt Johann in Tirol. In 6km take the ramp and at the roundabout take the first exit onto B170/Brixental strasse. In 9.4Km Panorama Camping is adjacent to the B170 main road, signposted, to the west of the village.

Sanitation:

Parking:

120, €29.50; Closed Nov - mid Dec

Custom

Arrive before noon, as this campsite is very popular because of its reasonable prices and excellent facilities, including sauna, bar-restaurant and powerful WiFi across the campsite. A reservation would be wise for popular periods, staff speak English. The characterful village is 1.5km walk. A ski bus calls at campsite entrance - check small printed timetable available at reception.

Activities and Facilities:

SÖLL — A3 | 22 | N47°30.061' E12°11.743' 734m

Stampfanger Strasse car park

Directions: Exit the A12/E45 junction 17 Wörgl Ost toward Lofer/Sankt Johann in Tirol on the B178. In 11km turn right onto Stampfanger at the crossroads, in the middle of the village, driving away from the village and church. The parking is 200m on the left at the ski lift.

Sanitation:

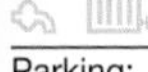

Parking:

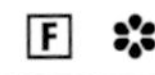

50

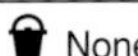
None

100m from the main Söll gondola, this is long established motorhome day parking in a large car park. There are no facilities but motorhomes were overnighting, and it is very busy with German motorhomes at weekends. Close by the swimming pool, a super, hot outdoor bubble pool is worth a visit. Nice 300m walk to village. Please leave this parking area spotless.

Activities and Facilities:

SÖLL

A3 | 23 | N47°30.484' E12°11.361' 750m

Camping Franzlhof, Dorfbichl 37, Söll
www.franzlhof.com

Directions: Exit the A12/E45 junction 17 Wörgl Ost toward Lofer/Sankt Johann in Tirol on the B178. Travel 10km and turn left at the cross roads in the middle of the village into the village. Drive past the church and follow the road round the bend to the right and then to the left. The campsite is on the northern outskirts, overlooking the village and slopes.

Sanitation:

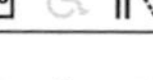

Parking:

50; €28; Closed Nov - mid Dec

Custom; 16amp elec metered

A small and pleasant campsite that is suitable for a week's holiday as Söll is well connected to the 'Ski Welt' area. Visit the automatic milk vending machine fitted to wall of wooden milk parlour. There is a nice swimming pool adjacent to the gondola.

Activities and Facilities:

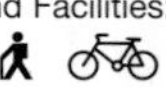

ITTER/HOPFGARTEN

A3 | 24 | N47°28.026' E12°08.368' 750m

Terrassencamping Itter, Brixentalerstrasse 11, Itter, www.camping-itter.at

Directions: Exit the A12/E45 junction 17 Wörgl Ost toward Lofer/Sankt Johann. In Tirol in 6km take the ramp and at the roundabout take the first exit onto B170/Brixental Bundesstrasse. Travel 2km and the campsite is on the left adjacent to the B170 near Itter.

Sanitation:

Parking:

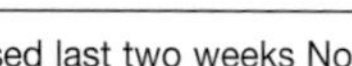

200; €31; Closed last two weeks Nov

Custom; Elec metered

A pretty campsite made up of sunny terraces with good drainage in rain and snow. The campsite has a restaurant-bar on site and English is spoken. The children's ski tow may be operating at weekends during winter and a swimming pool and children's adventure play area open in summer. Ski buses call at the campsite providing easy access to the 'Ski Welt' area.

Activities and Facilities:

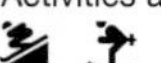

KITZBÜHEL

A3 | 25 | N47°27.609' E12°21.732' | 760m

Camping Schwarzee, Reitherstrasse 24, Kitzbühel, Tirol www.bruggerhof-camping.at

Directions: Exit Kitzbühel west on the B170 towards Kirchberg and turn off to Reith Bei Kitzbühel. Cross the railway line and take the next right and the campsite is on the left adjacent to Schwarzsee lake.

Sanitation:

Parking:

 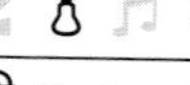

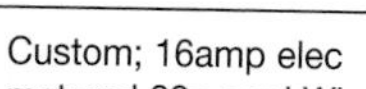

70; €43 — Custom; 16amp elec metered 80c per kWh

This is the only campsite in town; it is well kept, but statics occupy 90 percent of the pitches. Use of the extensive pool and wellness centre is included in pitch fees; this is normal for campsites in this valley. During winter, touring pitches are on the car park adjacent to toilets, showers, and sauna. Reservation needed for popular holiday periods. A 3km ski bus ride to Fleckalmbahn Gondola in Kirchberg connects to the top of Ehrenbach-hohe.

Activities and Facilities:

      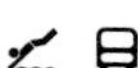

ST JOHANN IN TIROL

A3 | 26 | N47°30.646' E12°24.543' | 700m

Camping Michelnhof, Weiberndorf 6, St Johann in Tirol www.camping-michelnhof.at

Directions: Exit the A12/E45 junction 17 Wörgl Ost toward Lofer/Sankt Johann in Tirol on the B178. In 29km take the ramp to Lienz/Kitzbühel on the B161. In 400m, before the factory, turn left signed St.Johann Süd. Take the 3rd right onto Weiberndorf and the campsite.

Sanitation:

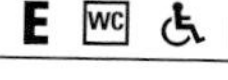 

Parking:

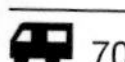  

70; €25 — Custom; Elec metered

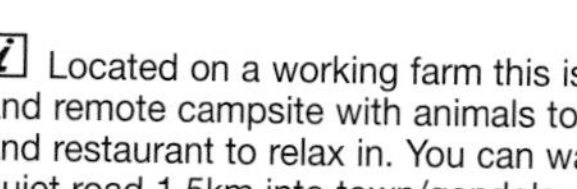

Located on a working farm this is a quiet and remote campsite with animals to pet, a bar and restaurant to relax in. You can walk up a quiet road 1.5km into town/gondola, or take the ski bus. This is the main gondola up the north side of Kitzbühel Horn Mountain.

Activities and Facilities:

 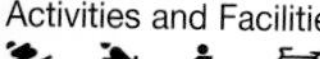    

KOESSEN

A3 | 27 | N47°39.226' E12°24.924' | 726m

Euro-Camp Wilder Kaiser, Kranebittau 18
www.eurocamp-koessen.at

Directions: From Köessen at the roundabout where the B176 and B172 cross, take the B176 south towards Sankt Johann in Tirol. In 1.4km, after passing through a quarry, turn left. Take the next left, keep left and the campsite is on the left in 1km near to the main gondola.

Sanitation:

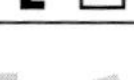

Parking:

200, €26; Closed last three weeks Nov - first week Dec

Custom; Elec metered

Surrounded by snow-capped mountains, in a lovely valley, this site feels isolated from the rest of Austria. Facilities include a sauna, summer pool and fascinating 'self cleaning' ladies loos. The English speaking staff are helpful. The resort is small, friendly and popular with weekending Germans, but is quiet mid-week. The gondola is a 200m walk; town centre is 1km. In summer, there is a 'Fun park' with a water park and activity centre www.hallodu.at

Activities and Facilities:

HOCHFILZEN

A3 | 28 | N47°28.707' E12°36.756' | 953m

Pillersee Ski Area, Mitterwarming, Hochfilzen

Directions: Located off the B164 halfway between Sankt Johann in Tirol and Saalfelden am Steinernen Meer. Turn off the B164 into Hochfilzen, cross the railway track and follow the road to the left, Warminger Str. follow this road for 1.2km along valley to the base of lifts. Warning; signposts in the village say it's at Kulture Haus, it's not!

Sanitation:

Parking:

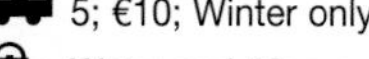

5; €10; Winter only

Water and 16amp elec included; No disposal

This new motorhome parking area is by the ski lifts of a small resort with intermediate slopes and providing a 'back door' ski entry down to St Jakob im Haus ski area. Also hosts Ski Langlaof competition and it has extensive cross-country trails. There is a ski bus to other areas. A local bar/restaurant is adjacent. Do not dump waste down toilet or this facility will close.

Activities and Facilities:

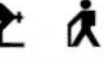

FIEBERBRUNN

A3 | 29 | N47°28.105' E12°33.247' | 820m

Tirol Camp, Fieberbrunn, Lindau 20
www.tirol-camp.at

Directions: Located off the B164 between Saalfelden am Steinernen Meer and Sankt Johann in Tirol. From Sankt Johann in Tirol drive 11km, pass though Fieberbrunn and turn right off the B164. The campsite is between the gondola and village centre.

Sanitation:

Parking:

150, €45; Closed mid April - mid May and mid July - first week Dec

Custom; Elec metered

This campsite offers extensive facilities including swimming pool, bar-restaurant, shop, sauna, and a wellness centre. The campsite grounds are well managed, even in heavy snow. The location is ideal, as it is only a 150m to the gondola station.

Activities and Facilities:

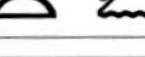

LEOGANG

A3 | 30 | N47°26.326' E12°43.216' | 833m

Leogang Hütten B164

Directions: Located off the B164 between Saalfelden am Steinernen Meer and Sankt Johann in Tirol. From Saalfelden am Steinernen Meer drive 10km on the B164, the parking area is next to Sports area/Azitbahn/ski lift adjacent to the B164 on the main route through town.

Sanitation:

Parking:

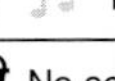

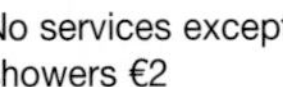

20; €4 plus tax

No services except showers €2

This is a top-secret Austrian spot (until now). Unsigned but official motorhome parking is free during the day and €4 per night plus tax, pay at information office adjacent. There are no services, but only 50m to gondola and you get a guest card to visit local sports facilities. From the Leogang ski lift it is possible to ski the Saalbach and Hinterglemm ski areas.

Activities and Facilities:

WAIDRING

A3 | 31 | N47°35.007' E12°34.980' | 741m

Camping Steinplatte, Unterwasser 43, Tirol www.camping-steinplatte.at

Directions: Located halfway between Sankt Johann in Tirol and Lofer, just off the B178. From Sankt Johann in Tirol drive 15km to Waidring and turn right off the B178 direction St Ulrich am Pillersee into the village. The campsite entrance is on your left in 300m.

Sanitation:

Parking:

70, €26 accepts ACSI Camping Card

Custom; Elec metered €0.80 per kWh.

This pleasant, clean, low-key, campsite accepts ACSI camping card for most of the winter season making it cheap. The intermediate ski slopes are 2km by ski bus, and there are ski buses to other slopes in the area. The village centre is a 1km walk.

Activities and Facilities:

BRUCK

B3 | 32 | N47°16.989' E12°49.002' | 755m

Woferlgut Sportcamp, Krossenbach 40, Bruck www.sportcamp.at

Directions: Exit Zell am See to the south onto the B311. Follow the B311 across the river and past the campsite on your left. Exit the B311 at the next exit to Bruck. Take the second turning on the left into Krössenbachstrasser. As the road draws parallel with the railway track turn left into the campsite.

Sanitation:

Parking:

120 €35 Custom; Elec metered €0.70

Located on the outskirts of Bruck village by a river, this is a clean and well-run campsite with staff who speak English. Good sports facilities are available all year, which include a gym, sauna and Turkish bath. In summer, there is a swimming pool and kids' club and an Aqua park at the lake opposite provides swimming, sailing and ball sports. This would be an ideal campsite for the summer or for people prepared to drive to the ski slopes each day.

Activities and Facilities:

ZELL AM SEE B3 33 N47°20.389' E12°48.539' 757m

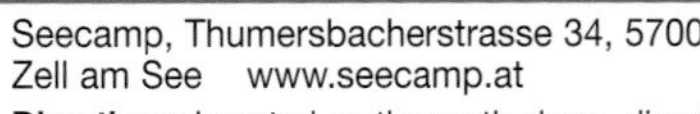

Seecamp, Thumersbacherstrasse 34, 5700 Zell am See www.seecamp.at

Directions: Located on the north shore, directions not really needed but from the E55/A10 take exit 46-47 Bischofshofen onto B311 and travel 47km to Bruck an der Grossglocknerstrasse. At the end of town take the slip road right and drive round the right hand side of the lake on Seeuferstrasse which becomes Thumersbacher Str in Thumersbach village. From the village continue round 1.4km to the top of Zell am See and the campsite is on the left.

Sanitation:

Parking:

160; €33 Custom; Elec metered

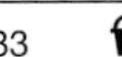

Located on the lakeshore the campsite and area has a beach atmosphere with swimming and boating. In winter, it can feel a little desolate. Zell am See is a 1.8 km walk or cycle along the lakeside path or by pleasure boats in summer. This lively town has interesting old buildings and plenty to do for non-skiers. Hiking trails are available summer and winter. In winter a ski bus to Zell am See stops outside campsite and another connects to Kaprun. If skiing at Kaprun we suggest you stay at Camping zur Muhle. 34

Activities and Facilities:

KAPRUN B3 34 N47°15.832' E12°44.732' 776m

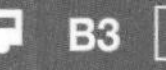

Camping zur Muhle, Umfahrungsstrasse B683, kaprun www.kaprun.at/muehle

Directions: Exit Zell am See to the south onto the B168. Turn off the B168 at the roundabout to Kaprun. Travel 3.6km driving through Kaprun and the campsite is just outside village on the left on the way to the ski station.

Sanitation:

Parking:

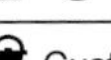

50; €25 Custom; Elec metered

This is a low-key campsite attached to a hotel, alongside a river. Most pitches are occupied by static or long-termers, in winter it is boggy, very quiet and under-used. The lively village of Kaprun has bars and shops; it is a 1km walk on the adjacent walking/cycling path. The campsite is on ski bus route to Kaprun ski station making it very convenient for skiing the Kaprun glacier, which is high, and snow sure. There are numerous walking, cycling, and cross-country skiing tracks through the village.

Activities and Facilities:

MARIA ALM

A3 | 35 | N47°23.861' E12°54.207' | 792m

Stellplatz Stegerbauer, Stegen 16,
Off Schattberg 11, Maria Alm
www.sbg.at/stegerbauer

Directions: Exit the village south on the B164 towards Hinterthal. The farm stop is on the right 700m outside village. Well sign posted from main road. Tricky access if heavy snow, and for large units.

Sanitation:

Parking:

6; €14 — Custom; Elec 6amp

Camping on a working farm; 1km bus ride from the Hochkoning ski slopes. Vans are parked in front of the main house during winter and on meadows in summer. Visitors receive a friendly welcome even though no English is spoken. Hochkonig ski area is mainly suitable for intermediates and beginners; it stretches from Maria Alm to Muhlbach and consists of several small villages spread along a gentle valley.

Activities and Facilities:

BAD GASTEIN

B4 | 36 | N47°08.044' E13°07.860' | 850m

Kur-Camping, Erlengrundstrasse 6, Bad Gastein
www.kurcamping-gastein.at

Directions: Turn off the B167 3km north of Bad Gastein signposted to 'Bad Bruck (Badesee)' opposite camping Bertahof. Follow Erlengrundstrasse 1.4km south towards Bad Gastein and the campsite in on the right.

Sanitation:

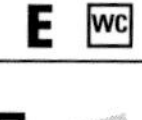

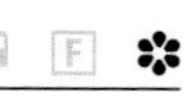

Parking:

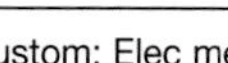

50; €31 — Custom; Elec metered

This campsite has 'Comfort' pitches with own water supply and disposal, but is more expensive than the other campsite in town, we suggest you check both before making a choice. There are warm thermal waters nearby which have outside pools and warm caves www.thermalgastein.com/www.gasteiner-heilstollen.com.

Activities and Facilities:

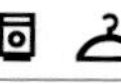

BAD GASTEIN

B4 | 37 | N47°08.623' E13°07.213' | 835m

Kur-camping Bertahof, Vorderschneeberg 5,
Bad Hofgastein
www.bertahof.at

Directions: The campsite is adjacent to the B167 3km north of Bad Gastein opposite the turning signposted to 'Bad Bruck (Badesee)'.

Sanitation:

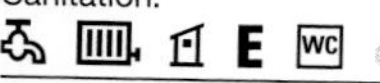

Parking:

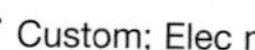

40 €30 — Custom; Elec metered

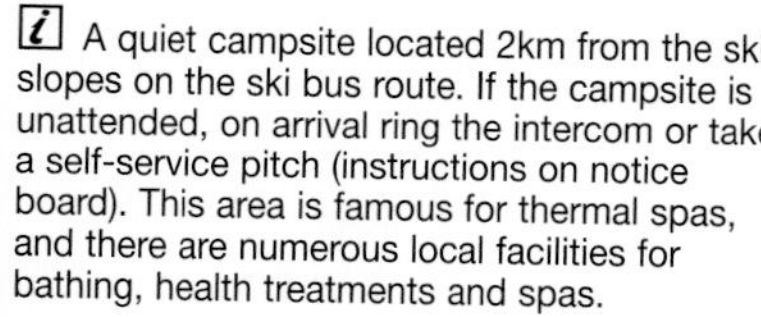

A quiet campsite located 2km from the ski slopes on the ski bus route. If the campsite is unattended, on arrival ring the intercom or take a self-service pitch (instructions on notice board). This area is famous for thermal spas, and there are numerous local facilities for bathing, health treatments and spas.

Activities and Facilities:

ST JOHANN IM PONGAU

B4 | 38 | N47°20.488' E13°11.889' | 843m

Camping Kastenhof, Kastenhofweg 6,
5600 Sankt Johann im Pongau
www.kastenhof.at

Directions: From the south on the B311, take the first turning to St Johann im Pongau. Travel 600m crossing the river and turn left. Take the next left into the campsite.

Sanitation:

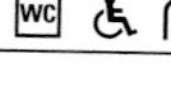

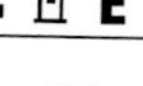

Parking:

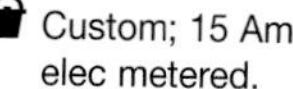

130; €29 — Custom; 15 Amp elec metered.

This is a large campsite in a quiet location convenient for ski bus to slopes. One of two campsites in the village, we recommend inspecting both before choosing. The historic old town is good for sightseeing, bars and, restaurants. Facilities onsite include free WiFi, a wellness centre and heated ski storage.

Activities and Facilities:

ST JOHANN IM PONGAU B4 39 N47°20.757' E13°11.533' 832m

Wieshof Camping, Wieshofgasse 8, Sankt Johann im Pongau
www.camping-wieshof.at

Directions: The campsite is adjacent to the B311, on the left if travelling north, on the southern edge of Sankt Johann Im Pongau.

Sanitation:

Parking:

70; €21 Custom; Elec metered €0.50; Showers €1

This site has generous, dry pitches, nicer views and is cheaper than other campsite in town but it suffers from road noise and is not so convenient for the ski bus. Their website has a useful links page and WiFi available onsite. The Liechtensteinklamm gorge walk may be worth visiting. www.liechtensteinklamm.at

Activities and Facilities:

PICHL A4 40 N47°23.386' E13°35.746' 807m

Camping Hotel Brunner, Gleiming 1, A8973, Pichl
www.hotel-reiteralm.at

Directions: Exit the E55/A10 junction 63 Ennstal onto the E651/B320 and travel east 16km.Turn right (1km before Pilch) to Gleiming/Forstau and the campsite is on the left in 100m.

Sanitation:

Parking:

50; €25 Custom; Elec metered €0.50

This pleasant family run campsite is located adjacent to the ski lifts connecting to the extensive 'Ski Amade' area, but people wanting nightlife you should stay at Schladming Campsite. Camping Hotel Brunner is highly recommended for skiers and the inspectors could not find fault with the site or the skiing! The campsite is attached to a hotel, which has a nice bar/restaurant and a clean toilet and shower block under the hotel, a key is provided.

Activities and Facilities:

RADSTADT

A4 | 41 | N47°23.245' E13°27.672' | 830m

Tauern Camping, A5550 Radstadt
www.tauerncamping.at

Directions: Exit the E55/A10 junction 63 Ennstal onto the E651 and travel east 4.3km. Take the exit toward Radstadt-West onto Salzburger Str, in 500m at the crossroads turn left onto Loretostr. Drive 300m, crossing over the E615, turn right onto Schlossstrasse, and drive 60m to the campsite. From the east, exit the E652 when it meets the B99 at Radstadt. Immediately turn sharp right then left onto Schlossstrasse follow this 500m to the campsite.

Sanitation:

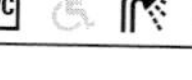

Parking:

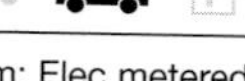

70; €25 — Custom; Elec metered €0.70 per kWh

Ideally situated, the campsite is an easy walk from the old centre of Radstadt and its castle. From spring to autumn you can go horse riding from the attached stables. The campsite is terraced making large vehicle access difficult. The ski bus stops outside the campsite taking skiers' the 2.5km to the Ski Amade slopes. The resort is crossed by walking, cycling and cross-country skiing trails.

Activities and Facilities:

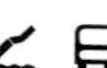

SCHLADMING

A4 | 42 | N47°23.910' E13°41.494' | 720m

Camping Gasthof Zirngast, Linke Ennsau 633, A-8970, Schladming www.zirngast.at

Directions: Traveling west from Liezen turn off the B320/E651 into Schladming at the first exit onto Coburgstrasse. At the roundabout turn right onto Langegasse and follow this road under the main road and across a river into Linke Ennsau. The campsite is on the right.

Sanitation:

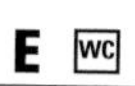

Parking:

50, €29 — Custom; Elec 4amp inc

The campsite is located 800m north of the village centre near the railway and is split either side of a quiet road. The bar, static homes and facilities are on one side, motorhomes on the other, so service motorhome before pitching. English is spoken, bottled gas is available, a swimming pool is nearby and a ski bus stops adjacent to site. The main gondola in village centre is part of the Ski Amade area. The local stellplatz has closed and 'no camping' signs have been erected.

Activities and Facilities:

Vicarious Books

ACSI DVD and Camping Card

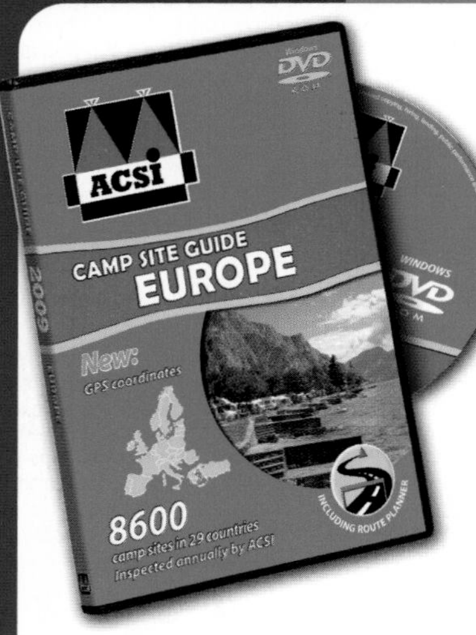

- Travelling with a Laptop? Leave Your Campsite Books Behind.
- 8600 Annually Inspected Campsites in 29 Countries.
- Seamless Mapping, for Planning and Navigation.
- GPS co-ordinates.
- Database Driven Campsite Selection. Wide Search Criteria.
- Buy Direct From The UK Agent.

only **£11.99** inc UK P&P

- Thousands of Discount Sites Across Europe.
- The Biggest Scheme Available.
- No Cheques, No Commitment.
- €11, €13 or €15 per night inc: 2 people, electric, a pet and showers.

2011 only **£11.99** inc UK P&P

Renewable Every January

To order, give us a call or visit our website to buy online.

0131 208 3333

www.VicariousBooks.co.uk

Driving in the Pyrenees

Arreau view from Col d'Aspin

FRANCE

Samöens

FRANCE

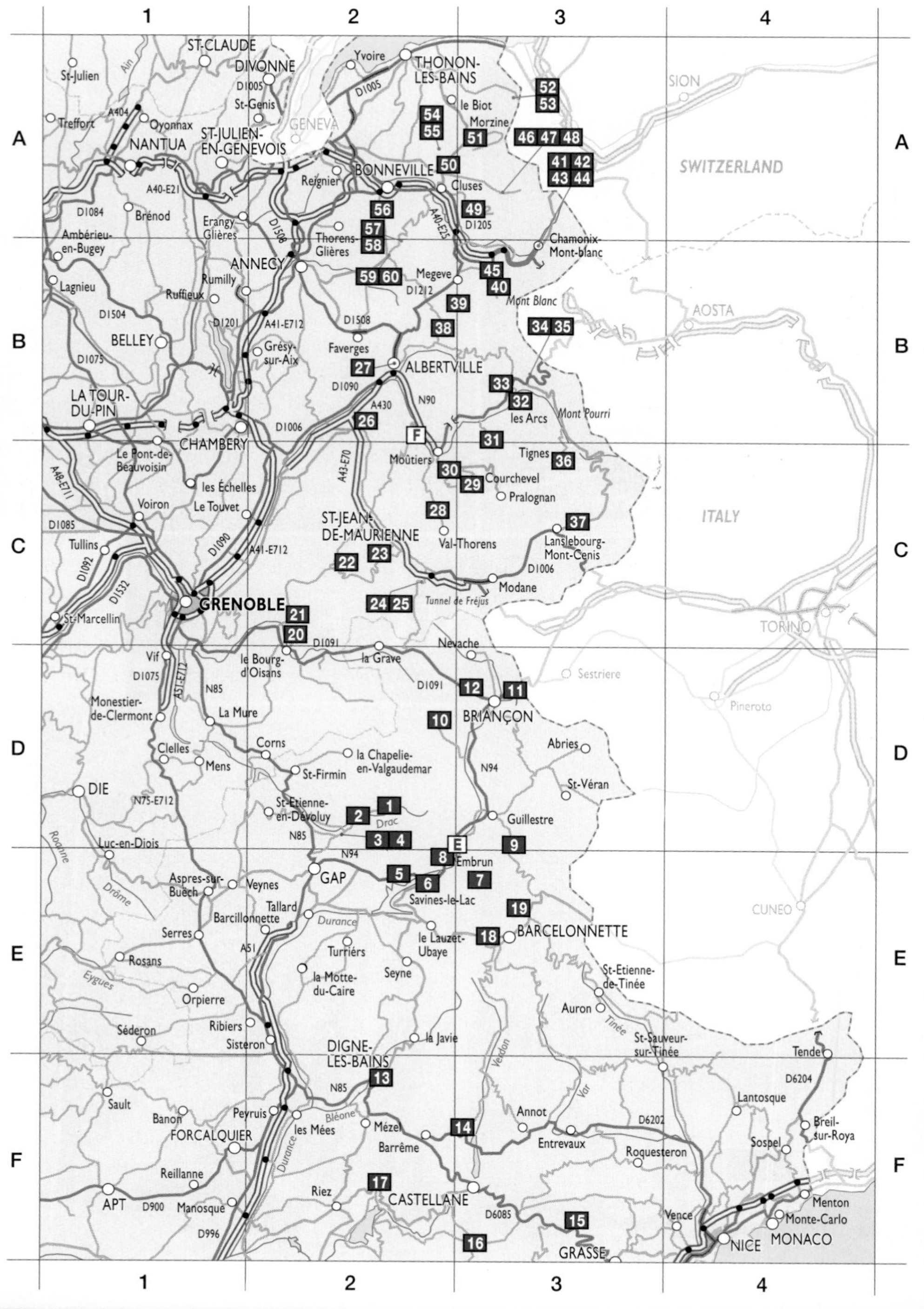
1
2
3
4
A
B
C
D
E
F
ST-CLAUDE
DIVONNE
THONON-LES-BAINS
Yvoire
SION
St-Julien
St-Genis
le Biot
Morzine
Treffort
Oyonnax
NANTUA
ST-JULIEN-EN-GENEVOIS
GENEVA
BONNEVILLE
Reignier
Cluses
SWITZERLAND
Brénod
Erangy Glières
Thorens-Glières
Chamonix-Mont-blanc
Ambérieu-en-Bugey
ANNECY
Megeve
Lagnieu
Rumilly
Ruffieux
Mont Blanc
AOSTA
BELLEY
Grésy-sur-Aix
Faverges
ALBERTVILLE
LA TOUR-DU-PIN
CHAMBERY
les Arcs
Mont Pourri
Le Pont-de-Beauvoisin
Moûtiers
Tignes
les Échelles
Courchevel
Pralognan
Voiron
Le Touvet
ST-JEAN-DE-MAURIENNE
Val-Thorens
Lanslebourg-Mont-Cenis
ITALY
Tullins
Modane
GRENOBLE
Tunnel de Fréjus
St-Marcellin
TORINO
Vif
le Bourg-d'Oisans
la Grave
Nevache
Sestriere
Monestier-de-Clermont
La Mure
BRIANÇON
Pinerolo
Corns
Clelles
Mens
St-Firmin
la Chapelie-en-Valgaudemar
Abries
St-Véran
DIE
St-Etienne-en-Dévoluy
Drac
Guillestre
Luc-en-Diois
Embrun
Aspres-sur-Buëch
Veynes
GAP
Savines-le-Lac
Tallard
Barcillonnette
Durance
CUNEO
Serres
le Lauzet-Ubaye
BARCELONNETTE
Rosans
Turriers
Seyne
la Motte-du-Caire
Eygues
St-Etienne-de-Tinée
Orpierre
Auron
Séderon
Ribiers
Sisteron
la Javie
DIGNE-LES-BAINS
Verdon
Tinée
St-Sauveur-sur-Tinée
Tende
Sault
Peyruis
Bléone
Annot
Lantosque
Banon
FORCALQUIER
les Mées
Mézel
Barrême
Entrevaux
Var
Breil-sur-Roya
Sospel
Roquesteron
Reillanne
APT
Manosque
Riez
CASTELLANE
Menton
Vence
Monte-Carlo
NICE
MONACO
GRASSE
Drôme
Rogne
A404
A40-E21
D1084
D1005
D1508
D1205
A40-E25
D1212
D1504
D1201
A41-E712
D1075
D1090
A430
N90
D1006
A43-E70
A48-E711
D1085
D1092
D1532
D1091
N85
A51-E712
N94
N75-E712
A51
D6204
D6202
D6085
D900
D996
1
2
3
4
5
6
7
8
9
10
11
12
13
14
15
16
17
18
19
20
21
22
23
24
25
26
27
28
29
30
31
32
33
34
35
36
37
38
39
40
41
42
43
44
45
46
47
48
49
50
51
52
53
54
55
56
57
58
59
60
E
F

French mountains offer something for everyone, lazy days in Provence lavender fields or skiing the Alps pistes or mountain biking along Pyrenean trails. The French Alps are the nearest alpine slopes to the UK and it is very easy to get to the ski slopes by road. The French Pyrenees are slightly further away but they are quieter, cheaper and make an ideal stop off en-route to Spain.

Driving and Roads

The French Alps and its ski resorts are one day's drive from Calais, if you use the quiet, but tolled, French motorways. When driving along narrow mountain lanes French driving etiquette is to give-way to traffic travelling uphill, this includes pulling over and reversing if necessary. The French Highway Code requires the sounding of horns on twisting roads with reduced visibility. The editors prevented a head on collision with an unseen truck by sounding their horn on a sunny drive in the Alps. The Michelin France Tourist and Motoring Atlas highlights difficult or dangerous sections of roads; motorhome and caravan towers should avoid these routes. High passes may be closed during winter and spring due to snow, drifts, or wind. Never drive down a route signed 'Route Barre' or 'Ferme' or open gates used to close off roads.

Mountain Biking

The French are very keen on cycling in the mountains, both on and off road. Often there are more spectators than there are riders; even for a minor race. During the Tour de France, it seems that every Camping Car in France is lining the mountain stages. See www.letour.fr. There are race stages through the Pyrenees and Alps but the route changes each year so ensure you have the current stage plan before camping out in the mountains.

Most resorts in both the Alps and the Pyrenees open for mountain biking during the summer, and the ski lifts are often running and carrying bikes to the summit. Servicing your bike's brakes before you visit the mountains is highly recommended. Trails can be on cross-country skiing tracks or forest roads, look for routes marked VTT or FCC and visit the Tourist Office to obtain routes, maps and confirm which lifts are open.

Walking

There are 180,000km of hiking and walking routes in France. There are three different classifications: Long distance routes are marked with red and white lines; circular walks are marked with red and yellow lines and short walks are marked with a single yellow line. If you have not planned your walk in advance the first trip should be to the local Tourist Office, which should have maps and walking leaflets. Many resorts also have orienteering courses for you to navigate your way to check points. Chamrousse has six Courses d'Orientation, you can purchase maps from the Tourist Office, and you will need a compass. As well as making the walk more interesting, it helps in improving or hones your navigation skills, an essential skill in the mountains. The Pyrenees has some fantastic walks including the Gorges de la Caranca, with suspension bridges for a little more excitement. Walk around the Cirque de Gavarnie to the largest waterfall in Europe and there are numerous walks from Pont d'Espagne.

Spas and Thermal water

Spas are big business in France with around 50 Spa resorts. The spa town Bareges at 1250m claims to have the highest thermal baths in France. The Pyrenees have plenty of spa towns. Bains de Dorres has municipal thermal pools with a €4 entrance fee; some of the pools were carved in the 1800s. Even with all the commercialism, there are still opportunities to enjoy naturally occurring hot water without the Spa complex so look on your maps for the thermal water symbol.

Skiing in France

France has two mountain ranges with ski resorts, the larger, busier, and more popular Alps, and the quieter, smaller, cheaper Pyrenees.

The Alps: The Alps offer something for everyone, all year round!

The Three Valleys (which consists of four Valleys) includes the resorts of Les Menuires, St Martin de Belleville, Val Thorens (the highest ski area in the Alps), Meribel, Brides-les-Bains, La Tania and the exclusive resort Courchevel. The resorts are interlinked and offer excellent skiing for all abilities.

The Portes du Soleil area links to Swiss ski resorts and competes with the Three Valleys to be the biggest ski area in the world. The main resorts on the French side are Avoriaz, Chatel, Morzine and Les Gets. Motorhomers will find they can ski back to the van at some resorts, but these are often the busiest parking areas. Researcher Andy Glasgow states 'tolerance, patience and firm diplomacy are required' and that is just in the car park!

The famous resort of Chamonix in the foothills of Mont Blanc is actually a group of resorts including Le Tour, Argentiere, Les Praz, Chamonix and Les Houches. The skiing is suited to adventurous intermediates and people seeking unbeatable off-piste touring. Unfortunately, the ski areas are not linked and getting around on the ski bus is quite involved, so be prepared to drive to your chosen slopes each day from your chosen base. Beginner skiers should head to Alpe d'Huez resort with its wide range of beginner slopes. Two beginner resorts are Sommand and Le Praz de Lys, they lie two sides of a resort but separated by a snow bound mountain pass. Absolute

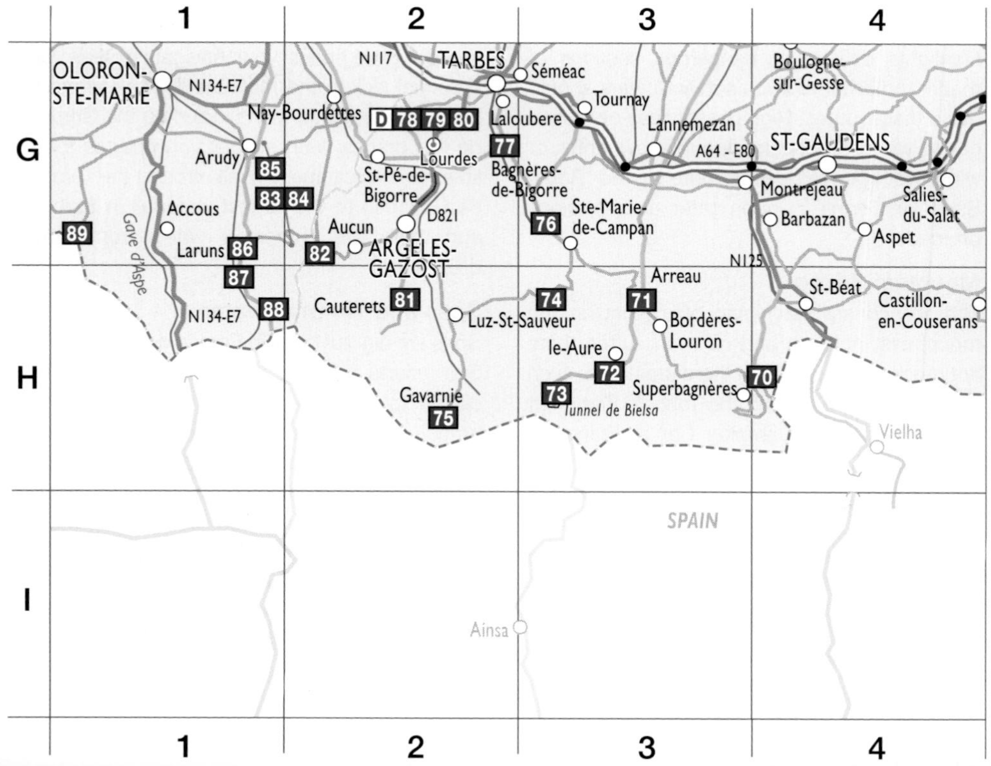

beginners should go to Vars Les Claux where there is a free lift adjacent to the motorhome parking area.

In summer it is possible to ski on the glaciers at L'Alpe-d'Huez, Les Deux-Alps, La Plagne, Tignes, Val d'Isere, Val-Thorens. The opening dates vary each year so check at your chosen resort before arrival.

The Pyrenees: For a different skiing experience, try the Pyrenees, the ski resorts are smaller than in the Alps but the slopes will be quiet during the week. Most resorts are not serviced by British tour operators and are not frequented by school parties.

Pyrenean skiing suits independent, intermediate skiers looking for somewhere unusual or quiet, adrenalin junkies are not going to challenge themselves on the slopes. For a variety of skiing head to Bareges and La Mongie which have 100km of slopes between them. Beginners should head to Cauterets and Font Romeu. Cross-country skiers should head to Cauterets and get the bus to Pont d'Espagne, there are 36km of cross-country trails on a former smugglers route with stunning scenery through the mountains to Spain.

The French are very keen for everyone to ski and most resorts have a traditional ski school with guides but many also have facilities for disabled skiers and these are in the Handiski scheme. These resorts have been assessed and have lifts suitable for disabled skiers as well as special equipment and trained guides. More information is available through the French ski school, www.esf.net

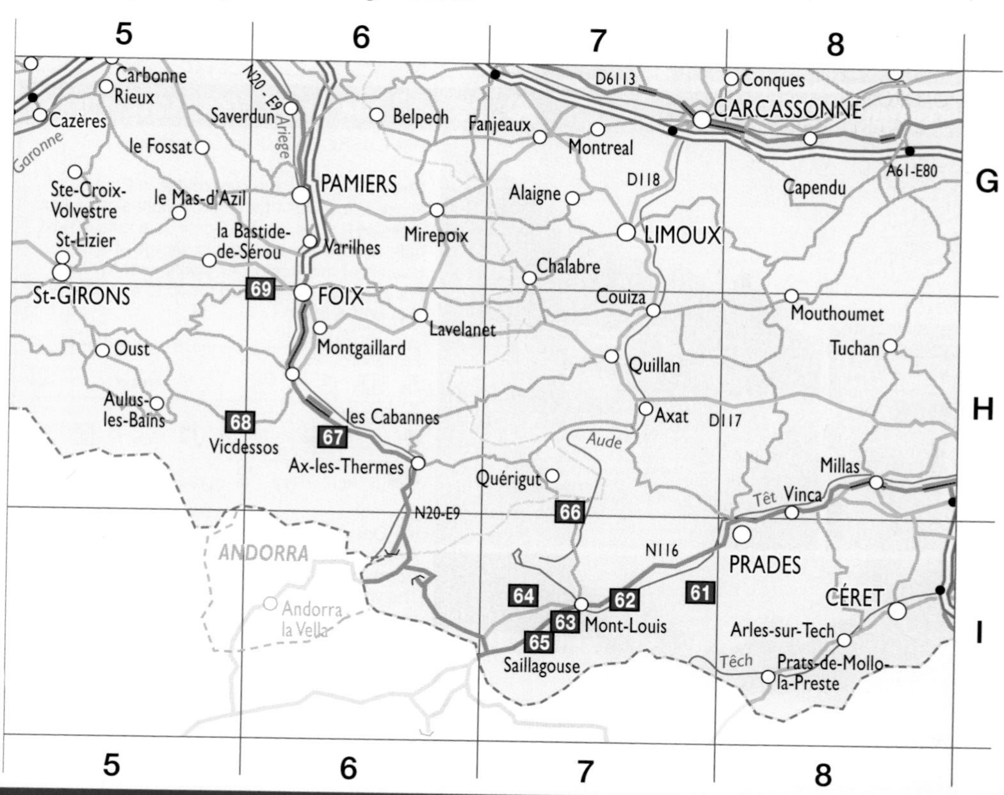

ORCIERES D2 1 N44°41.704' E006°19.562' 1850m

Parking P2 Casse Blanche - Orcières 1850

Directions: Turn off the D944/D475 into Orcieres. Follow sp 'P2 Casse Blanche'. The Aire is on top of a multi-storey car park.

Sanitation:

Parking:

 24; €12 per day

 Raclet; Included; CC or cash to warden

Very tight access to Aire located on dramatic top-level car park. Motorhomers with adventurous kids or sufferers of vertigo should take care! If full, go to St Leger, 6km. Built in the 1960s the ski complex is right in the middle of the beautiful Parc National D'Ecrins. The Aire and ski area is very popular and many motorhomers stay for a week. www.orcieres.com

Activities and Facilities:

PONT DU FOSSE D2 2 N44°40.200' E006°14.317' 1100m

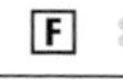

D944, 05260 Saint-Jean-Saint-Nicolas

Directions: From the river bridge in Pont du Fosse follow D944 for 900m. Ignore sign to Aire crossing 3.5 ton bridge. Continue and take next right turn adjacent to Toyota garage (the GPS given is at this turning for clarity as the road is not on GPS). Follow road round to right and Aire is at end in 500m.

Sanitation:

Parking:

5; April - Nov   Euro Relais; April - Nov

Open April - Nov, this is a useful summer Aire in woodland setting. Located in an old campsite adjacent to river, prone to flooding. The village is in the very centre of Parc National des Ecrins, www.valgaudemar.com, France's largest National Park with over 1000km of footpaths and central to small but excellent nearby ski areas.

Activities and Facilities:

ST-LEGER-LES-MELEZES D2 3 N44°38.526' E006°11.853' 1320m

Route d'Ancelle, 05260

Directions: D13. Exit St Leger southwest on the D13 towards Ancelle and the parking is on the left adjacent to the D13 at the ski lift, 400m from town centre.

Sanitation:

Parking:

10; Day parking None; WC next to office

This is not an Aire but a small, friendly ski resort only 10 minutes away from busy and usually full Orcieres Aire. Motorhomers have been welcome to stay overnight on the slope side car park in a dramatic valley setting. There is also a nice café and local bar. Great sledging. Service point available at campsite 'La Pause' for €5. www.st-leger05.fr

Activities and Facilities:

ST-LEGER-LES-MELEZES D2 4 N44°38.720' E006°12.288' 1340m

Camping La Pause, Route du Barry, 05260
Saint-Léger-les-Mélèze
www.camping-la-pause.com

Directions: From the roundabout in the centre of St Leger, head east onto Route du Barry and the campsite is 400m on the right.

Sanitation:

Parking:

28; €16 Service only €5; Elec €1 per amp

This is a small campsite/caravaneige and it is possible to service your motorhome here if you do not wish to stay the night. There is a spa room with Jacuzzi available for rent from €20 for 1/2 hour and a restaurant onsite. For local Tourist Information, see www.st-leger05.fr Chairlifts and snow cannons servicing the slopes.

Activities and Facilities:

Library image: S. Pirnie

CHORGES

E2 | 5 | N44°32.750' E006°16.800' 880m

Chemin La Butte, 05230 Chorges

Directions: From southeast on D94 turn right sp 'Chorges'. Signed. After 800m turn right into Place du Champ de Foire. Continue between Gendarmerie & Salle des Fetes. Aire on right in 150m.

Sanitation:

Parking:

20; 12hrs None

This area is very popular with mountain bikers and the Aire is adjacent to a BMX park. Follow the picturesque D9 towards Reallon for 15km and turn left at the roundabout to the ski resort ZAC Pra Prunier. In summer the lifts take visitors to a viewpoint and walkers and mountain bikers to the start of their trails. The huge local lake, Lac de Serre-Poncon, has a variety of water sports available in the summer.

Activities and Facilities:

Photos: Peter Gordon

SAVINES-LE-LAC

E2 | 6 | N44°31.483' E006°24.033' 800m

D954, 05160 Savines-le-Lac

Directions: The Aire is on the west side of the village beside the D954, Avenue Faubourg, signposted 'P' camping cars on entering the village.

Sanitation:

Parking:

17; €7 inc elec 12 noon - 12 noon; Pay at machine

Custom; €2

Located 100m from the lake and the modern village with Tourist Information centre. The old village was flooded during the making of one of the largest reservoirs in Europe. It takes half a day to drive around the lake. There is a municipal beach in the village (water was freezing in the summer!) and boat trips are available on the lake. The Rellion ski resort ZAC Pra Prunier is 13km north. In summer the lifts take visitors to a viewpoint and walkers and mountain bikers to the start of their trails.

Activities and Facilities:

Photos: Kev Hardwick

LES ORRES

E3 | 7 | N44°30.010' E006°33.371' 1564m

D40, 05200 Les Orres

Directions: Parking Champ Lacas. From Embrun, take the D40 through Les Orres to Le Melezet. The Aire is alongside the D40, well signed and located at the bottom of chairlift/ticket office on gravel parking area. Park in bottom car park as you will be moved from the top car park.

Sanitation:

Parking:

20 — Flot Bleu; €3; Showers available from Tourist Office at cost.

This is a small ski/summer walking resort with little nightlife. The adjacent 'Salle de Hors Sacs' is a common room with microwave, sinks, snack bar, information point and costs €1.50 a day. The north facing red runs hold surprises for unawares skiers. www.lesorres.com

Photos: Peter Gordon

Activities and Facilities:

EMBRUN

E2 | 8 | N44°32.757' E006°28.917' 780m

N94, 05200 Baratier

Directions: N94. Located at the east end of Lac de Serre-Poncon lake, adjacent to the N94 just South of Embrun when travelling towards Crots, just past the D40 roundabout, at the Intermarche Supermarket.

Sanitation:

Parking:

20 — Flot Bleu Pacific; €2

This Aire is central to all local ski resorts because it is at an Intermarche Supermarket and Bricolarge (DIY store). It is an ideal place to stock up but it is alongside a busy main road and there is no need to stop overnight. It also has LPG, and free WiFi at McDonalds - just log on. Laundrette onsite near fuel station.

Activities and Facilities:

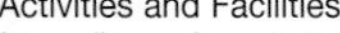

VARS LES CLAUX

D3 | 9 | N44°34.534' E006°40.675' 1600m

Allee trub, 05560 Vars

Directions: D902. Car park No5. Turn off the D902 in Vars les Claux by the Tourist Office and ski lift sp 'P5' and signed. Follow road to the top of the resort to P5.

Sanitation:

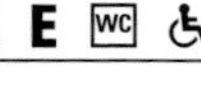  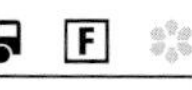

Parking:

  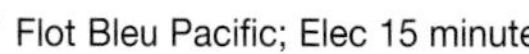

50 Flot Bleu Pacific; Elec 15 minutes

This is an excellent large Aire where there is always space. There is slope side access from the Aire so you can ski to and from your van and the adjacent 200m chairlift is free and ideal for beginners. You can also access the up and coming Vars/Risoul ski area. 1 hr free WiFi at Tourist Office in village centre. www.vars-ski.com

Activities and Facilities:

PUY ST VINCENT

D2 | 10 | N44°49.187' E006°29.198' 1600m

D804, 05290 Puy St Vincent

Directions: D804. Turn off the D4 in Puy St Vincent to 1600 Station. The Aire is next to the snowplough garage at 1600 station and five minutes to Ski Station.

Sanitation:

Parking:

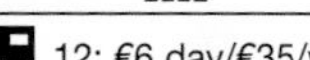 

12; €6 day/€35/week; Max 2 weeks

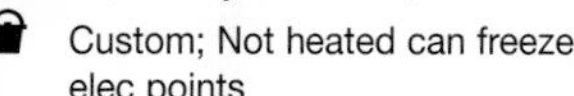

Custom; Not heated can freeze; 10 6amp elec points

A nice French family ski/summer walking resort in Ecrins Nature Park, with stunning views. Although busy during holidays, it is quieter than Montgenevre. The snowplough driver will dig you a space if needed! An easy walk uphill brings you to the centre with shops, bars, and ski lifts. The skiing has something for everyone. www.puysaintvincent.com

Activities and Facilities:

MONTGENEVRE

D3 | 11 | N44°56.074' E006°44.185' 1860m

Photo: Peter Gordon

N94, 05100 Col de Montgenèvre

Directions: N94. Head through Montgenèvre on the N94 towards Italy (1.5 km). The large purpose built Aire is 500m out of town, and well signed in town. Snow chains needed for Col du Lautaret if coming from Grenoble but also accessible via Frejus tunnel.

Sanitation:

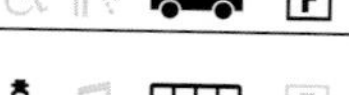

Parking:

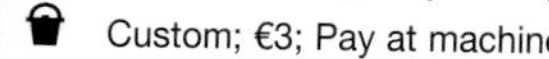

280; €10 per 24hrs inc 10 amp elec; Decreases daily; Pay on departure

Custom; €3; Pay at machine

The Aire is located on a snow prone pass and the Aire suffers huge snowdrifts but is busy at weekends, often full of Italian campers. The ski slopes are 100m and there is a ski bus. The skiing is fantastic with links to Italy and the Milky Way. The long red run down to Italy (and lunch) via Rocher de l'Aigle is highly recommended. A good walking resort during summer.

Activities and Facilities:

LA SALLE-LES-ALPES

D3 | 12 | N44°56.890' E006°33.334' 1400m

Photo: Peter Gordon

Chemin des Preras, 05240 La Salle-les-Alpes

Directions: In the Serre Chevalier ski area at Serre-Chevalier 1400. From the D1091 follow sp 'P Pontillas'. The Aire is at the ski lift Pontillas adjacent to the roundabout and a pond near the river. The service point is silver and visible from the roundabout. Parking is through the barrier, barrier card available from the Tourist Office.

Sanitation:

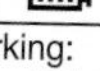

Parking:

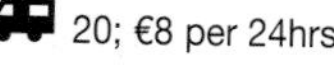
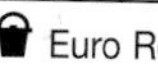

20; €8 per 24hrs — Euro Relais

The Aire is located at the bottom of the ski lift; some parking is beside the swimming pond. Of the four resorts in the area, this is the best one for snow boarders as there is a snow park and half pike. Many of the slopes are in sheltered woodland. The Aire is close enough to walk into town for supplies and nightlife. There is a local tennis club and riding stables. www.serre-chevalier.com

Activities and Facilities:

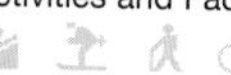

DIGNE-LES-BAINS

F2 13 N44°04.796' E006°15.637' 680m

D20, 04000 Digne-les-Bains

Directions: Ave des Thermes. From the N1085 turn off sp 'Les Thermes'. Follow the signs for 'Camping Les Eaux Chaudes' on D20 approx 3km from town. The Aire is near the thermes.

Sanitation:

Parking:

30 Euro Relais Junior; Token €2.50

This spa town is 'the capital of lavender' and the Aire is located 3km out of town adjacent to thermal baths. The sulphurous waters are accessible via Societe and there is a 35° swimming pool. www.thermesdignelesbains.com. The town has a fair in September celebrating the locally grown lavender. www.ot-dignelesbains.fr. Pleasant riverside 3km walk to town.

Activities and Facilities:

ST-ANDRE-LES-ALPES

F2 14 N43°57.921' E006°30.489' 1000m

Grand Rue, 04170 Saint-André-les-Alpes

Directions: Approaching St-André-les-Alpes on the N202 from the south, at the Gamm Vert roundabout take second exit signed 'Aire de Stationment'. The Aire is on the left in 100m, signed. The Aire is visible when driving through town.

Sanitation:

Parking:

20 Flot Bleu; €3; Tokens or CC

This is a large tarmac motorhome parking area in the village centre. St Andre les Alpes is on the route of the Train Provence, www.trainprovence.com, which winds through Provence from Nice to Digne Les Bains. The train runs four times a day and there are stops every 3 - 5km making it ideal for walking between stations. www.ot-st-andre-les-alpes.fr

Photo: motorhomeandaway.co.uk

Activities and Facilities:

CAILLE

F3 | 15 | N43°46.733' E006°43.997' 1140m

Photo: Ruth Grant

Rue St Pons, 06750 Caille

Directions: Turn off D6085 onto D79 sp 'Caille' and signed. Follow the road for 5km to Caille. At Caille, turn into the village sp 'Centre Ville' and drive through which is narrow in places. The Aire is adjacent to the road as you exit the village to the east.

Sanitation:

Parking:

3 Flot Bleu; €4

The Aire is in a pretty spot on the outskirts of this small village that has two restaurants and local shops. The D4085 is known as Route Napoleon, marked with flying Eagle symbol, and follows the Route that Napoleon took in 1815 on his return from exile to retake power.

Activities and Facilities:

COMPS-SUR-ARTUBY

F3 | 16 | N43°42.375' E006°30.392' 900m

Photo: Daren Fasey

D955, 83840 Comps-sur-Artuby

Directions: D955. Travel 400m south of Comps-Sur-Artuby on the D955 and the Aire is alongside the sharp bend in the road

Sanitation:

Parking:

19; 24hrs Custom; €3; Token from Pizzeria.

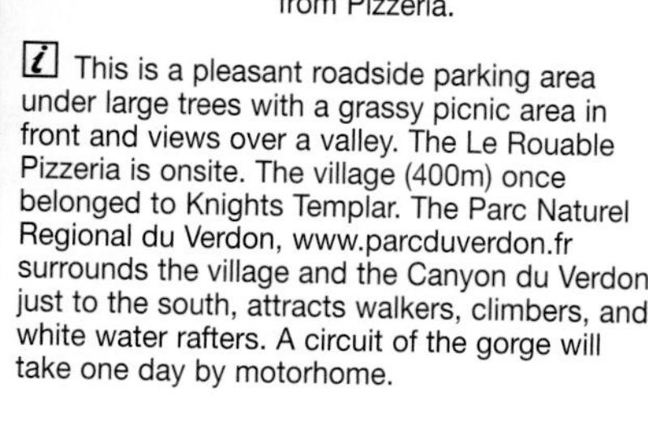

This is a pleasant roadside parking area under large trees with a grassy picnic area in front and views over a valley. The Le Rouable Pizzeria is onsite. The village (400m) once belonged to Knights Templar. The Parc Naturel Regional du Verdon, www.parcduverdon.fr surrounds the village and the Canyon du Verdon just to the south, attracts walkers, climbers, and white water rafters. A circuit of the gorge will take one day by motorhome.

Activities and Facilities:

MOUSTIERS STE MARIE

F2 | 17 | N43°50.597' E006°13.124' 600m

Photo: [illegible] Fasey

Chemin de Quinson, 04360 Moustiers-Sainte-Marie

Directions: D952. Between Camping Saint Jean; www.camping-st-jean.fr and Camping Le Vieux Colombier; www.lvcm.fr on the D952 just below Moustiers signed parking 5. New barriered entrance being installed.

Sanitation:

Parking:

30; €6 — Urba Flux; €2 coins

The Aire is just off the D952 in a wide-open valley and it is a lovely walk up into the lovely village with 360° views. The Parc Naturel Regional du Verdon, www.parcduverdon.fr surrounds the village and the Canyon du Verdon, just to the south attracts walkers, climber's and white water rafters. A circuit of the gorge will take one day by motorhome. A shuttle bus service runs in summer and a bus stop is beside D952. Walkers should visit tourist information before planning their routes.

Activities and Facilities:

PRA LOUP 1600

E3 | 18 | N44°22.054' E006°36.367' 1530m

D109, 04400 Uvernet-Fours

Directions: D109. From Barcelonnette take the D902 then the D908. Turn off the D908 to Pra Loup. The Aire is adjacent to the road just before entering Pra Loup next to the bottom gondola station 'Choupettes'.

Sanitation:

E

F

Parking:

F

20 — Flot Bleu; €3 for 15 minutes

This is a 1960s style resort with little charm but has good skiing. There is a free bus/ski lift adjacent to Aire. www.praloup.com. The resort housed the MTB European Championships and has a program of developing mountain bike trails. The gondolas take bikes up on the mountains. There is a local golf course.

Activities and Facilities:

JAUSIERS

 E3 19 N44°24.757' E006°43.745' 1200m

Photo: motorhomeandaway.co.uk

D900, 04850 Jausiers

Directions: On D900 Aire adjacent to D900 as enter village from Barcelonnette.

Sanitation:

Parking:

 4 Flot Bleu; CC; €3 for 15 minutes

This is a small parking area on the outskirts of the village adjacent to main road and river. You can cross the border to Italy via Col de Larche on D900. In summer, you can travel the scenic D64, Route de la Bonette from Jausiers through the Parc National du Mercantour to Nice. This is the highest road in France, and the second highest in Europe, but snow blocks the route between Nov - June. The road is narrow in places and requires confident driving.

Activities and Facilities:

ALPE D'HUEZ

 C2 20 N45°05.204' E006°04.750' 1860m

Route de l'Altiport, 38750 Alpe d'Huez

Directions: Parking des Brandes. Approach Alpe d'Huez on the D211, turning right sp 'Station Entree Est'. At the roundabout turn off sp 'Les Bergers' and 'Site archeologique de Brandes' onto Route de l'Altiport. Turn right sp 'Site archeologique de Brandes', and the Aire is signed to the right on the wall of Parking des Brandes. Follow this road to the car park, at the end of the runway.

Sanitation:

  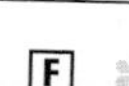

Parking:

 50; €10.40 per 24hrs; CC  Raclet

The Aire is in the village of Alpe d'Huez which has a large ski area with plenty of beginner green runs. More challenging runs are accessible via the ski lifts that pass over the village. Numerous summer walks start from the resort. Cyclists can enjoy mountain biking or ride the testing 21 hairpin bends of the Tour de France which has finished at the resort nearly every year since 1976. In spring and autumn, the resort is quiet with many facilities closed or operating reduced hours. www.alpedhuez.com

Activities and Facilities:

VAUJANY

C2 | 21 | N45°09.410' E006°04.803' 1250m

D43a, 38114 Vaujany

Directions: Turn right off the D43a as you approach Vaujany and follow road towards Espace Loisirs. The Aire is up this road in 100m.

Sanitation:

Parking:

10 Euro Relais Mini; Elec €5

In Alpe d'Huez ski area with plenty of ski lifts adjacent. The Vaujany side of the resort offers varied skiing. Across the mountain, Alpe d'Huez offers a wide range of beginner green runs. In summer walkers can use the cable cars to enhance their journeys taking in fantastic views whilst cyclists can enjoy mountain biking. www.alpedhuez.com

Activities and Facilities:

LA TOUSSUIRE

C2 | 22 | N45°15.453' E006°16.424' 1624m

Camping-Caravaneige du Col, D78, 73300 Fontcouverte-la-Toussuire
www.camping-du-col.com

Directions: D78. From St Jean de Maurienne take the D926 towards St Jean d'Arves. Turn off onto the D78 to Fontcouverte La Toussuire and follow the D78 on a scenic climb up to La Toussuire. The campsite is adjacent to the D78 before you enter the village.

Sanitation:

Parking:

40; €19; 10/6 - 1/9 15/12 - 22/4

Custom; Inc

This is a friendly campsite with a small pool open in summer. A ski bus stops outside the entrance. The skiing is spread around several undiscovered resorts so service is polite and food is reasonably priced in the mountainside restaurants. www.les-sybelles.com

Activities and Facilities:

ST-JEAN-DE-MAURIENNE C2 23 N45°16.769' E006°20.849' 580m

Photo: Peter Gordon

Place du Champ de Foire, 73300 Saint-Jean-de-Maurienne

Directions: Place du Champ de Foire. Heading south from La Chambre (E70 junction 27) enter town on the D906. At the roundabout, once you have entered town turn left sp 'Toutes Directions' 'Gare S.N.C.F'. At the next roundabout turn left sp 'A.N.P.E' and 'Centre de Secours'. Take the next left by the zebra crossing into the car park.

Sanitation:

Parking:

10 Flot Bleu; €4; 2 x €2 coins

The Aire is five minutes walk from the pleasant mountain town with all necessary facilities. A Hyper Casino is two minutes walk so this is an ideal place to stop and stock up before visiting the local slopes in winter, or when driving the D926 scenic route in summer. The car park is used for other things, such as fairs.

Activities and Facilities:

VALLOIRE C2 24 N45°10.179' E006°25.800' 1385m

Library image: S. Pirnie

Camping Ste Thecle, Route des Villards, 73450 Valloire
www.valloire.net

Directions: In Valloire follow the D902 one-way system and sp 'Mairie Eglise' 'Autres Directions'. Next to the church on the one-way system turn left sp 'Camping'. Follow this road out of town north, cross over the river and the campsite is adjacent to the river on the other side opposite the tennis courts.

Sanitation:

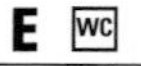

Parking:

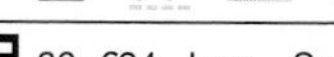
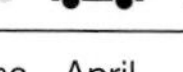

80; €24; June - Sept, Dec - April

Custom

This is an excellent mid-priced campsite. Old buildings and churches dominate the village centre with lovely bars. A mini train links the campsite to the town (5 minutes walk) and all the chairlifts. The skiing is wide ranging and stretches over several peaks surrounding the village. www.galibier-thabor.com

Activities and Facilities:

VALLOIRE

C2 | 25 | N45°10.179' E006°25.800' 1385m

Route des Villards, 73450 Valloire

Directions: From the D902 follow the one-way system and sp 'Mairie Eglise' 'Autres Directions'. Next to the church on the one-way system, turn left sp 'Camping'. Follow this road heading north out of town and cross over the river and the campsite is adjacent to the river on the other side opposite the tennis courts. The service point is outside the campsite.

Sanitation:

Parking:

None — Custom

Excellent free service point but parking in centre is vague.

Activities and Facilities:

AIGUEBELLE

B2 | 26 | N45°32.625' E006°18.327' 400m

Rue des Ecoles, 73220 Aiguebelle

Directions: From the A43/E70 take exit 24 and drive on the D1006 into the centre of Aiguebelle and turn left into Rue Carret between the supermarket and Tourist Office. The Aire is at Place du Champ de Foire, near the railway station and park.

Sanitation:

Parking:

Grass parking in summer — Custom

Tuesday is market day, it's best to arrive after 2pm. Facilities in town a bit limited but adequate for a short stay and ideal in winter to stop and restock before heading to the ski resorts. There is noise from the railway all night.

Photo: Peter Gordon

Activities and Facilities:

ALBERTVILLE

B2 | 27 | N45°40.443' E006°23.828' 400m

Photo: Charlie and Angie Anderson

Montée Adolphe Hugues, 73200 Albertville

Directions: D105. From the north turn off D1212 at the roundabout sp 'Albertville'. Turn left onto D105 sp 'Venthon'. Cross over the river, and continue up hill on the D105 to Venthon. The Aire is in a car park on right, opposite the cemetery on outskirts of town. It is well signed, Flot Bleu, from main road.

Sanitation:

Parking:

6; 24hrs   Flot Bleu; €3.50; CC

The Aire is five minutes from town and Conflans, a medieval town worth a visit, is five minutes further up the road. Albertville hosted the opening and closing ceremonies of the 1992 winter Olympics, and has a museum dedicated to the event. www.albertville.com

Activities and Facilities:

LES MENUIRES

C2 | 28 | N45°18.900' E006°32.367' 1760m

D117, 73440 Saint-Martin-de-Belleville

Directions: D117. Follow D117 through valley towards Val Thorens. The Aire is on left side as you drive up valley in the resort of Les Menuires below 'Les Bruyeres' hotel. The Aire has moved 200m along road at 'Preyerand'.

Sanitation:

   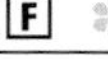

Parking:

 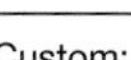 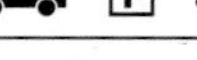 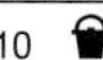 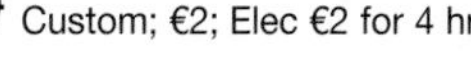

40; €10   Custom; €2; Elec €2 for 4 hrs

A good popular Aire that is busy during holidays. This is the most popular choice for motorhomers in the three valleys and the easily reached resort of Val Thorens is both high and excellent. Hopefully the new position of the Aire will mean that more spaces are available. Pay credit card on exit.

Activities and Facilities:

LA TANIA-COURCHEVEL

C3 | 29 | N45°25.895' E006°36.030' 1350m

Photo: Peter Gordon

D98, 73600 La Perrière

Directions: D98. From Moutiers take the D915 turning off onto the D91A towards Courchevel. After St Bon Tarentaise turn off onto the D98 to La Tania. At the roundabout, past the ski jump, turn left. The Aire is 100m uphill from the Flot Bleu service point (N45°25.932'E006°35.736').

Sanitation:

Parking:

6 Flot Bleu; €2; Below Aire

This is a nice family resort with excellent links to Meribel/Courchevel. The Aire is 100m from the village and is often full with long-term skiers' motorhomes. The large adjacent car park is also the ski bus terminal to other local resorts.

Activities and Facilities:

LE PRAZ – COURCHEVEL

C2 | 30 | N45°25.831' E006°37.485' 1300m

Photo: Colin Read

S. Pirnie

D91a, 73120 Saint-Bon-Tarentaise

Directions: D91A. From Moutiers take the D915 and then the D91A. Pass through village of Le Praz on D91a towards Courchevel. The Aire is on left in parking Jean Blanc, just after bend leaving village. The Flot Bleu is near the entrance to extensive parking amongst cars.

Sanitation:

Parking:

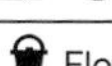

 20  Flot Bleu; €3; coins

This is a large level car park, 250m from the village. There are fine views and you can ski in and out down to main lifts in village, which has excellent links to Courchevel/Meribel.

Activities and Facilities:

LE PLAGNE

B3 | 31 | N45°30.392' E006°41.205' 2000m

S. Pirnie

D223, 73210 Mâcot-la-Plagne

Directions: D220. From Aime take the D220 to La Plagne. Pass the service point on the left (N45°30.543'E006°40.824'), and the Aire is 500m higher up in the car park.

Sanitation:

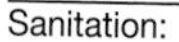

Parking:

40   Flot Bleu; 3 x €0.50

This is a nice ski Aire next to slopes, the Ticket Office is 100m away. The skiing is ideal for intermediates and there are links to Les Arcs when open. Spar supermarket 100m via the main entrance.

Activities and Facilities:

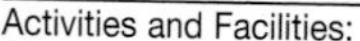

LES ARCS

B3 | 32 | N45°35.795' E006°47.520' 1600m

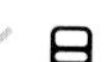

D119, 73700 Les Arcs

Directions: D119. From Bourg St Maurice take the D119 and follow sp 'Les Arcs 1600'. The Aire is in a large car park adjacent to the road, signed.

Sanitation:

Parking:

10   Flot Bleu

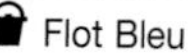

There are views of Mont Blanc from the Aire and a free ski bus runs between Arc 1600, Arc 1800, Arc 1950 and Arc 2000. Snow cannons guarantee the return to Arc 1600 and there are 30 shops in the resort. There is tolerated parking at the base of Pre St-Esprit ski lift. www.lesarcs.com

Activities and Facilities:

BOURG ST MAURICE

B3 | 33 | N45°37.311' E006°47.012' 800m

Camping Le Versoyen, Route Les Arcs, 73700, Bourg St Maurice
www.leversoyen.com

Directions: D119. Exit Bourg St Maurice on the D119, Route to Les Arcs, and the campsite is in 300m on the right.

Sanitation:

Parking:

26; €19

Custom; Elec €6 6amps or €8 10amps

This is an excellent winter campsite and is popular with skiers some staying all season. It is located 100m from Super U and Intermarche (LPG) supermarkets and there is a swimming pool next door and WiFi onsite. There is a free shuttle bus to funicular and ski passes can be purchased at the campsite.

Activities and Facilities:

LA ROSIERE

B3 | 34 | N45°37.482' E006°51.369' 1800m

D1090, 73700 La Rosiere

Directions: N1090. From Bourg St Maurice take the D902 towards Val d'Isere, then the D1090 towards La Rosiere. The Aire is signed on left just before the village behind the sapeurs-pompiers (fire station).

Sanitation:

Parking:

12

Flot Bleu; Token; €10

This is a popular Aire with an expensive service point. The Aire can become quite boggy. The wide sunny ski slopes and easy red runs are ideal for timid skiers. The ski resort of La Thuile in Italy is over the top of the mountain.
www.larosiere.net

Activities and Facilities:

LA ROSIERE

B3 | 35 | N45°37.398' E006°51.291' 1740m

Camping de La Foret, 73700 La Rosiere Montvalezan
www.campinglaforet.free.fr

Directions: N1090. From Bourg St Maurice take the D902 towards Val d'Isere, then the D1090 towards La Rosiere. The campsite is on left just before the village.

Sanitation:

Parking:

€20 Custom; Elec 4amp inc

Nice family friendly resort with sunny South facing slopes and a link to Italian resort La Thuile over the top of the mountain. www.larosiere.net. The campsite is ideal for longer stays.

Activities and Facilities:

TIGNES LES BREVIERES

C3 | 36 | N45°30.379' E006°55.326' 1568m

Allée du Géant, 73320 Tignes

Directions: Off D902. From Bourg St Maurice take the D902 towards Val d'Isere. After 8km, turn right Sp 'Les Brevieres'. Drive through the village to large car park at base of lifts. The short drive through the village is narrow. Arrive early or after 4pm, as during the day the car park is busy with cars and buses.

Sanitation:

Parking:

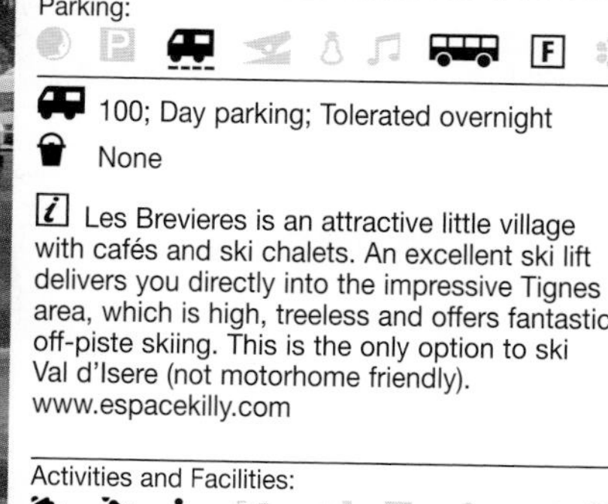

100; Day parking; Tolerated overnight
None

Les Brevieres is an attractive little village with cafés and ski chalets. An excellent ski lift delivers you directly into the impressive Tignes area, which is high, treeless and offers fantastic off-piste skiing. This is the only option to ski Val d'Isere (not motorhome friendly). www.espacekilly.com

Activities and Facilities:

LANSLEVILLARD

C3 | 37 | N45°17.438' E006°54.457' 1337m

Caravaneige de Lanslevillard
www.camping-valcenis.com

Directions: D902. From the D1006, (in winter this is the only main route clear of ice), turn off onto the D902 towards Lanslevillard. The campsite is on the left as you enter the village adjacent to the D902.

Sanitation:

Parking:

40; €6.40 pp Custom; €5.50; Cash

In summer the ski resort becomes a walking and mountain biking area, ask the Tourist Office for the guide with 60 walks and supporting maps. Lanslevillard is a nice village with swimming pool and historic church trail. The ski piste/ticket office is a 100m walk or free ski bus ride. www.valcenis.com

Activities and Facilities:

LES SAISIES

B2 | 38 | N45°45.749' E006°32.024' 1650m

D218b, 73620 Hauteluce

Directions: D218B. Designated motorhome parking in parking 'du Col', adjacent to the D218b as you exit the town towards Flumet.

Sanitation:

Parking:

40; €7.50; Pay at machine Flot Bleu, €2

A large well organised Aire with tarmac surface in an increasingly popular resort. The area has hosted international cross-country skiing events and the trails attract many skiers. The downhill skiing is tree-lined and good for beginners. The restaurant across the road from Aire offers good food at reasonable prices and is eccentric. www.lessaisies.com

Activities and Facilities:

PLAINE-JOUX B2 39 N45°57.077' E006°44.349' 1340m

Photo: motorhomeandaway.co.uk

D43, 74480 Passy-Plaine-Joux

Directions: At plateau d'Assy, car park at skiing and paragliding area. Large parking area before restaurants and paragliding centre on road to le Lac Vert. Note a camping fee is payable on grass fields past the campsite sign.

Sanitation:

Parking:

15 Flot Bleu; €2; Tokens

There are fantastic views of Mont Blanc and the route to this Aire is considered one of the best scenic drives in the area. Paragliding adjacent and in winter there is a very small ski resort. One of the chalets is the Information Centre for the Reserve Naturelle de Passy, which borders the village.

Activities and Facilities:

LES CONTAMINES-MONTJOIE   B3 40 N45°48.160' E006°43.291' 1164m

Caravaneige Gite d'etape du Pontet, Route de Notre Dame de la Gorge, 74170, Les Contamines Montjoie www.campinglepontet.fr

Directions: Route de Notre Dame de la Gorge. From St Gervais les Bains take the D902 south past Les Contamines Montjoie. At the roundabout on the edge of the village turn left and the campsite is at the bottom of the Pontet lift.

Sanitation:

Parking:

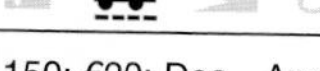
150; €20; Dec - April

Custom; Elec €2.90 2amp

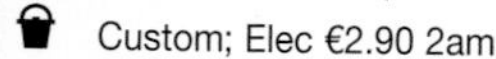
A simple campsite, prone to boggy conditions, but it is in an unbeatable location for great skiing under Mount Blanc. The huge mountain system appears to encourage good snow falls. The long red run from Col du Joly, via La Ruelle, down to Belleville is worth an early start to be the first down. Beginners best avoid the icy runs down to the campsite. A pleasant walk goes up the valley from the campsite to an old restored church and café. www.lescontamines.net

Activities and Facilities:

LES HOUCHES (CHAMONIX)

A3 | 41 | N45°54.942' E006°46.017' 866m

Route de la Plaine Saint-Jean, 74310 Les Houches

Directions: N205 Aire de Fontaine. Turn off the N205 just before les Houches ski area sp 'Aire de Fontaine' 'Servoz'. Follow sp 'Aire de Fontaine'. This is a main route service area adjacent to N205.

Sanitation:

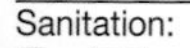

Parking:

Not recommended · Custom

A handy service point conveniently located when entering or departing the Chamonix region.

Activities and Facilities:

CHAMONIX MONT BLANC

A3 | 42 | N45°54.120' E006°50.234' 1050m

Camping les Deux-Glaciers, Route des Tissieres, 74400 Chamonix Mont Blanc
www.les2glaciers.com

Directions: N205. Adjacent to the N205 1km southwest of the centre of Chamonix. Approach from Les Houches and turn off the N205 sp 'Le Glacier du Mont Blanc et des Bossons'. The campsite is in 200m.

Sanitation:

Parking:

30; €15; Closed mid Nov - mid Dec

Custom; Elec €2.50 2amps or €7 10amps

Chamonix has six separate areas spread over 10km; they are not interlinked. A ski bus stops at campsite but it would be better to use own transport and therefore the area suits caravanners or motorhomers with their own cars.

Activities and Facilities:

CHAMONIX MONT BLANC

A3 | 43 | N45°54.964' E006°52.151' 1000m

Photo: Charlie and Angie Anderson

D1506, 74400 Chamonix

Directions: D1506. In Parking Grepon, signed off the D1506 in Chamonix at large roundabout. Height bar approx 3.25m.

Sanitation:

Parking:

300; €11 — Custom

Located in the town centre, making it ideal for nightlife in this famous resort, but skiers would have a long walk and ski buses to catch. The ski areas, spread around the valley, are suited to adventurous intermediates and people seeking unbeatable off-piste touring. Campsites are located in the valley bottom whilst the gondola base stations are home to hard-core boarders in self-converted vans.

Activities and Facilities:

ARGENTIERE LE TOUR

A3 | 44 | N46°00.235' E006°56.758' 1480m

Place du Tour, 74400 Chamonix

Directions: From Chamonix take the D1506 9km to and through Argentiere and then turn off to Le Tour. Follow the road to the base of 'Le Tour' Gondola.

Sanitation:

Parking:

Day parking — None

This is a lovely setting with fine views of Mont Blanc and under Le Tour glacier. There is a snack bar and ski pass office. The skiing is ideal for intermediates. From the café, you can watch off-piste skiers and weary skiers attempt the near vertical routes.

Activities and Facilities:

ST-GERVAIS-LES-BAINS

B3 | 45 | N45°53.250' E006°42.783' 800m

Photos: Charlie and Angie Anderson

Photo: Sally Bethell

Rue Panloup, 74170 Saint-Gervais-les-Bains

Directions: D909. From Megeve drive 3km on the D1212 and turn right at the roundabout and follow the D909 for 6.9km to Saint-Gervais-les-Bains. After crossing the bridge over the river, turn immediately right. The Aire is signed behind the Patinoire (skating ring), located in centre of town.

Sanitation:

Parking:

15 Raclet; €2; Token

Very handy service point with parking, though many motorhomes park at base of gondola 200m away. The gondola goes to Mt d'Arbois so this is a good place to ski to the Megeve ski station from. For something more relaxing the town is famed for hot springs which are located 4km north at Le Fayet. The Tramway du Mont Blanc, www.compagniedumontblanc.com, also stops in the town before ascending 2386m to Nid d'Aigle.

Activities and Facilities:

SAMOENS

A3 | 46 | N46°04.620' E006°43.133' 700m

Camping Le Giffre, 74340 Samoens
www.camping-samoens.com

Directions: Exit Samoens southwest on the D4 towards Morillon. Camping Le Giffre is adjacent to the roundabout before the river bridge.

Sanitation:

Parking:

 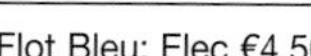

300; €23 Flot Bleu; Elec €4.50

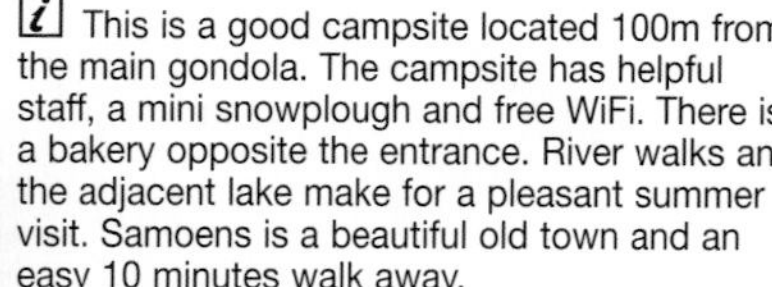

This is a good campsite located 100m from the main gondola. The campsite has helpful staff, a mini snowplough and free WiFi. There is a bakery opposite the entrance. River walks and the adjacent lake make for a pleasant summer visit. Samoens is a beautiful old town and an easy 10 minutes walk away.

Activities and Facilities:

SAMOENS

A3 | 47 | N46°04.620' E006°43.133' 700m

Camping Le Giffre, 74340 Samoëns

Directions: Exit Samoëns southwest on the D4 and travel 800m towards Morillon. Camping Le Giffre is adjacent to the roundabout before the river bridge. The service point is outside Campsite Le Giffre.

Sanitation:

E

Parking:

None — Flot Bleu; €5; CC

This is a service point only but tolerated overnight parking may be possible at the ice skating rink in the town centre. N46°04.970' E006°43.421'. Photo shows motorhome parking at the market place in Samoens town.

Activities and Facilities:

SAMOENS

A3 | 48 | N46°04.338' E006°42.159' 820m

D254, 74340 Samoëns

Directions: Exit Samoen southwest on the D4 and travel 800m towards Morillon. Pass Camping Le Giffre and cross the river bridge and continue 1.8km southwest on the D254 to Vercland. The Aire and service point are at the bottom of the Vercland ski lift.

Sanitation:

Parking:

F

5 — Flot Bleu; €5

This is a remote Aire with only a local bar/restaurant and chairlift for company. There is also parking on the opposite side of road near to a large boulangerie. All other facilities are in the village 3km along the D4.

Activities and Facilities:

FLAINE

 A3 49 N46°00.404' E006°41.375' 1600m

D106, 74300 Arâches-la-Frasse

Directions: D106. From Cluses follow the hairpin bends up the D106 to Flaine and park in car park P1.

Sanitation:

Parking:

€4

None

There are no facilities but parking overnight is allowed. At the entrance to the car park, there is the ticket office, toilet, and sandwich room with a sink and drinking water tap. There are several signs saying that motorhomers cannot empty their cassette in the toilets, so don't. The parking is only a short walk to the ski slopes and lifts. www.flaine.com

Activities and Facilities:

Photo: Peter Gordon

LES GETS

 A2 50 N46°08.993' E006°39.495' 1100m

Rue du Front de Neige, 74260 Les Gets

Directions: D902. Approach Les Gets from Taninges. The Aire is located adjacent to the D902 at bottom of lift at parking 'Les Perrieres'. At the roundabout take the first exit and the service point is straight on and the parking is on the right after the roundabout.

Sanitation:

Parking:

30; €14 1 day, €20 2 days and daily decreases; €50 7 days

Flot Bleu; CC

This Aire is pleasant and quiet in summer but in winter it is a popular ski Aire so an early arrival is essential as it can become overcrowded, thus tolerance, patience, and firm diplomacy are required. There is a supermarket adjacent and it is an 800m walk uphill to the attractive village.

In 'Portes du Soleil' ski area, the Aire is next to a ski lift, at the bottom of ski slope so you can ski to your motorhome door.

Activities and Facilities:

Photos: Peter Gordon

MORZINE

A3 51 N46°10.456' E006°42.623' 1000m

Photos: Peter Gordon

Route de la Manche, 74110 Morzine

Directions: Drive south from Thonon les Baines on Lake Geneva up the Dranse valley via the D902, an easy drive up to the 1000m resort. Drive through the town following sp 'Cascade de Nyon'. Parking is at Les Eaux Vives. Once over the river bear right and at roundabout take road to the cemetery. Aire is at the end of the road adjacent to the river.

Sanitation:

Parking:

Unknown Raclet; Token from Mairie

It is a long 10 - 15 minutes walk into town from the Aire. The Marie located opposite the Post Office by the bus station. During the day, it is possible to park at the sports centre, which has easy access to the Avoriaz Gondola and to the centre of town. The resort is popular with snow boarders as the slopes are suited to all boarding abilities.

Activities and Facilities:

CHATEL

A3 52 N46°15.447' E006°49.773' 1200m

Camping l'Oustalet, Route des Freinets, 74390 Chatel.
www.oustalet.com

Directions: Turn southwest off the D22, in Chatel centre onto the D228A towards Linga. The campsite is on the right in 1.5km.

Sanitation:

Parking:

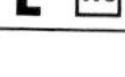   

€24 Custom; Elec €3.80 2amps or €9 10amps

Chatel valley is very attractive and has interesting wooden buildings, barns, and churches. The ski bus is necessary as the slopes are spread around the 'Portes du Soleil' area. The resort is low and one of the first to lose snow.

Activities and Facilities:

CHATEL

A3 | 53 | N46°15.447' E006°49.773' 1200m

Camping l'Oustalet, Route des Freinets, 74390 Chatel

Directions: Turn off the D22 in Chatel centre onto the D228A towards Linga (southwest). The campsite is on the right in 1.5km. The Aire is outside Camping de l'Oustalet.

Sanitation:

Parking:

15; €10 inc service — Flot Bleu; €6

This is a rural ski resort/summer walking area with access to Portes de Soleil ski area and skiing into Switzerland. Chatel valley is very attractive and has interesting wooden buildings, barns, and churches. The ski bus is necessary as the slopes are spread around the 'Portes du Soleil' area. The resort is low and one of the first to lose snow.

Activities and Facilities:

SOMMAND

A2 | 54 | N46°09.690' E006°33.306' 1500m

D308, 74440 Mieussy

Directions: D308. From Mieussy take the D308 northeast to Sommand. The Aire is adjacent to the main road. In winter, the Col de la Ramaz is blocked and there is no access to Praz de Lys.

Sanitation:

Parking:

40; €0.50 local tax — Custom

Of the two resorts either side of the closed Praz de Lys pass, the one on the other side of the pass is better for motorhomes. This is a nice ski area with gentle skiing suitable for beginners and intermediates and has plenty of cross-country skiing. www.prazdelys-sommand.com

Library image: S. Pirnie

Activities and Facilities:

LE PRAZ DE LYS

 A2 55 N46°08.656' E006°35.577' 1500m

D308, 74440 Taninges

Directions: D308. From Les Gets travel 4km southwest on the D902. Turn right onto the D307 sp 'Praz de Lys' and in 800m turn right onto the D328. Then in 1.8km take the D308 to Praz de Lys. The Aire is adjacent to the main road in 4km. In winter, the Col de la Ramaz is blocked and there is no access to Sommand.

Sanitation:

Parking:

40; €0.50 local tax Custom

Of the two resorts either side of the closed pass this side is better for motorhomes. There are a few local cafés in 100m and the ticket office is 15 minutes walk but quicker on skis depending on ability! This is a nice ski area with gentle skiing suitable for beginners and intermediates and has plenty of cross-country skiing. www.prazdelys-sommand.com

Activities and Facilities:

LE REPOSOIR

A2 56 N46°00.676' E006°32.096' 980m

Photo: Pat and Philip Wilde

D4, 74950 Le Reposoir

Directions: D4. From Cluses travel 11km southwest on the D4 to Le Reposoir and the Aire is in the village centre on road to Chartreuse, signed.

Sanitation:

Parking:

 5  Toilets at Mairie 100m

Le Reposoir is a lovely village amongst forest with restaurants and limited shops on the road to the Col de la Colombiere. The Aire is in the ski area adjacent to the ski lift.

Activities and Facilities:

LE GRAND-BORNAND   A2 | 57 | N45°56.405' E006°25.681' 1000m

Caravaneige d l'Escale, 74450 Le Grand-Bornand
www.campinglescale.com

Directions: During winter, take the D4 from St Jean de Sixt as the D4 from Cluses is closed. In the village take the first road on right after the roundabout and the campsite is adjacent to the next roundabout.

Sanitation:

Parking:

 142; €28; Closed Oct - Nov

Custom; Elec €3.80 2amp

This Caravaneige is located in the town centre with good nightlife. This is a luxury campsite with free WiFi and an indoor pool and it is an ideal site for longer stays. There is a ski bus that delivers skiers to the slopes.

Activities and Facilities:

LE GRAND-BORNAND  A2 | 58 | N45°58.529' E006°27.638' 1296m

D4, 74450 Le Grand-Bornand

Directions: D4. During winter, take the D4 from St Jean de Sixt as the D4 from Cluses is closed. Follow D4 through Le Grand Bornand for 7.5km to La Mulaterie, and the Aire is in Le Chenaillon suburb at bottom of 'La Mulaterie' ski lift. Service point 200m signed at WC at bottom of Chatalet lift, to the left of ticket office window.

Sanitation:

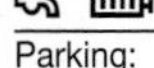    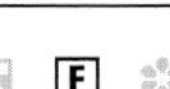

Parking:

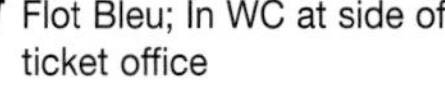 10; 48hrs Flot Bleu; In WC at side of ticket office

This ski resort and village are next to the better known but more expensive La Clusaz. The main lifts are only 100m away from the parking but it is a fair way from the nightlife of Le Grand Bomand.

Activities and Facilities:

LA CLUSAZ

B2 | 59 | N45°54.565' E006°27.111' 1200m

Caravaneige du Plan Fernuy, Route des Confins, 74220 La Clusaz
www.plandufernuy.com

Directions: Turn east off the D909 at the roundabout (with a wooden hut in the centre) in La Clusaz sp 'Vallee des Confins'. Follow this road for 1.8km and the campsite is on the right.

Sanitation:

Parking:

40; €28; Open Jun - Sept and Dec - April

Custom; Inc; 4 amp elec; €4

This Caravaneige is Ideal for longer stays or if the car park is unsuitable. There is a free ski bus from the campsite every 30 minutes and Le Clusaz town centre is 2.3km away. The campsite offers free WiFi.

Activities and Facilities:

LA CLUSAZ

B2 | 60 | N45°54.667' E006°27.891' 1200m

Chemin des Chenons, 74220 La Clusaz

Directions: Turn east off the D909 at the roundabout (with a wooden hut in the centre) in La Clusaz sp 'Vallee des Confins' and 'Plateau de Beauregard'. Follow this road for 2km, pass Caravaneige du Plan Fernuy and turn right (straight on) sp 'P Les Chenons' on a hairpin bend. The day parking is 100m at the base of the Fernuy Gondola.

Sanitation:

Parking:

Day parking None

There is a nice café and gluvine bar. Set up in the snow this is an ideal place to rest after the demanding red run down that tests your calf muscles. The Ticket Office is at the base of the gondola and a ski bus can take you to town.

Activities and Facilities:

CASTEIL

I7 | 61 | N42°32.017' E002°23.517' 760m

Photo: Rita Remminghoff

D116, 66820 Casteil

Directions: D116. From the N116 travel 7km south on the D116 passing through Corneilla de Conflent. The small parking area reserved for motorhomes is in the woods on left just after sign for village but before village, signed.

Sanitation:

Parking:

5 Custom; WC & Tap in adjacent height barriered car park

This is a small parking area under trees. From here walk uphill through the woods for 30 minutes to the Abbaye St Martin du Canigou, and enjoy the views of the Romanesque Abbey. Priests and nuns lead tours in French - a translation is available from the gift shop. http://stmartinducanigou.org. There are 2 restaurants in village but no shops and the Tourist Office has WiFi.

Activities and Facilities:

THUES-ENTRE-VALLS

I7 | 62 | N42°31.333' E002°13.283' 800m

Photo: Rita Remminghoff

Photo: Jan Dennett

Rue de l'Ubac, 66360 Thuès-Entre-Valls

Directions: N116. Turn off the N166 and cross over the river (3.5t weight limit) to Thuès-Entre-Valls for 'Gorges de la Caranca' parking. Then follow the signs in the car park to the motorhome parking.

Sanitation:

Parking:

€4 per day Custom

The Gorges de la Caranca are accessible from here, they provide entertaining but challenging walking with suspended bridges across the gorge and metal walk-ways with hand rails. You can also catch the tourist train that follows the route of the N116 offering passengers amazing views of the Pyrenees from open carriages and the chance to visit other villages along the valley.

Activities and Facilities:

MONT-LOUIS

 I7 | 63 | N42°30.467' E002°07.367' 1680m

Boulevard Vauban, 66210 Mont-Louis

Directions: Turn off N116 into car park sp 'Parking Entree' to right hand side of arched entrance into town. Pass through barriers and Aire is at rear of car park. Do not drive through arch into town.

Sanitation:

Parking:

€4; 18hrs - 10hrs; Pay at machine

Custom

This fortified town is located at a strategic meeting point of three valleys and has UNESCO World Heritage Site status. Building started in 1681 to help provide defences along the border with Spain, troops still occupy parts. The parking area is adjacent to the massive ramparts. The town is also home to Four Solaire, a solar furnace that uses the sun's light to generate heat and power. http://mont-louis.net

Activities and Facilities:

BOLQUERE (PYRENEES 2000)

 I7 | 64 | N42°30.983' E002°03.533' 1780m

Rue du Belvedere, 66210 Bolquère

Directions: Turn off D618 (Egat to Mont Louis road) at roundabout into Ave du Serrat de l'Ours, sp 'Bolquere Pyrenees 2000'. Take 2nd turning left into Rue du Belvedere. Aire at rear of Pizzeria/Creperie. The service point is located at the Casino supermarket on the D618 Mont Louis to Egat road north of the village of Bolquere. N42°30.867' E002°03.733'

Sanitation:

Parking:

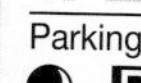

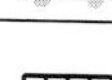

10 Custom; WC disposal onsite; Flot Bleu at Cassino Supermarket

This is a good skiing area popular with families and can get busy at weekends. Pyrenees 2000 has links to the Font Romeu ski area providing 23 sunny slopes. www.pyrenees2000.com www.font-romeu.fr

Activities and Facilities:

SAILLAGOUSE I7

65 N42°27.467' E002°02.250' 1300m

Lieu-dit village, 66800 Saillagouse

Directions: Lieu-dit village. Travelling through the centre of town on the N116, the Aire is located in a small car park behind the Marie across the main road and river from Hotel de Ville.

Sanitation:

Parking:

5 Flot Bleu Fontaine; Tokens

The village is near the Spanish border and en-route to Andorra. There are shops, restaurants, a bank and comical statues in the centre. You can catch the tourist train that follows the route of the N116 offering passengers amazing views of the Pyrenees from open carriages and the chance to visit other villages along the valley. The nearby village of Dorre has municipally run outdoor thermal pools, entrance €4, www.bains-de-dorres.com. The village of Llo also has a thermal spa. www.saillagouse.fr

Activities and Facilities:

PUYVALADOR H7

66 N42°39.076' E002°04.622' 1780m

Rue Ecureuils Rieutort, 66210 Puyvalador

Directions: At Puyvalador turn west off the D118, main route, sp 'Station de Ski de Puyvalador' and travel 5km following signs to the ski station. Aire on left in parking No. 3.

Sanitation:

Parking:

20 Custom; In poor condition tap removed

This is remote parking at a ski station. The small resort has 17 tree-lined quiet slopes suiting intermediate skiers. To the south there are several ski resorts within an easy drive by visiting Formigueres, les Angles and Bolquere, so you can ski a different resort every day. www.puyvalador.com

Activities and Facilities:

LES CABANNES

H6 | 67 | N42°47.084' E001°40.970' 540m

09310 Les Cabannes

Directions: Turn off the N20 sp 'D522' 'Les Cabannes' and follow the D522 to Les Cabannes. As you enter Les Cabannes turn right off the D522 sp 'Gendarmerie' and 'Aire Camping Car'. Follow the road, turn right at the T-junction and the parking is in 100m.

Sanitation:

Parking:

20; €2 per 24hrs; Pay at machine

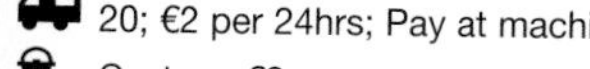

Custom; €2

To the east on the N20 lies Carriere de Trimouns, an open cast Talc mine producing 8 percent of the world's talc. The mine is open to the public in summer. Further south is the ski resort and thermal spa resort of Ax les Thermes. To the west on the N20 are La grotte de Niaux and the Parc de la Prehistoire both famed for their prehistoric drawings. www.ariege.com

Activities and Facilities:

LES ANGLES - PLA DEL MIR

H5 | 68 | N42°33.787' E002°04.008' 1600m

Pla del Mir, 09220 Auzat

Directions: At the ski station parking near the zoo. The turning is to the south of the village. On the road Pla del Mir.

Sanitation:

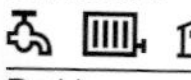
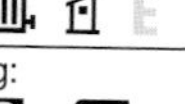

Parking:

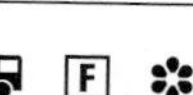

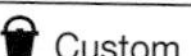

4 Custom

Directly at the bottom of the ski runs. The Aire has fabulous mountain views. The ski resort is ideal for intermediate skiers and has 16 red runs. There is 35km of cross country trails. In summer the animal park with native pyrenees animals, open 9hrs- 18.00hrs, adj. A bike park opens at the resort from 26 june -5 sept www.bike-park-66.com. There are 11 walks in the area. Further details of all activities at www.lesangles.com

Activities and Facilities:

SERRES-SUR-ARGET H6 69 N42°58.150' E001°31.133' 540m

Photo: motorhomeandaway.co.uk

Photos: Keith and Sue Lawrence

D21, 09000 Serres-sur-Arget

Directions: The route offering the widest road is; exit Foix towards Serres-sur-Arget on the D17. In 8km turn sharp right off the D17 onto the D21 sp 'Serres s/A' ans 'Salle Polyvalente'. Follow the D17 into the village and the parking is behind the Salle Polyvalente (village hall) in the village.

Separated custom service point signed (wooden) in lay-by adjacent to main road.

Sanitation:

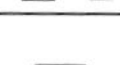

Parking:

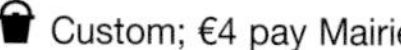

5 Custom; €4 pay Mairie

There is a small lake and park below the parking area otherwise it is a quiet little French village. There are numerous mountain roads from the village; the D17 is the 'Route Verte', it winds through forests to the Sommet de Portel. Foix, 13km west, is an attractive town, dominated by its castle; it is worth a visit for the fantastic views. Foix has a market on Fridays.

Activities and Facilities:

BAGNERES DE LUCHON H4 70 N42°47.706' E000°35.920' 620m

Photo: Rita Renninghoff

Allée du Corps Franc Pommiès, 31110 Bagnères-de-Luchon

Directions: Allee du Corps France Pommies. Approaching from north on the D125, go straight over the roundabout with the bottle/basket water feature and travel 1.2km to the top of town. Turn left sp 'D125' 'Espagne' and 'Accueil Camping Car' on very small sign at road level. Take the next left and follow this road 150m and the Aire is on the left opposite the sports ground.

Sanitation:

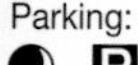

Parking:

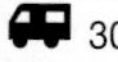

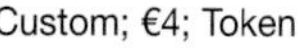

30; €4 Custom; €4; Token

The town is famous for its hot springs and thermal baths 10 min walk from the motorhome parking. A Lidl is nearby. The ski resort of Superbagneres links to the town by gondola on the other side of town from the motorhome parking. The gondola carries mountain bikers and walkers to the summit in summer. Road cyclists can test their skills on the famous Cols popular with Tour de France cyclists.

Activities and Facilities:

ARREAU

H3 | 71 | N42°54.437' E000°21.549 | 700m

Avenue de la Gare, 65240 Arreau

Directions: Avenue de la Gare. Turn off D929 into Ave de la Gare sp 'Office du Tourisme' and 'Pailhac' and cross the river bridge. Aire in car park on left within 150m.

Sanitation:

Parking:

5; €2pp   Custom

This is a small and pretty mountain village. Col d'Aspin, a popular Tour de France climb lies to the west on the D918. Take the D929 14km south to the ski resort of St Lary Soulan and then on to the Bielsa Tunnel to Spain.

Activities and Facilities:

SAINT-LARY-SOULAN

H3 | 72 | N42°49.348' E000°19.397' | 800m

Photo: Peter Gordon

Route de Vieille Aure, 65170 Saint-Lary-Soulan

Directions: From Arreau head south on the D929 for 9km and turn left in the square in Vieille Aure to join the D19 then in 90m bear right to stay on the D19 Rue de Soulan. Travel 1km and go straight over the roundabout into Route de Vieille Aure and the Aire is in 100m at the sports stadium.

Sanitation:

Parking:

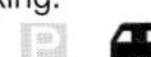  

54; 7pm - 8am; €6   Euro Relais; €2

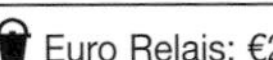

This Aire and town with all amenities makes a good stopping off point en-route to Spain via the Bielsa tunnel. The cable car to the ski slopes is 500m from the parking and there is a thermal spa in town. The slopes offer 100km of intermediate ski runs and a half pike. In summer, St Lary 1700 converts into a mountain bike park. www.saintlary.com. If you need any ski gear, visit Snowproblémo, 22 Rue Vincent Mir.

Activities and Facilities:

PIAU ENGALY

H3 | 73 | N42°47.150' E000°09.467' 1860m

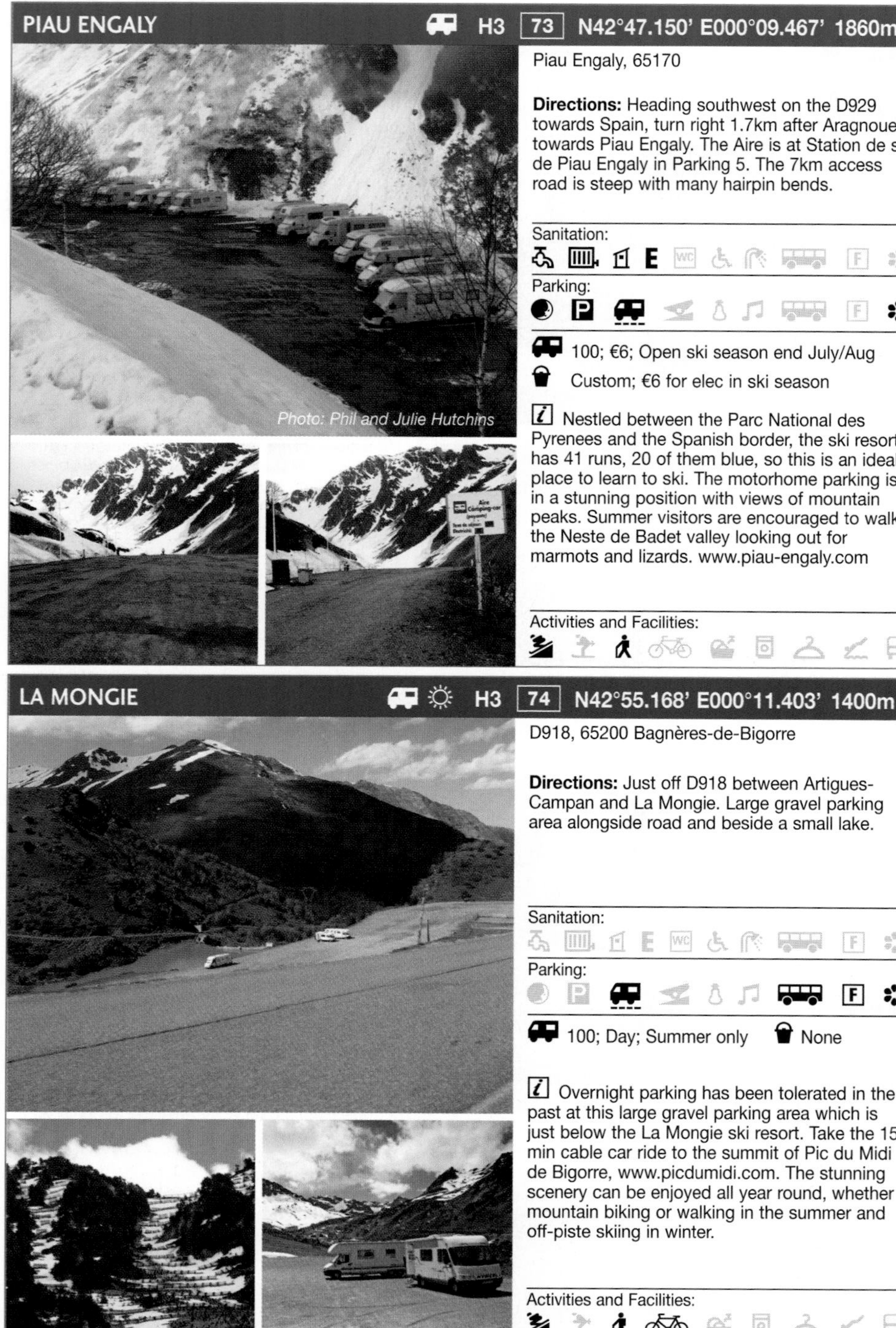

Photo: Phil and Julie Hutchins

Piau Engaly, 65170

Directions: Heading southwest on the D929 towards Spain, turn right 1.7km after Aragnouet towards Piau Engaly. The Aire is at Station de ski de Piau Engaly in Parking 5. The 7km access road is steep with many hairpin bends.

Sanitation:

Parking:

100; €6; Open ski season end July/Aug

Custom; €6 for elec in ski season

Nestled between the Parc National des Pyrenees and the Spanish border, the ski resort has 41 runs, 20 of them blue, so this is an ideal place to learn to ski. The motorhome parking is in a stunning position with views of mountain peaks. Summer visitors are encouraged to walk the Neste de Badet valley looking out for marmots and lizards. www.piau-engaly.com

Activities and Facilities:

LA MONGIE

H3 | 74 | N42°55.168' E000°11.403' 1400m

D918, 65200 Bagnères-de-Bigorre

Directions: Just off D918 between Artigues-Campan and La Mongie. Large gravel parking area alongside road and beside a small lake.

Sanitation:

Parking:

100; Day; Summer only

None

Overnight parking has been tolerated in the past at this large gravel parking area which is just below the La Mongie ski resort. Take the 15 min cable car ride to the summit of Pic du Midi de Bigorre, www.picdumidi.com. The stunning scenery can be enjoyed all year round, whether mountain biking or walking in the summer and off-piste skiing in winter.

Activities and Facilities:

GAVARNIE

H2 | 75 | N42°44.317' W000°01.167' 1470m

D923, 65120 Gavarnie

Directions: D923. Follow sp through Gavarnie towards Gedre ski station turning right in the village sp 'Station de Ski'. There are large level gravel parking areas each side of the road 1.7km past the village; signed.

Sanitation:

Parking:

€5 July - Sept   Custom

The parking is in a stunning position in the Parc National des Pyrenees, surrounded by mountain peaks and the most fantastic views. From the village there is a good, well-signed, popular walk to Cirque de Gavarnie and its waterfalls, the return trip takes 2 - 5hrs depending on ability and number of stops taken. A walking map is available at the Tourist Office for €1. The small ski resort is open in winter with 45km of ski runs. www.gavarnie.com

Activities and Facilities:

CAMPAN

G3 | 76 | N43°01.099' E000°10.687' 640m

D8, 65710 Campan

Directions: D8. From Bagneres de Bigorre travel south on the D8 Route d'Aste (minor road) and follow road into Campan. Service point and parking adjacent to this road by the war memorial, metal cross. Alternatively, drive south along the D935 and turn left as you enter the village and the Aire is 75m ahead.

Sanitation:

Parking:

  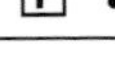

5; 48 hrs max   Custom

Campan is a quaint village with 'Moumaques' (puppet) makers in village centre. It is located between the spa town of Bagneres de Bigorre to the north and the ski resort of La Mongie to the south. There are numerous walks in the area.

Activities and Facilities:

Photo: Judy Crane

BAGNERES-DE-BIGORRE

 G2 77 N43°04.396' E000°09.139' 500m

Photo: Harry Ridsdale

65200 Bagnères-de-Bigorre

Directions: Zone industriele. Heading south towards Bagnères-de-Bigorre on the D935 turn left at the roundabout sp 'Zones d'Activites' onto the D8. In 500m turn right off the D8 after crossing the river. Take the next left and the motorhome parking is in 200m. Well signed from main road.

Sanitation:

Parking:

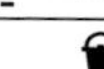  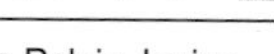

10 — Euro Relais Junior

The motorhome stop is located in an industrial but quiet area on the outskirts of this famous spa town. The thermal baths are located to the south of the town in a 100ha park called Parc Thermal de Salut, www.aquensis.fr. The town has a large market on Saturdays and is an ideal place to stock up before heading into the mountains. The tourist office offers information on local walks and guides in summer and the ski bus departs from the tourist office in winter.

Activities and Facilities:

 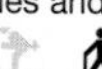   

LOURDES 1

G2 78 N43°05.296' W000°03.161' 400m

Photo: Penny and David Hurst

Esplanade du Paradis, 65100 Lourdes

Directions: Boulevard du Gave. Heading south from Lourdes centre on the D914 pass the Marie (grand building/gardens) and in 200m turn right sp 'La Grotte' and 'P Arrouza'. At the traffic lighted crossroads go straight on following sp 'La Grotte' and 'P Arrouza'. Once you are parallel with the river you will see the parking on the other side. Turn left at the junction opposite Hotel Contaro and follow road across the river bridge to Aire.

Sanitation:

Parking:

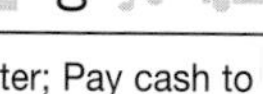 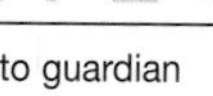

50; €10 inc water; Pay cash to guardian

Custom; €5

This parking area is to the south of Lourdes, adjacent to a park beside the river ideal for walking dogs and exercising children. The Mountain Streams Green Route is a 27km cycle path along the route of the old railway, the start is just to the south of the car park. The Sanctuaries Notre Dame de Lourdes can be walked to by following the river into town.

Activities and Facilities:

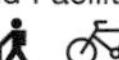    

LOURDES 2

G2 | 79 | N43°05.900' W000°02.517' 400m

Photo: Malcolm and Janet Webb

Photo: Susan Bratt

Boulevard du Lapacca, 65100 Lourdes

Directions: Boulevard du Lapacca. Located 250m due south of the train station. From Tarbes, take the N21 to Lourdes. At the roundabout, follow the N21 around Lourdes. Turn off the N21 onto D937 sp 'Bagneres'. At the roundabout go straight over, sp 'Centre Ville'. Turn right at the roundabout sp 'La Grotte' and 'Gare S.N.C.F' into Boulevard du Lapacca. The parking area is on your left just after the coach park.

Sanitation:

Parking:

20; €7; March - Oct | None

In 1858 the Virgin Mary was seen in the cave Grotte de Massabielle, the Sanctuaries Notre Dame de Lourdes were built soon after and Lourdes receives around 5 million visitors/pilgrims each year. Follow the road to the west of the parking to the Sanctuaries, and along the riverside is the cave. You can be blessed, holy water can be collected from taps around the complex, and there are pools where you can be dunked and 'cured'.

Activities and Facilities:

LOURDES 3

G2 | 80 | N43°06.620' W000°02.310' 400m

Photo: James and Judith White

Photo: Keith and Sue Lawrence

Avenue François Abadie, 65100 Lourdes

Directions: At the Leclerc supermarket. Adjacent to the N21 on the right hand side as you approach Lourdes from Tarbes.

Sanitation:

Parking:

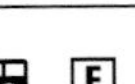

 10 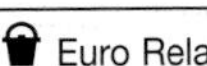 Euro Relais

Very handy stop for stocking up with provisions before heading into the mountains. The motorhome parking is an easy 1.5km walk from the religious centre of Lourdes where there are numerous opportunities to light candles and purchase religious memorabilia.

Activities and Facilities:

CAUTERETS

H2 | 81 | N42°53.577' W000°06.769' 940m

Route de Pierrefitte, 65110 Cauterets

Directions: Route de Pierrefitte. Follow the D920 to Cauterets. The motorhome parking is adjacent to the D920 sp 'Camping Cars' as you enter the village.

Sanitation:

Parking:

50; €8 inc 4amp elec; Pay at machine

Custom

The motorhome parking is adjacent to Cauterets ski lift, the 25 slopes are predominantly blue and also red runs. Drive to Spain navigating a series of hairpin bends with waterfalls at virtually every one before ending at the car park, Pont d'Espagne. In summer, there is a shuttle bus from Cauterets. The path Chemin des Cascades takes you to the falls, several other footpaths venture into the Parc National des Pyrenees from the car park. The Mountain Streams Green Route is a 27km cycle path along the route of the old railway from Cauterets to Lourdes, the route begins on the D920 adjacent to the Aire. www.cauterets.com

Activities and Facilities:

ARRENS-MARSOUS

G2 | 82 | N42°57.483' W000°12.433' 860m

D918, 65400 Arrens-Marsous

Directions: Exit the village northeast on the D918 towards Argeles Gazost. In 600m turn right beside La Balaguere building and the Aire is signed with a small sign on road edge and it is 50m from the road to the parking area.

Sanitation:

Parking:

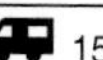 15  Custom

The parking is a pleasant area on edge of village with a small mini market nearby. Situated in the Val d'Azun, www.valdazun.com, the area is famed for its cross-country ski routes whilst in summer it is popular with walkers and Tour de France spectators. The road to Gourette is closed in winter and is not recommended to motorhomes and caravans the rest of the year.

Activities and Facilities:

GOURETTE-LES-EAUX-BONNES 1

G2 | 83 | N42°57.445' W000°19.837' 1400m

Gourette Nord, 64440 Eaux-Bonnes

Directions: Parking du Cardet. In Gourette turn off the D918 just by the roundabout on the hairpin bend sp 'Aire de Camping Car'. Follow this road driving under a bridge between two blocks of flats and the Aire is in front of you, signed.

Sanitation:

Parking:

30; 72hrs all year   At Parking de Ley.

This motorhome parking is in town at the bottom of the ski slopes. There are 28 ski runs at this resort, in the summer they are open to mountain bikers via the Cotch ski lift. Past Gourette the road closes at Col d'Aubisque in winter, and is not recommended to motorhomes and caravans at all. The pass is a very popular stage of the Tour de France.

Activities and Facilities:

GOURETTE-LES-EAUX-BONNES 2

G2 | 84 | N42°57.778' W000°20.357' 1400m

D918, 64440 Eaux-Bonnes

Directions: D918. Parking de Ley. Outside campsite in large car park off the D918.

Sanitation:

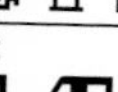

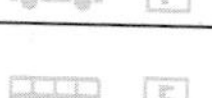

Parking:

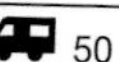

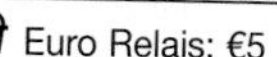

50   Euro Relais; €5

This Aire is located out of town near the campsite. There are fantastic views of the surounding mountains from here and there is a streep 300m path into the village. Past Gourette the road closes at Col d'Aubisque in winter, and is not recommended to motorhomes and caravans at all. The pass is a very popular stage of the Tour de France. Eaux Bonnes on the D918 is worth stopping at to wander along the Promenade d'Imperatrice, which clings to the mountainside overlooking the town. www.gourette.com

Activities and Facilities:

SEVIGNACQ-MEYRACQ ARUDY G1 85 N43°06.414' W000°25.216' 400m

D232, 64260 Sévignacq-Meyracq

Directions: From Laruns heading north on the D934, turn left 100m, signed, after the D287 turning to Arudy, the turning is a small lane and is technically straight on as the D934 bends to the right. In 350m, turn first left sp 'Camping Car'. Drive 280m following signs past marble works to site. Not suitable for large units.

Sanitation:

Parking:

20; €7; March - Oct Custom; Elec €1.5

Lovely grassy, shaded parking adjacent to the river. Facilities on site include a laundry. Arudy, which may be closer on foot than by road, is a charming small town, www.arudy-tourisme.com, and the tourist office has details of numerous day walks.

Activities and Facilities:

LARUNS G1 86 N42°59.350' W000°25.500' 530m

Rue du Bourguet, 64440 Laruns

Directions: Avenue de la Gare. Signed from D934. Aire in town centre car park (but not signed) 100m east from the town square. Drive through car park to the large motorhome parking area.

Sanitation:

Parking:

30 Euro Relais; Tokens

Situated in the lower part of the Ossau valley it is possible to watch Griffon vultures and red kites from the car park. North of Laruns at Aste Beon is La Falaise aux Vautours a very interesting visitor centre with a live camera in the vulture nests. The D934 follows the river valley to the ski resort of Fabreges and crosses the border into Spain and then to the ski resort of El Formigal. The waste drain is awkward to get to if car park is full; and market day is Sunday. www.ossau-pyrenees.com

Activities and Facilities:

LES EAUX-CHAUDES

H1 | 87 | N42°57.117' W000°26.417' 700m

D934, 64440 Laruns

Directions: D934. This is a small lay-by located in the small village, beside the D934 road to Spain in the Ossau valley, 14km from the Fabreges ski resort. The Euro Relais is beside a small toilet building so obscured from view if coming from Spain.

Sanitation:

Parking:

Poss. Euro Relais

This is a small lay-by beside the D934 road to Spain in the Ossau valley 14km from the Fabreges ski resort. Although parking is possible it is only suitable for small motorhomes and then only whist servicing or for a quick night halt. Look out for Isards antelope, which often graze the grassy slopes above the river. The village has hot (chaude) springs and the spa is open May - Oct. www.ossau-pyrenees.com

Activities and Facilities:

ARTOUSTE-FABREGES

H1 | 88 | N42°52.067' W000°23.650' 1260m

D431, 64440 Laruns

Directions: D431. Follow the D934 towards Spain (11km). At the south end of Lake de Fabreges turn left onto the D431 sp 'ARTOUSTE-FABREGES' and 'Station de Ski'. There is parking on the gravel areas and tarmac car park overlooking the lake.

Sanitation:

Parking:

4; €3.25 Euro Relais; Token from Laruns; €3.30

Photo: Rodney Martin

When parking here you must not obstruct local residents. There is a small ski resort, La Station de ski d'Artoust, with 17 runs. The mini mountain railway, Le Petit Train d'Artouste, travels east up to Lac d'Artouste at over 2000m is open in summer. www.ossau-pyrenees.com

Activities and Facilities:

ARETTE-PIERRE-SAINT-MARTIN G1 89 N42°58.733' W000°44.883' 1620m

64570 Arette

Directions: The motorhome parking is located at the ski station 3km from the Spanish border. Turn off the D132 sp 'Station de Ski Pierre St Martin'.

Sanitation:

E

Parking:

P

24; July - Aug Custom; €7

This ski resort is right on the Spanish border up the D132, a small hairpin scenic road. In winter, only attempt to get there if you have a suitably equipped vehicle and are a competent driver. In summer, the resort opens for walkers and mountain bikers. The Tourist Office has guidebooks and maps with 200km of mountain biking routes and walks. Sheep's milk and cheese is a local speciality. www.lapierrestmartin.com

Activities and Facilities:

Bavarian church

Mittenwald alpine meadow

GERMANY

Zugspitze glacier skied from Garmisch-Partenkirchen

Mittenwals gorge

GERMANY

The Bavarian Alps may not be high on your 'must visit', mountain areas, but you will soon discover Germany's alpine wonderland has it all; bountiful beer, amazing architecture, stunning scenery, lovely swimming lakes, walking, mountain biking and a whole host of small ski resorts. Getting around could not be easier on the toll free roads as you tour along the 200km Austrian border. History vultures will be flying high at Hitler's Eagle's Nest; see page 122 for details of how to get there and the best places to camp. Hopeless romantics may wish to start or end their scenic drive along 'Romantische Strasse' taking in elaborate country houses and German castles; page 110. Bavaria also has some pivotal pilgrimage sites including the Wieskirche, page 110 and octagonal Chapel of Grace with its Black Madonna on page 128. Cash is king in Germany and very few places take credit or debit cards so you will have to make regular visits to cash machines.

Driving and Roads

Germany is a good driving country with only a few things to note.

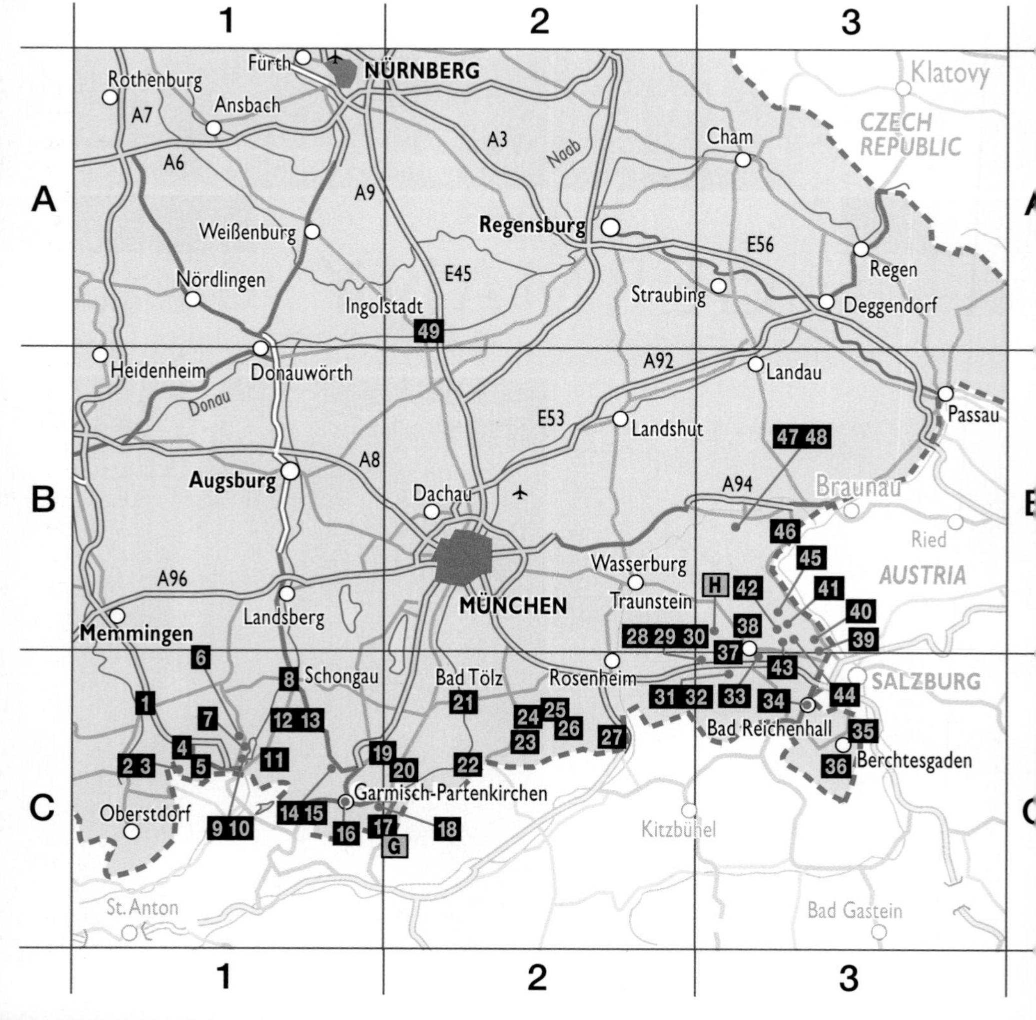

Motorways across Germany are toll free; frequently two lanes only and often have very fast cars on them. Do not 'middle lane' on motorways, it is very dangerous, and you are likely to be chastised. See www.bmv.de for detailed information on road rules. Vehicles over 3.5t are frequently restricted to the inside lane only, so look out for signs. Ausfahrt, exits, can have very short slip lanes with unbelievable steep bends. There have been a few reports of burglary at motorway service stations, for the sake of £25 we recommend you buy Bord Atlas that lists 3000 German stopovers off the motorways. www.vicarious-shop.co.uk

Germany's alpine ski resorts are easy to get to, there are no expensive tunnels or tricky mountain passes to climb. Being Germany the resorts are well run and the roads are kept clear of snow. The Romantic Road (Romantische Strasse) runs from Fussen in southern Bavaria to Wurzburg 340km to the north. It's Germany's most popular tourist route linking some of the most picturesque medieval towns in Bavaria, it is well worth considering as a contrasting route north after exploring the Bavarian Alps.

Umwelt zones are pollution control areas in towns and cities, and the scheme is growing quickly. All vehicles entering an Umwelt zone must display a sticker (red, yellow, or green) or face a €40 fine. The sticker must be stuck inside, on the bottom right corner of the windscreen. Some towns exclude red stickered vehicles, this will increasingly include yellow. The sticker is valid for the entire life of the vehicle as long as the number plate is unchanged. Umwelt zones stickers cost €29,90 see www.umwelt-plakette.de. Stickers can also be issued at local Dekra vehicle registration offices for €5. www.dekra.de has a Dekra station search facility. Just type in a postcode or town name and the details of the nearest Dekra office is displayed.

Euro 2 engines. Red stickers are awarded to Euro 2 and Euro 1 diesel cars/motorhomes with retrofit particulate filters.

Euro 3 engines. Yellow stickers are awarded to Euro 3 and Euro 2 diesel cars/motorhomes with retrofit particulate filters.

Euro 4/5 engines. Green stickers are awarded to Euro 4/5 and Euro 3 diesel cars/motorhomes with retrofit particulate filters.

Petrol engines. Green stickers are awarded to cars/motorhomes with petrol engines fitted with closed-loop catalytic converters, excluding some older models.

Visit www.umwelt.nrw.de and click 'English' then 'low emissions zones' for a good explanation of how engines are given a euro rating.

Mountain Biking & Cycling

There are over 7,000 km of clearly signed cycle routes across Germany. A pictogram is used to mark the routes, it also depicts the terrain, from flat to steep and even details routes most suitable for children and bikes with trailers. Mountain biking trails are marked on orange signs with the letters MTB. There are two long distance cycle routes; one is 418km from Lake Constance to Schonau, the other is 22km from Munich to Austria. Both routes are on undulating designated cycle routes and can be enjoyed in shorter sections.

Walking

Walking is very popular in Germany and paths are well marked. Ski lifts provide transport up the mountains for walkers in summer, often there are numerous walks around the summit or down the mountain. Around Garmisch-Partenkirchen the many footpaths are clearly marked and estimated in hours rather than distance. Researchers Sue and Keith Lawrence state 'be warned, the person who measured them was very fit and it is a good idea to double the estimated time.' Paths can also be rugged and dramatic, so always check the map, leaflet or with the tourist office before departing.

Spas and Thermal Water

There are two types of spa in Germany, Bad and Thermal. Medicinal spas with curative facilities are often prefixed with the word Bad (bath). Thermal baths are leisure based day facilities, consisting of saunas and steam rooms as well as a pool complex. The treatments available will be cosmetic such as facials and massages. Etiquette is very important; you must shower before entering the pools, sauna or steam room. Most people wear flip-flop type footwear; these are worn everywhere except when swimming or in the sauna. Many people will also be wearing bathrobes as well as having towels. Most Germans will remove their swimming suits in saunas and steam rooms, but towels are taken into Saunas, as naked flesh must not touch the wooden benches. For a truly extreme German spa experience visit Rupertus Thermal Baths, (www.rupertustherme.de) in Bad Reichenhall. Researcher Andy Glasgow describes them: 'hot and cold, bubbly and still, salty and fresh, outside, inside and underground - water bathing in every possible way'.

Skiing in Germany

Germany's ski resorts are a well-kept secret, having chosen to keep them low key, family-friendly and affordable. The resorts are mostly small with a couple of gondolas serving a mountain and a collection of drag and chairlifts off the main peak. Munich skiers bring the slopes alive at weekends but you are likely to have the place to yourself during the week.

Spitzingsee: The lakeside setting, easy access and good lifts make this a top Bavarian resort. It is very busy at weekends but quiet on weekdays. The skiing here is quite good by Bavarian standards with enough to hold a good skier's attention for two to three days. A gondola takes you to the top and four draglifts serve the eastern side of the lake. The new bubble chair takes you up to 1506m then 10 drag lifts serve a good section of short, black, red, and blue runs. A red run drops down the other side to **Rottach Egern** you return by bubble chair. Rottach Egern has a steep, marked black run down a narrow tree-lined valley; enquire locally before attempting and go properly equipped. The 6.5 km long toboggan run is a 'must do', a reasonable amount of locals do it fuelled by schnapps. When Rottach Egern is busy or snowbound, rather than try and park at the main car park at the gondola station, you may prefer to use one of the numerous local car parks and catch the ski bus.

Lenggries: 6km south of Bad Tolz the extensive ski area of Brauneck/Lenggries spreads over the mountain. A gondola, chair and drag lifts make it a large ski area by Bavarian standards. Good road links make it an easy drive to the resort and at the large car park in the resort a sign in German states "If you wish to stay overnight in the car park ask for permission at ski lift offices". See www.brauneck-bergbahn.de for further information.

Walchensee: The Herzogstandbahn cable car whisks you up the Fahrenberg mountain with a couple of drags at the top and a red and blue run. The home run down the valley has a black run detour halfway down. Walchensee is very close to Mittenwald that has a smaller ski area.

Garmish Partenkirchen: Hitler merged the two towns of Garmish and Partenkirchen in 1930 to site his Winter Olympics; today the area offers the best skiing in Germany. The town is now a popular, upmarket destination for Munich weekenders. Downhill skiing spreads over three areas; Zugspitze (2050m), Hausberg (1340m) and Kreuzeck (1650m) All are linked with cross-country skiing along the main valleys and around Mittenwald. The mighty **Zugspitze:** (www.zugspitze.de) and its glacier loom over Garmish Partenkirchen. A dramatic cog railway provides a ski connection from Garmish up 2982m to Zugspitze. The assent increases from 15% to 25% in the long tunnel through the inside of the mountain, but you'll arrive late in the morning so it is better to ski the mountain itself from the more convenient Austrian side with its faster cable car. The Wankbahn Gondola, pronounced Vank, is open in peak holiday periods and takes you up to the 1780m Wank mountain with nice views and walks in winter and summer.

Sledging

Germany is the home of sledging with many dedicated sledge chairlifts and long runs down. Traditional wooden sledges can be bought from German shops for €30 for an adult sledge. Sledges can be rented for the day. The sledging hill close to Bad Tolz, page 115, has free parking and charges €15 for as many goes as you can manage. The run is 3.5km and a chairlift whisks you up hill for more - sledgtastic! The guide 'Rodeln in den Bayerischen Alpen' details sledge runs and is available for €10 from bookstores.

KEMPTEN

1C | 1 | N47°43.775' E10°19.150' | 680m

Illerdamm, 87437 Kempten

Directions: Motorhome parking, located at Kempten football club and sports stadium on the east side of the river. Follow signs in town to 'Illerstadion'. From the B19/B12 junction on the east side of the ring road head south on the B19. Take the first right onto Kaufbeurer Strasse sign posted 'Zentrum'. Follow this road for 500m taking the 2nd turning on the right (if you get to the bridge over the river you have gone too far). Follow the road north along the river and the parking is on the right opposite the river bridge.

Sanitation:

Parking:

10; €5 ticket machine; max 3 days.

Sani Station; €1; Coin.

This is a small and peaceful motorhome parking area with a practical service point. Kempten itself is not very interesting but is a large, ordered city with useful facilities and there are pleasant parks along the riverbanks. This is a good place to stop when heading north/south on a long drive.

Activities and Facilities:

WERTACH

1C | 2 | N47°36.601' E10°26.833' | 900m

Camping Grüntensee, Grüntensee Strasse 41, 87497 Wertach
www.camping-grüntensee.de

Directions: From Wertach head northeast towards Nesselwang on the OAL1 Grüntensee Strasse. This road runs parallel and to the south of the lake. Camping Gruntensee is on the left of road.

Sanitation:

Parking:

100; €22.50 Custom; Elec €0.50.

This campsite, with its excellent facilities and the adjacent ski lift make this a convenient place to stop whilst skiing on the local Retitewanne Mountain. A couple of lifts take you to the top where there is one black run otherwise there are gentle runs through the trees suitable for beginners. In summer there are water sports on the lake.

Activities and Facilities:

    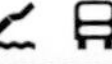

WERTACH 1C 3 N47°36.601' E10°26.833' 900m

Grüntensee Strasse 41, 87497 Wertach

Directions: From Wertach head northeast towards Nesselwang on the OAL1 Grüntensee Strasse. This road runs parallel and to the south of the lake. The motorhome parking is on the left adjacent to camping Grüntensee.

Sanitation:

Parking:

20; €15. Custom; Elec €0.50.

Stellplatze attached to campsite. There are water sports on the lake in summer and the adjacent ski lift makes this a convenient place to stop whilst skiing on the local Retitewanne Mountain. A couple of lifts take you to the top where there is one black run otherwise there are gentle runs through the trees suitable for beginners.

Activities and Facilities:

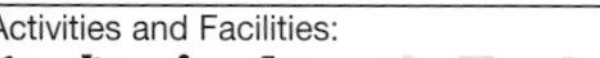

NESSELWANG 1C 4 N47°37.211' E10°29.875' 900m

Maria-Trost-Allee, 87484 Nesselwang

Directions: Nesselwang Parkplatz Alpspitzbahn. Exit the A7/E532 at exit 138 Nesselwang on the St2007 toward Marktoberdorf/Rückholz. At Nesselwang follow signs to 'Alpspitzbahn' up to the cable car station and the huge parking area directly adjacent to cable car station.

Sanitation:

Parking:

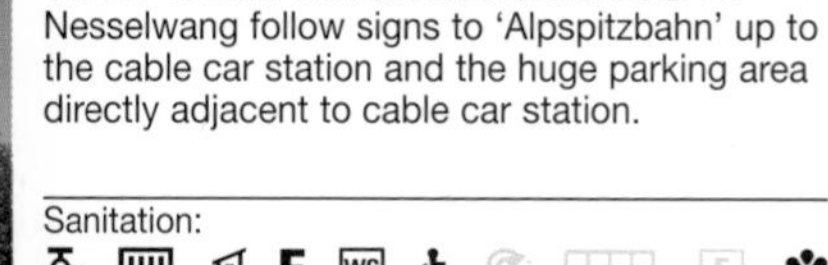

100; €8 Sani Station; Water €1; Elec meter

This parking area is adjacent to the gondola that transports walkers in summer and skiers in winter. The village, with shops and bars, is a 700m downhill walk. A single gondola takes you up a pleasant, typical Bavarian mountain to a ski area served by a couple of local lifts and frequented by local skiers. This is a good stelplatze and a good base to visit ski slopes. Adjacent to great sledge run.

Activities and Facilities:

PFRONTEN-WEISSBACH 1C 5 N47°35.917' E10°33.159' 890m

Am Weiscle 22, 87459 Pfronten

Directions: Heading south towards Austria on the B309/B310, take the second turning on the left when you enter Weissbach onto Am Weisele, signed off main road in village. Follow the road round to the left and the parking is on the right.

Sanitation:

E

Parking:

10; €9; Honesty box Custom

This is private motorhome parking run by the adjacent hotel. In winter, the cosy 5m x 3m clubhouse gets packed with ruddy-faced skiers enjoying a beer from the beer vending machine. This is a convenient stopover for summer touring or winter skiing, as the local ski bus whisks you to local slopes on the Breitenberg Mountain. The skiing is typically Bavarian, low-key, family friendly and not over-taxing, and is delightful for a day or two. The village with a few bars is within 500m walk.

Activities and Facilities:

ROSSHAUPTEN 1C 6 N47°39.522' E10°43.156' 790m

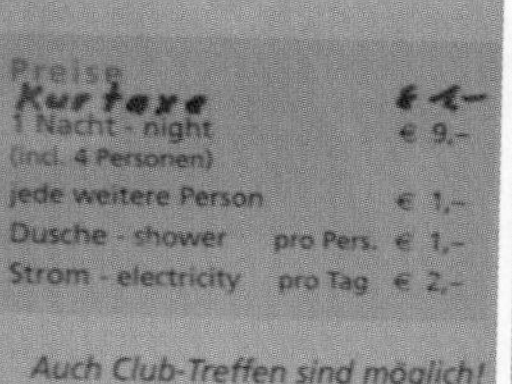

Ausberger Strasse 23

Directions: From the north, exit the B16 onto Rosshaupten as you enter the village. The parking is at the motorhome and caravan dealership at the main road junction - look for the flags.

Sanitation:

E

Parking:

25; €11 Custom; Elec €2

Located on the northern outskirts, 500m from the village centre at a motorhome and caravan dealership. The parking area is open all year round.

Activities and Facilities:

ROSSHAUPTEN (WIRTHAUS AM TIEFENTAL) 1C 7 N47°38.591' E10°43.820' 790m

Camping Warsitzka, Tiefental 87669 Rieden am Forggensee

www.camping-forggensee.de

Directions: From Rosshaupten head 1km south on the B16. Cross over the lake inlet on the bridge and the motorhome parking is on the left alongside the lake.

Sanitation:

Parking:

20; €11.50; Easter – Oct

Custom; Elec €2; Shower €2.50

This summertime motorhome parking is in a very nice location adjacent to lakeside with boating and swimming, cycling is also a popular pastime. Camping Warsitzka adjacent to the stellplatze focuses on season pitches. Fussens with its city attractions is a 15-minute drive or a 9km walk away.

Activities and Facilities:

SCHONGAU 1C 8 N47°48.513' E10°53.873' 680m

Lechuferstrasse, 86956 Schongau

Directions: In Schongau follow signs through town to 'Festplatz' taking the ST2014 to the river bridge and turn right before it crosses the river. Follow Lechuferstrasse along the north bank 400m to the parking.

Sanitation:

Parking:

50 Sani Station; Water €1; Coin

Riverside parking with a new service point, clean toilets and an adjacent café. This parking makes a good base for touring "Romantic Strasse" area of Bavaria, so is always popular. Located just north of the main ski areas it is also a useful place to stop, re-fuel, and defrost if the weather has been particularly harsh.

Activities and Facilities:

FUSSEN

1C 9 N47°34.914' E10°42.078' 780m

9 Abt Hafner Strasse, 87629 Füssen
www.wohnmobilplatz-fuessen.de

Directions: Heading south on the B16 toward Füssen, 300m after the junction with the B310, turn right at the roundabout, signed. In 300m take the second turning on the left and the parking is 200m on the left past the motorhome dealers, this parking is also adjacent to Lidl and Aldi. This is a popular stellplatze so best to arrive around 1pm.

Sanitation:

Parking:

60; €11 Custom; Elec €1 1.62 kwh; Water 100l €1; Showers €0.50.

Excellent motorhome parking with good facilities and reasonable charges. The office is open 8am-10am and 6pm-8pm, if closed check office window for reserved pitches notice, then find pitch and occupy it immediately as parking is very popular. Lidl and Aldi adjacent (closed 2pm sat all day sun). The town is worth the visit for the couple of churches, a good castle and town museum. Also, see entry 10

Activities and Facilities:

FUSSEN

1C 10 N47°34.956' E10°42.205' 780m

2 Abt-Hafner Strasse, 87629 Fussen
www.caravanzentrum-allgaeu.de

Directions: Caravan Zentrum Allgau. Heading south on the B16 toward Füssen, 300m after the junction with the B310, turn right at the roundabout, signed. In 300m take the second turning on the left and the motorhome parking is at the motorhome dealers. This is popular so best to arrive around 1pm.

Sanitation:

 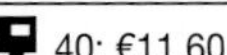 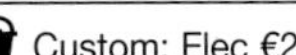

Parking:

40; €11.60 Custom; Elec €2

Pleasant parking at motorhome dealers, with accessory shop and workshop. A safe and easy cycle path takes you 1km to the city. The medieval centre has nice nightlife with beer halls and restaurants. Another path leads via a forest and roadside path to the famous castles 2km to the southeast. A Ski bus stop is 250m away; the skiing is reasonable and accessed via one chair lift and several draglifts. Also, see entry 9

Activities and Facilities:

HOHENSCHWANGAU

1C | 11 | N47°33.454' E10°44.453' 800m

ST2016, Colomanstrasse

Directions: Adjacent to ST2016 in village, follow signs to main parking area P2.

Sanitation:

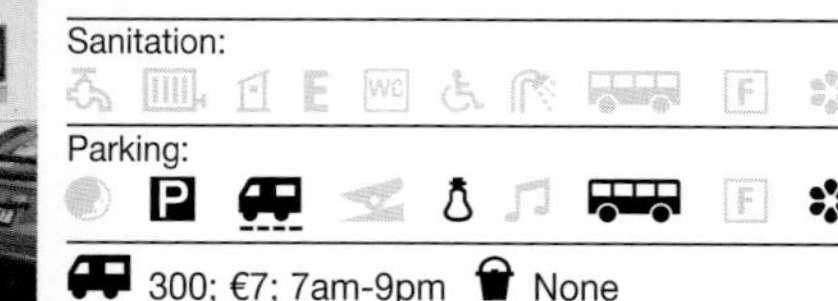

Parking:

300; €7; 7am-9pm None

Huge car park specifically built for visitors to two famous castles, Schloss Hohenschwangau and Schloss Neuschwanstein. Ticket office and transport up to the castles is adjacent. A short cycle ride takes you to lovely Schwansee lake with picnic area and lake bathing area - it's a world away from the hustle and tourist bustle of the castles.

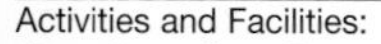

Activities and Facilities:

WEISKIRCHE

1C | 12 | N47°40.951' E10°53.967' 660m

Weis, 86989 Steingaden

Directions: From Steingaden take the ST2059 east towards Wildsteig. After 2.6km turn right and head south for 2.5km. Follow signs for 'Weiskirche'. The designated parking is on right as you the approach church.

Sanitation:

Parking:

20; day only; €2 first hour, 50c per hour after

None

Weiskirche "meadow church" is Bavaria's most popular pilgrimage church - a UNESCO World Heritage Site - packed to the hilt with Rococo gold carvings and paintings. Church has free entry and more gold carvings than the eye can take in. This is a landmark in architecture (according to books on the subject) and marks a highlight in the Rococo style. www.wieskirche.de

Activities and Facilities:

BAD BAYERSOIEN

 1C | 13 | N47°41.259' E10°59.890' | 780m

Trahtweg, 82435 Bad Bayersoien

Directions: Approaching the village from the south on the B23 the farm is located to the left of the B23, 250m from the lake. Take the exit towards Bad Bayersoien and turn right under the B23. Immediately take the first turning on the right, Trahtweg, and the farm is on the left. Well signed from main road.

Sanitation:

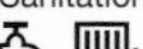   

Parking:

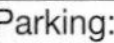    

 8; €9; coins 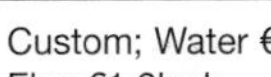 Custom; Water €1; Elec €1 2kwh

Located on a quiet and peaceful farm beside a meadow. There is nice cycleway to the village and to the local swimming lake. This stopover is close to the famous "meadow church" of Weiskirche with its riotous Rococo gold carvings and paintings and good motorhome day parking.

Activities and Facilities:

OBERAMMERGAU

  1C | 14 | N47°35.715' E11°03.860' | 820m

Eugen-Papst-Strasse, 82487 Oberammergau

Directions: Heading south exit the B23 taking the first exit to Oberammergau and travel 1km into town. 200m after crossing the river take the 2nd turning on the right, follow the road to the right and the parking is at the tourist office in 400m. Follow signs for Tourist Office.

Sanitation:

Parking:

20; Day only, 6am - 10pm None

Very convenient, free motorhome daytime only, parking 5 minutes walk from the historic centre. The large Peter and Paul church is an excellent example of Bavarian Rococo church building. Entry is free as is the helpful video tour system used to explain the dazzling decoration. Every kind of pilgrimage related souvenir is available in the many shops lining the main streets.

Activities and Facilities:

OBERAMMERGAU

1C | 15 | N47°35.360' E11°04.360' | 820m

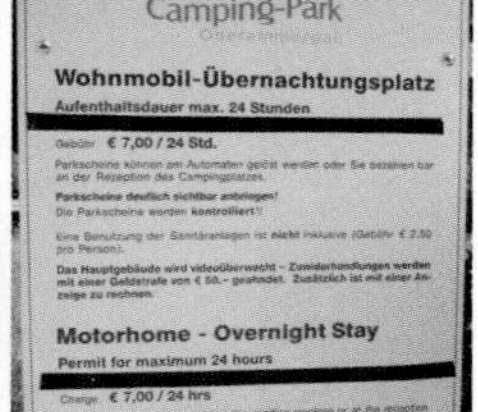

Lindermoos, 82487 Oberammergau

Directions: Heading north exit the B23 at the first turning to Oberammergau. Take the second turning on the left and drive past the campsite entrance. The parking is adjacent to a campsite and a ticket machine is located at the car park entrance.

Sanitation:

Parking:

30; €7; 24hrs   None

There are nice views from the parking area and a pleasant, car free, cycleway leads right into the heart of the village. The Large Peter and Paul church is an excellent example of Bavarian Rococo church building. Entry is free as is the helpful video tour system used to explain the dazzling decoration. Every kind of pilgrimage related souvenir is available in the many shops lining the main streets.

Activities and Facilities:

GARMISH-PARTENKIRCHEN

1C | 16 | N47°30.320' E11°06.492' | 730m

Wankbahnstrasse, 82467 Garmisch-Partenkirchen
www.alpencamp-gap.de

Directions: From the 2 from the north turn left onto Münchner Strasse signed for Wankbahn chairlift. Take the first left onto Wankbahnstrasse and follow to the chairlift. The Motorhome parking is adj to the chairlift.

Sanitation:

Parking:

 50; €10 + €2 pp tax; Pay in bar

Custom; Water €2; Showers €1; Elec meter

Privately run this is an excellent stellplatze. The adjacent Wankbahn Gondola is open all year but only operates at weekends during summer and only takes walkers, but there are nice walking trails. A free ski bus (with guest card) takes you to the town centre and Garmish's local ski slopes. Whilst the parking is excellent it might suit skiers to drive to the large car park at the base of local slopes enabling an earlier hassle-free start.

Activities and Facilities:

MITTENWALD

2C 17 N47°26.256' E11°15.852' 940m

Bahnhof, Albert Schott Strasse, 82481

Directions: This parking is located centrally in town adjacent to the railway station. Follow sp 'Bahnhofplatz P1'. The card controlled entry barrier system was not in use and the barrier remained open during the day. Owner collects parking and electric fees at 8am and 8pm daily. This town is famous in Bavaria for beauty and rare painted buildings.

Sanitation:

Parking:

30; €10; owner collects

Custom; 16amp elec meter

Leutascher gorge is a five-minute cycle ride away; entry costs €2, there is a dramatic walk up the gorge or take the longer circular walk (goblin) up to the panoramic bridge. Get a guest card from the parking owner and catch the free bus to ski lift station. The Karwendel cable car accesses the unskiable Karwendel range. The Kranzberg-sessel lift takes you to the top of the local mountain, the slopes are unchallenging but are scenic and fun.

Activities and Facilities:

KRUN

1C 18 N47°29.417' E11°15.297' 980m

Am Tennsee, 82493 Krun
www.camping-tennsee.de

Directions: Driving towards the Austrian border on the E533/B2 1km before the exit to Krun, turn right opposite Barmsee lake, signed, and drive to the campsite.

Sanitation:

Parking:

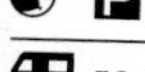

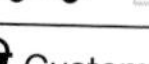

50; €17.50 peak season Custom

This stellplatze is in a beautiful Alpine valley setting with the added luxury of being able to use the adjacent campsite facilities, including showers and drying room. The local ski slopes are a 5 minutes/5km drive.

Activities and Facilities:

GROSSWEIL (FREILICHTMUSEUM)  1C 19 N47°39.840' E11°17.046' 760m

Ander Glentlieten 4

Directions: 57km south of Munich exit the A95/E533 at junction 10 and drive 1.5km into centre of Grossweil on the ST2062. Turn right at the crossroads and follow signposts for 'Freilichtmuseum' museum out of village, 2km southeast up country road to museum - designated motorhome night parking right at top of slope through bus/car parking area.

Sanitation:

Parking:

25; 6pm - 9am only None

Nice quiet parking area. Motorhome parking is restricted to evenings between 6pm and 9am only. The local agricultural museum is popular with German tourists. The small village is a 2km downhill walk or cycle.

Activities and Facilities:

EINSIEDELN (Nacthparkplatz am Alchensee) 2C 20 N47°34.143' E11°18.220' 900m

ST2072/B11

Directions: Just south of Einsiedeln turn off the B11 onto the ST2072 lakeside road. The parking is well signposted and at the start of lakeside road.

Sanitation:

Parking:

70+; €5; Max 3 days.

Custom; Water 100l €1; Elec 1.6kwh €1; Coin; No waste disposal

This is excellent parking adjacent to an attractive lake in a national park. The lake has a lovely 11km cycleway along a quiet private road. The shoreline is dotted shallow sandy bathing spots with grassy banks. Skiers in winter and walkers in summer can take the Herzog stand bahn cable car up the Fahrenburg mountain. Also close to Mittenwald's smaller ski area.

Activities and Facilities:

BAD TOLZ

2C | 21 | N47°45.811' E 11°33.009' | 700m

Konigsdorfer Strasse

Directions: In Bad Tolz by the ST2072 river bridge on the west bank, follow Königsdorfer Str. north along the river and parking Isarpromenade is on the right in 500m and is well signed.

Sanitation:

Parking:

40; 48hr; 50c 1 1/2 hours.

Holiday Clean; Water €1; Coin.

This riverside location is popular at weekends and during the annual festival in August. There is an easy, safe cycleway along the river to a lake or town centre. This attractive Bavarian town, on the river Isar, acquired its wealth from salt trade. The tourist office has a guided walk leaflet written in English detailing the main sights. 6km south is the extensive ski area of Brauneck/lenggries. Popular ski resort with extensive sledging and blue ski runs 2km.

Activities and Facilities:

FALL

2C | 22 | N47°34.250' E11°32.031' | 790m

Durrachstrasse, Gemeinde Lenggries

Directions: Travel 21km south from Bad Tolz on the B13 until you reach Sylvensteinsee lake and turn right onto the B307 and drive 2.3km. After crossing large lake bridge, take the first turning on the left, clearly signed 'Nacht Parlplatz'. The best parking area is to the left of WC's. Check weather reports before visiting in winter, if snow falls, you may be stuck until spring.

Sanitation:

Parking:

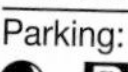

20; 4€; 24hr

Sani Station behind WC; €2; coin

Pleasant wooded parking with individual bays and lay-bys that is exceedingly busy at weekends and public holidays. There is a lovely lake bathing beach 100m away, and numerous cycle paths. In the adjacent village there is a bar with an outdoor beer garden. This parking is amongst the mountains of the German Austrian border and should not be used if snow is expected as you may be stuck until spring.

Activities and Facilities:

ROTTACH-EGERN 2C 23 N47°40.491' E11°46.539' 790m

Talstation, Wallbergstrasse, 83700 Rottach

Directions: From Rottach follow the B307 south. Take the last turning on the left sign posted 'Talstation' and follow signs up the mountain to the bottom of main gondola.

Sanitation:

Parking:

 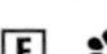

 10  None

Day parking only. Apart from the off piste ski runs there is a 6.5km (4 mile) long toboggan run that the Glasgows highly recommend. The gondola gives access to a five-mile walk on a medium incline or gentle walks offering sunny views. A paragliding school will launch you off the top of the mountain in tandem for a fee; see gleitschirmschule-tegernsee.de. The Tegernsee lake area is very touristy and popular with well-heeled German tourists.

Activities and Facilities:

GMUND AM TEGERNSEE 2C 24 N47°44.911' E11°44.253' 700m

Max-Obermayer Strasse, Fisherweg, 83703

Directions: Parking at north end of lake on east side of river, signposted, "see" parking. Driving south on the B318 pass through Gmund am Tegernsee and cross the bridge, in 100m turn right and the parking is 100m on the left.

Sanitation:

  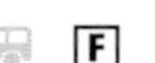

Parking:

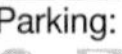   

 50  None 

This is a free day parking area a short and pleasant walk to a bathing area on the Tegernsee Lake. Other car parks along lake make charges and other restrictions; this one is free and unrestricted. The Tegernsee lake area is very touristy and popular with well-heeled German tourists.

Activities and Facilities:

SCHLIERSEE 2C 25 N47°44.227' E11°51.748' 800m

Schonauerstrasse, 83727 Schliersee

Directions: Turn off the B307 in the centre of Schliersee onto Leitnerstrasse, signed motorhome parking and to 'Hotel Reiter'. Then take the second left onto Schonauerstrasse. The Reiter family provides a small, gravelled, motorhome parking area.

Sanitation:

Parking:

3 None

Local "Gasthaus Reiter" runs this private motorhome parking. Whilst not obliged to use restaurant Reiter you show your appreciation by having a beer or coffee there. Please leave area tidy. Schliersee lake has easy bathing, sailing and boat trips and is more commercial and popular than the higher beautiful Spitzingsee lake.

Activities and Facilities:

SPITZINGSEE 2C 26 N47°39.940' E11°53.281' 1100m

Spitzingstrasse ST2077, 83727 Schliersee

Directions: From Schliersee head south on the B307 and drive through Neuhaus then turn right to 'Spitzingsattel'. Follow the ST2077 road and the stellplatze is very well signposted as you emerge after long uphill climb to Spitzingsee Lake. On lakeside adjacent to ski lift.

Sanitation:

   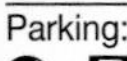 

Parking:

  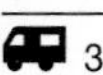

30; €9; Easter - Oct and weekends during ski season Custom; Closed in winter

Parking adjacent to Germany's highest lake with mountains filling in the backdrop. You can cycle or walk around the wildlife packed lake or take the adjacent gondola up the mountain for stunning views, a mountain stroll or skiing in winter. Busy at weekends but nice and peaceful even in peak season on weekdays. The service point is likely to be frozen in winter so arrive with full water and empty waste tanks.

Activities and Facilities:

KIEFERSFELDEN

 2C **27** N47°37.729' E12°11.352' 490m

WSG Wasserskilift, Guggenaur Weg, 83088
http://wakeboard-kiefersfelden.de

Directions: Exit the A93 at junction 60 following signs to Kiefersfelden onto the ST2589. In 1km at the end of the road turn right onto the 171/ST2089 towards Rosenheimer. In 400m take a sharp right (third turning) and follow road for 600m to a small water-skiing and wakeboarding lake adjacent to a railway line.

Sanitation:

Parking:

10; 3 days; €5 None

Motorhomes may park overnight with permission from the water-ski centre. The parking area is open all year and a convenient place to take a break during a long trip. You can relax, bathe and buy a cold beer and during the summer watch the beginners learn to water-ski. This might be a lively place at weekends with water-skiers.

Activities and Facilities:

PRIEN AM CHIEMSEE

3C **28** N47°51.548' E12°21.880' 570m

Harrasser Strasse 19 83209

Directions: Exit the A8 at junction 106 towards Prien a Chiemsee. Head north on the ST2092, in 2.5km at the roundabout turn right to Harras. Follow Harrasser Strasse for 4km and the large parking area is located at side of boat harbour for the lake steamer.

Sanitation:

Parking:

50; day only; €3.50 whole day None

Paddle steamers alight from the adjacent harbour on a two hour round trip calling at all the beauty spots. Get off at Frauenchiemsee Island and visit its large tower, convent and brewery. The little train (steam in summer, weekends only) chugs 2km into town and a Lidl is at the main station. Although the area is very touristy, the lake is majestic so pack your costume, as it is a popular, clean, and warm bathing lake.

Activities and Facilities:

PRIEN AM CHIEMSEE

3C | 29 | N47°51.241' E12°22.049' | 570m

Harrasser Strasse 83209

Directions: Exit the A8 at junction 106 towards Prien am Chiemsee. Head north on the ST2092, in 2.5km at the roundabout turn right to Harras. Follow Harrasser Strasse for 3.5km and the parking is at the boat club car park on the right 100m past the Yachthotel Chiemsee. Boat club car park used for motorhome parking between 6pm and 10am only.

Sanitation:

Parking:

10; 6pm-10am; €10 Custom; Elec €3

The boat club allows motorhomes to park between 6pm and 10am only but arrive at 6pm as popular. A nice grassy lawn bathing area is only 1km away. An outdoor sink is attached to clean toilet block. Take the steam railway to town (steam in summer, weekends only) and a Lidl is adjacent to the main railway station.

Activities and Facilities:

PRIEN AM HARRAS

3C | 30 | N47°50.430' E12°22.396' | 570m

Camping Harras, Harrasser Strasse 135, 83209 Prien am Chiemsee

Directions: Exit the A8 at junction 106 towards Prien am Chiemsee. Head north on the ST2092, in 2.5km at the roundabout turn right to Harras. Follow Harrasser Strasse for 1.8km and the campsite is on right adjacent to the lake before entering village.

Sanitation:

Parking:

10; 1 April - 5 Nov €10, (1st July - 31 Aug €29 inc elec)

Custom; Elec €2.50; Shower €0.80.

This lakeside campsite is set on a small peninsula, it also has motorhome parking on gravel with no lake views. There is a cycle track to village and a small harbour adjacent.

Activities and Facilities:

UBERSEE - STEGEN

3C 31 N47°48.570' E12°29.532' 570m

Almfischer 11

Directions: Exit the A8 at junction 109 and head south on the ST2096. Follow the road for 3.4km to the hamlet of Stegen and take Almfischer, the second turning on the left. Take the next turning on the right in 400m and the farm is at the end of the road. Well signposted off ST2096.

Sanitation:

Parking:

15; €10

Custom; Elec €0.50 per kwh (long lead needed)

Situated amidst rural German farmland with good drainage if wet. Conveniently close to the main road and lake Chiemsee. Visited in a thunderstorm so pictures don't do justice.

Activities and Facilities:

UBERSEE - STEGEN

3C 32 N47°48.753' E12°29.303' 570m

Stegen, 83236 Ubersee

Directions: Exit the A8 at junction 109 and head south on the ST2096. Follow the road for 3.4km to the hamlet of Stegen and take Almfischer, the third turning on the right. The farm is 200m on the right, well signposted.

Sanitation:

Parking:

10; €10

Custom; Elec €0.50 kwh; Shower €1

Farm stopover with cattle, horses and chickens and clean gravel/grass parking. Look at both farms in the village and choose yourself. Visited in a thunderstorm so the pics don't do it justice.

Activities and Facilities:

SIEGSDORF

3C 33 N47°50.020' E12°39.220' 700m

Camping Gaststatte Josef Reitthaler, Aigen 4, 83313 Siegsdorf

Directions: Exit the A8 at junction 112 towards Traunstein. In 350m take the first right onto Hochberg strasse/TS29, signed to Hochberg/Wernleiten. This is a steep minor road and campsite Gaststatte is well signposted along the way and is on the left as you clear trees on hillside.

Sanitation:

Parking:

5; €10 inc showers

Custom; Elec €3.50; Water €2; Cash

This farm campsite has a restaurant and small grassy stellplatze (motorhome parking) outside the main farm. The ski resort of Aschau im Chiemgau is a 19km drive.

Activities and Facilities:

BAD REICHENHALL

3C 34 N47°44.071' E12°52.531' 450m

Hammerschmiedweg, 83435 Bad Reichenhall

Directions: Having approached Bad Reichenhall from the north, follow the B20/B21 southwest alongside the river. Turn right into Hammerschmiedweg off B20/B21 behind blue coloured petrol station. Follow signs for Rupertthermе motorhome parking, located beside the river.

Sanitation:

Parking:

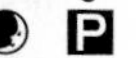

30; €13 inc elec, €37 3 days; €61 5 days

Ticket via machine (coins and notes) then obtain elec (16amp) key from adjacent garage (€20 deposit); Drinking water 100l €1

Brand new, ultra modern, motorhome parking five minutes gentle cycle to the famous Rupertus thermal baths. Pay €14.50 for 4 hours (with Guest Cart) and indulge yourself in hot and cold, bubbly and still, salty and fresh, outside, inside and underground - water bathing in every possible way. A few minutes away is a lovely park with a drinking fountain supplying free, medicinal, mineral water.

Activities and Facilities:

BERCHTESGADEN - OBERAU 3C 35 N47°39.030' E13°04.215' 800m

Renothenweg 15, 83471 Berchtesgaden

Directions: Head towards Oberau on the B319 then the BGL9. The village is 200m after the B319/BGL9 junction and you must follow many small signs that lead, right, off main road into the small village. Unfortunately, the gravel road up to the parking is completely unsuitable for large motorhomes.

Sanitation:

Parking:

15; €8; Owner collects at 19.30hrs

Custom; €1; Elec €1.5 pay owner

Level pasture parking with stunning valley views and sunsets over the Alps.

The easiest way to visit Hitler's Eagle's Nest, open May - Oct, is by catching a bus or the cable car from Berchtesgaden. There is bus parking/stop 4km east of Berchtesgaden at Obersalzberg on the B319 but from Berchtesgaden it is very steep - 1st gear for 2 km; only undertake if your faith is in your clutch and brakes.

Activities and Facilities:

KONIGSSEE 3C 36 N47°35.694' E12°59.149' 550m

Campingplatz Grafenlehen, Konigssee
Fussweg 71, 83471
www.camping-grafenlehen.de

Directions: From Berchtesgaden travel 4km south on the B20/Königssee Strasse towards Konigssee. Turn right by the McDonalds and before the road ends and turns into large car parks for the lake. In 300m turn right into the campsite.

Sanitation:

Parking:

50; €23 Custom; Inc

Open all year campsite with full ski facilities. 100m walk to lifts serving runs under Hitler's Eagle's Nest. The ski slopes overlook Konigsee lake and you can see Hitler's Eagle's Nest perched on a mountain top. The main gondola serves 3 drags and 1 chair on the 'Jenner' 1874m. Konigssee lake is a popular tourist destination in the summer with pleasure boaters on the lake, hikers walking the surrounding parkland and pilgrims visiting St Bartholomä Catholic church.

Activities and Facilities:

TINNERTING   3C 37 N47°51.141' E12°36.413' 500m

Tinnerting 3, 83278 Traunstein

Directions: Exit the A8 at Junction 110 Bergen towards Vachendorf. Drive 3.2km on the ST2096 to Axdorf and turn left at the crossroads into Tinnertinger Strasse then take the first left onto Büchling. Follow the road for 800m down narrow country lane towards small hamlet of Tinnerting and take the first turning on the right and the farm is in 100m.

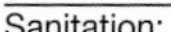

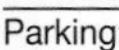

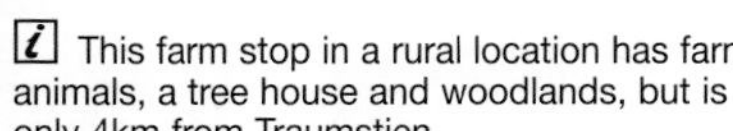

Sanitation:

Parking:

5; €15.50 inc elec — Custom

This farm stop in a rural location has farm animals, a tree house and woodlands, but is only 4km from Traumstien.

Activities and Facilities:

TRAUNSTEIN, WOLKERSDORF  3B 38 N47°52.988' E12°36.017' 580m

Schmidhamer Strasse 31, 83278 Traunstein
http://gruenaeugl.de

Directions: From Traunstein head west towards Seebruck on the ST2095. Turn right onto Dorfstrasse and drive 1km to Wolkersdorf, drive through the village bearing left onto the TS2 and follow signs to 'Wolkersdorf' industrial area. Drive 700m and the parking is behind Camping and Freizeit GmbH Grünäugl motorhome/caravan dealers with large flags and vans on forecourt.

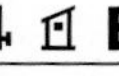

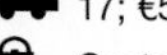
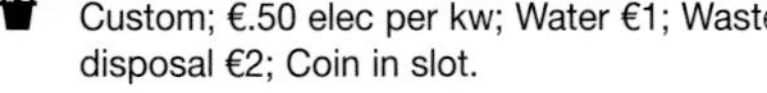

Sanitation:

Parking:

17; €5

Custom; €.50 elec per kw; Water €1; Waste disposal €2; Coin in slot.

Good night halt and useful selection of bits and pieces for motorhomes in dealership shop.

Activities and Facilities:

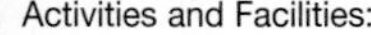

FREILASSING

3B | 39 | N47°50.473' E12°59.060' | 500m

Aumuhlweg

Directions: Turn off the B20 at the east side of town signposted 'Freilassing' and Waging am See' on to the ST2104. Drive 200m on the ST2104 towards Freilassing crossing the river then take the first turning on the right. Turn immediately left into the parking area.

Sanitation:

Parking:

4; 4 days   Custom

Small motorhome only parking area alongside the main road near to the sports facilities. Close to Austrian border and 7km from Salzburg. Service point 300m away signed from the parking.

Activities and Facilities:

GAUSBURG

3B | 40 | N47°53.584' E12°56.653' | 400m

Paulbauernhof Farm, Gausburg 47, 83416 Surheim   www.paulbauernhof.de

Directions: From Laufen follow the B20 south. After 3km turn right signposted to Niederheining. Follow this road through Niederheining and in 2.3km turn right to Gausburg and the farm is on the left in 500m just before the railway track. Low railway bridges from other directions.

Sanitation:

E

Parking:

11; €7   Custom; 10amp elec €1.50; Long lead required

This dairy farm stopover has meat and homemade dairy products for sale. The Glasgows received a warm welcome, found a good set up with grass and gravel parking amongst trees in a pleasant location. There is a BBQ area and small common room for beer drinking in evening. Close to Austria, and an easy 10km drive to Salzburg.

Activities and Facilities:

PETTING

3B | 41 | N47°54.716' E12°48.551' | 500m

Farm Schneiderhof, Seestrasse 11a, 83367, Petting
www.stellplatz-schneiderhof.de

Directions: From Waging am See take the St2104 and travel 6km towards Petting. Exit the St2104 and take the flyover left on the TS23/ Seestrasse to Petting. The farm 'Schneiderhof' is 300m on the right, signed, just as you enter the village.

Sanitation:

Parking:

2; €14; May - Oct Custom; Elec €0.50 kwh.

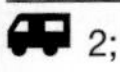 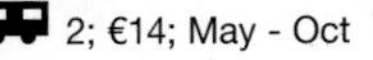 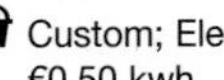

Situated in the pretty village of Petting which has a nice lowlands Bavarian feel - a bit like a cross between Somerset and the Alps - with painted flower-decked buildings, quaint churches and lush farmlands. This farm stop has pleasant views and is well equipped with pot washing area, good toilets and shower area.

Activities and Facilities:

EBING

3B | 42 | N47°54.468' E12°47.166' | 500m

Ebing 2, 83329, Gemeinde, Waging am See

Directions: From Waging am See at the roundabout on the ST2105 town bypass take the TS27 and travel south 3.2km towards Telsendorf. Turn left towards the village of Parschall and follow the road for 1.1km to Parschall and Ebing is in 500m further on the left, but not signed until you arrive.

Sanitation:

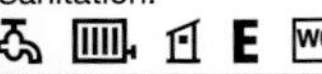   

Parking:

5; €15 inc elec; May - Oct Custom

 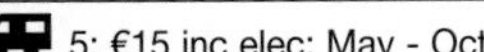 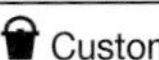

Motorhomes and tents can pitch up on a well kept grassy area at this pleasant farmyard. A communal eating and drinking area is available for rainy days.

Activities and Facilities:

AICH/PETTING

3B | 43 | N47°53.506' E12°46.456' | 500m

Aich 5, 83367, Petting

Directions: From Waging am See at the roundabout on the ST2105 town bypass take the TS27 and travel south 5.9km towards Telsendorf. After 5.3km pass the turning to Petting on the left and take the second right in 600mm signed off main road with 'camping sign'.

Sanitation:

E WC

Parking:

P

5; €12; Reduction low season; Easter – Oct

Custom; Elec €0.40 kwh.

This is a traditional farm surrounded by arable crops, which has nice open views of the countryside. The motorhome parking is adjacent to a restaurant and BBQ area.

Activities and Facilities:

PETTING-STUBERN

3B | 44 | N47°53.377' E12°47.089' | 500m

Stubern 1

Directions: From Waging am See at the roundabout on the ST2105 town bypass take the TS27 and travel south 7.4km towards Telsendorf. Turn left to Helming and in 200m turn left again in Helming to Stubern. The farm is in 600m down narrow country lane. Follow GPS no signs until you arrive.

Sanitation:

E WC 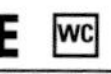  

Parking:

 P    

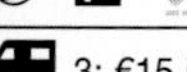 3; €15 inc elec  Custom 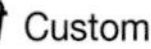

This is a very remote Bavarian farm, offering 100 percent peace and quiet. The Glasgows received a nice family welcome and mused at some wacky goats. The motorhome parking is amongst trees at the front of the farm, and the facilities very basic with no emptying point.

Activities and Facilities:

KIRCHANSCHORING 3B 45 N47°56.616' E12°49.338' 450m

Pollner 1

Directions: From Laufen head 4.8km northwest along the border on the B20. Turn left at Kolomann/TS25 (signs for Waging am See/Kirchanschöring). Travel 4.1km on the TS25 through Kirchanschoring and stay on the TS25 towards 'Lampoding', signed. After crossing the railway line take the 4th turning (100m after emerging from trees) on the left into Pollner strasse and the farm is 300m on the right.

Sanitation:

Parking:

10; May - Sep; €12

Custom; Elec €0.40 Kwh

Gasthof with attached, recently renovated, camping and stellplatze. Village is nice and home to Meindl walking boots factory with nice shop in centre.

Activities and Facilities:

BURGHAUSEN 3B 46 N48°09.274' E12°48.495' 400m

Berghamerstrasse 1

Directions: Travelling south toward Burghausen on the B20. Before entering the town, exit the B20 to the right onto Burgkirchener Strasse towards the ST2107 and Burgkirchen an der Alz. Follow this road for 2.8km turning left at the roundabout adjacent to McDonalds. In 1.2km at the end on the road turn right onto Berghamer Strasse and the motorhome parking is on the left in 400m adjacent to a BBQ area.

Sanitation:

Parking:

 16; 21 Days; €5; Apr - Oct

Holiday Clean; Water €1; Elec by coin slot.

Council run motorhome parking open Apr – Oct, pay at nearby hotel. Located on the outskirts of town at a huge grill/BBQ area, this is a pleasant green space with walks along the Salzach River, which forms the border with Austria. There is a bus route into the historic village and large castle.

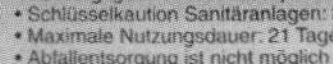

Activities and Facilities:

ALTOTTING — 3B — 47 — N48°13.380' E12°40.850' — 400m

Doltplatz, Burghauser Strasse

Directions: From the east side of town exit the ST2107 where it crosses the ST2607 and turn into Altotting onto Burghauser Strasse. Go straight across the first roundabout and follow signs 'P Doltplatz', on the left in 800m. It is a large gravel car park with separate motorhome parking.

Sanitation:

Parking:

8; Max 3 days

Custom; Water €1; 8hr elec €1

Large dusty car park with separate parking for eight motorhomes; there are toilets onsite and good electric points. It is an easy walk into the old town. This parking would always be second choice to the other parking area in town but during festivals and pilgrimages to see the Black Madonna in the octagonal Chapel of Grace, you may have no other choice.

Activities and Facilities:

ALTOTTING — 3B — 48 — N48°13.815' E12°40.465' — 400m

Rosenweg/Wohrstrasse

Directions: Travelling south exit the B299 to Altotting just after the B12 junction. Go straight across the first roundabout onto Muhldorfer Strasse. In 1km turn left at the crossroads into Raitenharter Strasse. In 200m take the first right onto Pater-Joseph-Anton-Strasse and follow signs for parking 'Wohrstrasse' 400m on the left.

Sanitation:

Parking:

10; max 3 Days

Custom/Holiday San; Water €1; 10hr elec €1

This is the better of the two motorhome parking areas in town. It has grassy/gravel marked bays, separated by mature trees. There is good sanitation and electric points. A five minute stroll gets you to the historic centre which has been the spiritual centre of Bavaria for over 1250 years. Every year more than a million pilgrims come to see the Black Madonna in the octagonal Chapel of Grace.

Activities and Facilities:

INGOLSTADT 2A 49 N48°45.669' E11°25.244' 375m

Jahnstrasse

Directions: From the west on either the B13 or the IN2 turn right onto the Westliche Ringstrasse ring road and then take the first left into Friedhofstrasse towards the old town. Drive 400m and follow the main road around to the right into Jahnstrasse and the parking is 500m on the right signposted 'Hallenbad' The motorhome parking is in a separate area to the rear of the car park. Enter through barrier and take ticket - pay on leaving.

Sanitation:

E WC

Parking:

P

9; €3 inc elec; Max 3 days

Holiday Clean; Water €1

The parking is just 100m from the lovely old city, with famous churches and breweries. Pick up a historic walk leaflet in English from the town hall (Rathaus) or have an afternoon beer in the popular marketplace, selling Bavarian food and beer until 8pm. The motorhome parking is in a separate area but has small bays, max 8m, and is deservedly popular, filling up most nights. If you want to use the service only, you get 30 minutes free when you take a ticket at the entrance barrier.

Activities and Facilities:

Zugspitze glacier skied from Garmisch-Partenkirchen

Passo d'Eira

Cervina

ITALY

Mountain biking

Start off of piste decent St Martino to gondola station

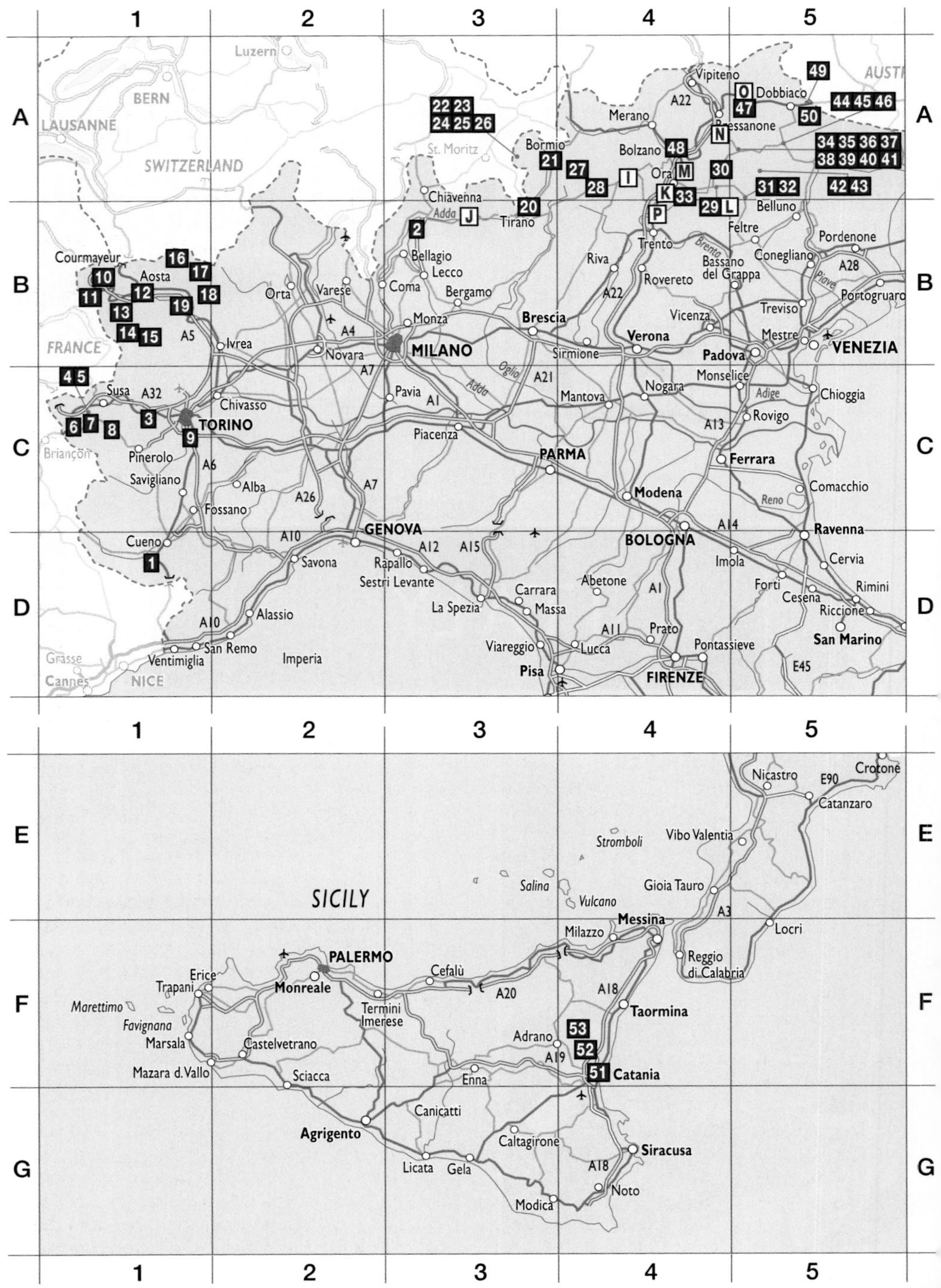
1
2
3
4
5
A
B
C
D
E
F
G
Luzern
BERN
LAUSANNE
SWITZERLAND
St. Moritz
AUSTR
FRANCE
Vipiteno
Dobbiaco
A22
Merano
Bressanone
Bolzano
Ora
Bormio
Chiavenna
Adda
Tirano
Belluno
Feltre
Pordenone
Trento
Brenta
Riva
Bassano del Grappa
Conegliano
A28
Piave
Rovereto
A22
Portogruaro
Treviso
Vicenza
Mestre
VENEZIA
Padova
Verona
Sirmione
Brescia
Bergamo
Bellagio
Lecco
Coma
Monza
Varese
Orta
Courmayeur
Aosta
A5
Ivrea
Novara
A4
MILANO
A7
Pavia
A1
Oglio
Adda
A21
Mantova
Nogara
Monselice
Adige
Chioggia
Rovigo
A13
Susa
A32
Chivasso
TORINO
Briançon
Pinerolo
A6
Savigliano
Alba
Fossano
A26
A7
Piacenza
PARMA
Ferrara
Modena
Comacchio
Reno
A14
BOLOGNA
Ravenna
Cueno
A10
GENOVA
A12
A15
Savona
Rapallo
Sestri Levante
Imola
Cervia
Abetone
Carrara
Massa
A1
Forli
Cesena
Rimini
La Spezia
Riccione
Alassio
A10
A11
Prato
San Marino
Pontassieve
Viareggio
Lucca
San Remo
Ventimiglia
Imperia
Grasse
Cannes
NICE
Pisa
FIRENZE
E45
Nicastro
E90
Crotone
Catanzaro
Stromboli
Vibo Valentia
Salina
Vulcano
Gioia Tauro
SICILY
Messina
A3
Milazzo
Locri
PALERMO
Reggio di Calabria
Erice
Trapani
Monreale
Cefalù
A20
Marettimo
Termini Imerese
A18
Taormina
Favignana
Marsala
Castelvetrano
Adrano
A19
Catania
Mazara d. Vallo
Sciacca
Enna
Canicatti
Agrigento
Caltagirone
Siracusa
Licata
Gela
A18
Noto
Modica
1
2
3
4
5
6
7
8
9
10
11
12
13
14
15
16
17
18
19
20
21
22
23
24
25
26
27
28
29
30
31
32
33
34
35
36
37
38
39
40
41
42
43
44
45
46
47
48
49
50
51
52
53
I
J
K
L
M
N
O
P

Italy is the best country in Europe for freewheeling tourists, there is so much to see and do its hard to know where to start, it even has warm winter sun especially on Sicily, the editor's favourite winter destination. There are plenty of campsites and lots of motorhome Aires so getting around is easy see www.vicarious-shop.co.uk for the latest guides. As Italy has such excellent food, it is good to get up into the mountains for a spot of walking, mountain biking or skiing before a long leisurely lunch. When you look around the slopes, you cannot help but wonder if looking good and eating well is more important than the physical activity. Generally, the ski slopes are only busy late morning at weekends as lying in and long lunches are popular. See www.italiantouristboard.co.uk for further information.

Driving and Roads

Travelling down Italy you will notice the road conditions continually deteriorate the further away from the industrial north you get. Motorways tend to have tolls, but the minor roads that run parallel are often more interesting and challenging. Cycling clubs are common and fly along the minor roads on Sundays. Road drainage appears uncommon in southern Italy. Road signing can be difficult to interpret so take some time to get it right; a straight on sign often looks to be indicating left or right. The south is less busy than the north but Italians love their cars so there is always some traffic.

Some ski resorts are only accessible by crossing high mountain passes, these can become blocked after light snow or wind, always check with tourist office on day of departure. All tourist offices receive daily updates for mountain pass conditions and a three-day snow forecast.

There are rumours that the Italians are mad drivers with one hand always on their horn. OK they are expressive with their horns, but it is an unofficial language that is easy to learn. One short beep from a following car is a warning that they are overtaking or simply I am here. Two beeps means ciao and they are generally saying hello to someone they know. A progression of beeps or one long beeeeeeeep usually means you or something is in the way. Either they have nearly driven into you or there is a parked car blocking the route.

Italians drive at two speeds: Fast and slow, those going slowly are happy to drift along and are not concerned by confused tourists. The speedy variety drive with intent often displaying full beam or flashing lights, as a general rule everyone gets out of their way and lets them through.

Parking is a sport in Italy and any space is fair game, even if it blocks the road. If a route is blocked the standard practice is to give a long blast on your horn, shopkeepers and passers by soon inspect the situation then summon the owner, who will soon move the car. This stresses no one and the queue of traffic will revel in beeping with you, it is a cultural thing, and when in Rome! Tailgating is something you have to accept. If you need to stop and think, when navigating towns, putting your hazard lights on will be enough to encourage people to drive around you. After dinner cruising is common, and really blocks towns, so try to avoid driving between 7-10pm

Mountain Biking

Cycling is popular in Italy. The Italian tourist offices are very helpful and often have maps and guides so it is always worth visiting the local office once you arrive. The Dolomites have numerous mountain biking routes; see www.infodolomiti.it where detailed descriptions are available on routes of an hour or more. The area around Bormio transforms into a mountain bikers summer utopia. The gondolas take cyclists and bikes up the mountains. Visit www.Altarezia.eu routes with GPS co-ordinates are downloadable for a small charge.

The Aosta valley has over 1000km of bike routes on un-surfaced former mule tracks, farm roads, and forest paths. Visit www.regione.vda.it/turismo/sport_eventi/sport simply click onto your chosen activity. Some day routes are detailed and can be found under bike itineraries. Lifts stay open during the summer at Pila and La Thuile, so downhill mountain biking and walking can be enjoyed.

Walking

Information panels throughout the Dolomites display walks of around two hours or more. Some starting points and walk overviews are displayed on www.dolomitipark.it under 'Tours'. The Dolomites are accessible from the towns of Belluno and Feltre. The visitor centre at Belluno (Piazza dei Martiri 8) is worth visiting before entering the park. The Aosta valley website provides detailed information on many outdoor activities, including walking (described as trekking), horse riding, mountain biking, water sports and numerous snow based activities. See www.regione.vda.it/turismo/sport_eventi/sport simply click onto your chosen activity. There are long walks plus over 300 one-day excursions with details and satellite maps.

Spas and Thermal Water

Modern-day Romans still partake in Wellness and using thermal spas is part of Italian culture. Naturally occurring warm thermal waters rise to the surface all over Italy but one of the best known is found in the Bormio Mountains. Bormio has been a spa town since Roman times, it has two thermal pool complexes, for more information visit www.bormioterme.it

Ski Info

The Milky Way: The Milky Way ski area connects to 400km of slopes and several resorts including Sestriere, Italy's first purpose built multi sports resort, dating from 1930s. The circular tower blocks, which look to be 1960s design, were actually built in the 1940s. Sauze d'Oulx hosted the 2006 winter Olympics, so invested in new chairlifts and gondolas throughout the area. British skiers dominate the slopes here in winter. Cesana Torinese is the Glasgows first choice for skiing in the area.

Aosta Valley: A series of resorts flank the Aosta Valley, which is located at the Italian end of the Mont Blanc tunnel providing easy access to Italy from France. The interlinked villages provide access to some excellent intermediate and off piste skiing. **Courmayeur** is a pricy ski resort but you can ski in sunshine all day. Ski the sunny Checrouit in the morning and follow the sun round to Val Veny in the afternoon. The intermediate slopes are not only for sliding on as posing in Prada is just as popular with Italians at weekends. The resort of **Cervina** has excellent skiing and connects to Zermatt in Switzerland via a 3480m gondola. Make the effort to be first up in the morning to ski on breathtaking snow and then treat yourself to some of Cervinas lively nightlife. At **Gressoney** it is important to check the ski lifts are going to be open, as they can be closed if quiet mid-week.

Italian/Swiss border: The resort of **Livigno** is high and snow sure with extensive slopes located on both sides of the valley. It is only accessible via a very exposed mountain pass, this can be blocked after light snow or wind; always check with Tourist Office on day of departure. Livigno is a duty free province of Italy with half price booze and fuel so officers from the customs post at the pass may stop and search you. **Bormio** is excellent for intermediate and beginner skiers and has a beautiful old town. Visit the Tourist Office for the free ski bus timetable and ask about weekly events held in the main square.

Dolomites: Both **Predazzo** and **Cavalese** offer convenient skiing from the Trento valley without having to cross any snow prone passes. The resort and parking area are empty except during holidays and at weekends when your vehicle may become boxed in during the day. All tourist offices receive daily updates for mountain pass conditions and a three-day snow forecast. At **Cortina d'Ampezzo** get to the top of Pomedes, 2303m, early in the morning for some dramatic, steep cruising on fresh snow. There is a breathtaking black run between cliffs - don't even think about the consequences of losing it! The Glasgows saw people having a morale-boosting pep talk before setting off! **San Vigilio de Marebbe** has loads of skiing for all levels, and the motorhome parking is slope side, you can ski out with a 50m walk back. This is an excellent resort for beginner boarders as there are no drag lifts just chairs and gondolas. There is also direct access to Kronplatz a single mountain with 31 gondolas and chairlifts feeding the summit from all sides. Just choose clockwise or anti clockwise and spend the day heading down to nice bars/restaurants and then back to the summit, then back down; it is strangely relaxing! **San Martino di Castrozza** is a secret valley with a small, attractive four-star resort surrounded by fantastic peaks the Italians are trying to keep to themselves, shame we discovered it.

Sella Ronda (Dolomites): Arabba is a nice village with low-level nightlife. You can choose to ski Mount Marmolada or the Sella Ronda circuit, the Glasgows first choice for skiing is the Sella Ronda. The steep local slopes can dismount the best of skiers, especially on the steep icy slopes as you return to the village. Arabba is smaller, prettier and better than **Canazei**. At an altitude of 2778m **Passo Falzarego** is at the top of the Mount La Gazvio and the start of an easy ski down on a red run known as the 'Hidden Valley'. At the bottom you connect with a horse drawn sledge rope tow (€2), which delivers you a short distance from the taxi station (€5 each, best to share), which takes you back to the pass and the motorhome parking. Several modestly priced cafe/restaurants tempt you to halt as you drop down into the 'Hidden Valley' keep an eye out for the WW1/WW2 mountain gun emplacements cut into the rock high above you! Passo Falzarego is an easy excursion from Cortina and if crystal clear weather were promised you'd be a fool not to spend a chilly night here and be the first down the mountain.

Etna: Etna is the largest volcano in Europe and one of the most active in the world. It makes for an interesting visit at any time and is accessible all year via a cable car and land rovers. The Etna effect, because Etna is a single large volcano in the middle of a warm ocean it causes its own unpredictable weather. It is often cloudy on the eastern side of the island so expect to wait a few days for clouds to clear before you climb the summit. On the mountain the weather can change rapidly and conditions can become bleak, so always pack for all conditions no matter how glorious the day. Any snowfall might be sudden and substantial, add wind and drifting snow and you may be stuck for a few days. So go prepared with chains, shovels, and provisions. The lava that covers the slopes of Mount Etna is sharp and irregular and good walking boots should be worn. Ski rental is available at the base station; it might be wise to rent skis, as the lava under the snow is sharp. Mount Etna has a modest selection of gondolas and chairs with runs amongst recent lava flows. Skiing Etna should not be underestimated; with rapidly closing in cloud, active volcano, and sharp irregular rock base beneath the snow, all make for challenging skiing. The area reeks with sulphur fumes and you have to admire the optimism of the resort to try again as previous ski lifts can been seen, partially buried in newly cooled lava. Guides are available for off piste skiing, ski mountaineering and walking subject to ability of individuals and the volcanoes activity. Visit www.funiviaetna.com for more information on visiting Etna.

Cervina top station with Matterhorn behind

BORGO SAN DALMAZZO

 D1 | 1 | N44°19.769' E007°29.505' 638m

Strada Comunale Del Cimiterio, Piemonte

Directions: From the Tende Tunnel travel north 26km on the E47/SS20 to Borgo San Dalmazzo. The Aire is on the right adjacent to swimming pool, 50m from the roundabout, 100m from village. Signed 'Area Camper' in town and at entrance.

Sanitation:

Parking:

 20   Custom

This is the first/last nice Aire when travelling the Tende tunnel route. Situated in a big village with historic centre, old church and museum. There is a supermarket by the roundabout and other local shops in the village. The ironmonger adjacent to church sells snow shovels for €14, top item!

Activities and Facilities:

COLICO

   B3 | 2 | N46°08.530' E009°22.465' 200m

Lake Como north via Montecchio Nord.

Tel: 0341 941782

Directions: From the south or north turn off the SS36 and take the SP72 into Colico. Travelling north drive past the train station and turn left by the MEGA building into Via al Monteggiolo, travelling south drive past the Q8 and turn right into Via al Monteggiolo, signed. Then turn left onto Viale Padania and over the railway track on a bridge. Follow Via Padania west alongside the railway, 75m past the station parking veer right onto Via Alle Torri. At the marina turn right onto Via Montecchio Nord, the Aire is 400m on the left.

Sanitation:

Parking:

  15; €13 inc elec.   Custom; Inc.

This private Aire is located on the banks of Lake Como. In the summer, there is shaded parking, a warden, sailing and canoe hire, there is also a bar and restaurant. This is a good winter night halt when travelling north to the Bormio Livigno region, but phone first to check it is open.

Activities and Facilities:

AVIGLIANA

 C1 | 3 | N45°04.379' E007°23.399' 620m

Via Suppo

Directions: Exit the E70/A32 9.5km west of Torino at Avigliana Est toward Avigliana. In 900m turn right at the roundabout then in 350m turn left at the roundabout. At the next roundabout (if unable to go under the railway), turn right alongside the track. In 600m turn left and cross the track and continue through town on Corso Laghi for 2.3km, then turn right onto Via Pontetto 150m from the lake and the Aire is 300m on the right. Well signed from main road, do not worry about height restriction signs on motorway as not along route to Aire.

Sanitation:

Parking:

20 None

Avigliana is located on the Val di Susa; this is an excellent location for skiers as it is at the base of valley for travelling in the Milky Way ski area or travelling to France via pass. The Aire has a solid tarmac base and is located on the outskirts of the village and 200m from the lake. The town is nice, the lakes are lovely, there are good walks, and non-ski activities.

Activities and Facilities:

SAUZE D'OULX

  C1 | 4 | N45°01.694' E006°51.865' 1498m

Via Monfol

Directions: From Sauze d'Oulx (do not go into town) travel north towards Monfol on the SP214. Located up a short winding road from Oulx, in car park on the right near Segg. S Comba chairlift.

Sanitation:

Parking:

20; Day None

Suitable day parking for visiting this ski area but 24 hour parking may be tolerated. 300m walk to centre of cheap and cheerful resort. Ski slopes are 200m by foot or bus. Try to avoid centre of Oulx after fresh snow as steep, polished granite cobbles make it slippery. There is a ski school in winter, in summer there is a mountain bike school, horse riding and walking guides.

Activities and Facilities:

SAUZE D'OULX

C1 | 5 | N45°03.718' E006°52.102' 1032m

Camping Gran Bosco - S.S. 24 Monginevro - Km75 - Salbertrand (TO), ITALY
www.campinggranbosco.it

Directions: From Turin take the A32/E70 towards Bardonecchia and exit at Junction 7, Oulx Est 2km after the toll booths (campsite adjacent) and go back towards Turin on the SS24 main road for about 2km and the campsite is on the left.

Sanitation:

Parking:

€26 — 6 amp Elec; Service only €3

Located in a valley bottom this touring campsite has modern facilities include a bar, restaurant, play area and games room. Touring pitches are on a grassy area with trees providing shade; the rest of the site has long stay pitches. Walking is popular in summer. The Sauze d'Oulx ski resort is a 6km drive and you will need your own transport. It is an easy drive to the French resorts of Sansicario, Sestriere, Cesana, Claviere, Monti Della Luna and Montgenevre, all are interconnected by ski lifts.

Activities and Facilities:

CESANA TORINESE

C1 | 6 | N44°56.880' E006°47.695' 1363m

Viale Bouvier adjacent to Hotel Chalet Casa Cesana

Directions: From Claviere on the French/Italian border head northeast to Cesana Torinese on the SS24. In Cesana Torinese turn right onto Viale Terzo Alpini, which becomes Viale Bouvier, travel 750m passing the supermarket and the Aire is on the left.

Sanitation:

Parking:

 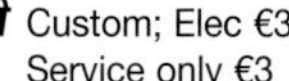

10, €10 — Custom; Elec €3; Service only €3

This is a very nice private Aire, follow instructions on the notice and pay at the adjacent hotel. Located by the river at the southern end of the village, it is a 10-minute walk to the village square; the Tourist Office has internet access. The village is best avoided at weekends as it comes alive catering to skiers from Turin and Milan. This small resort/village site is in the middle of the Milky Way ski area, and the Aire is only 5 minutes walk from the gondola station.

Activities and Facilities:

SESTRIERE

C1 | 7 | N44°57.876 E006°52.963 1693m

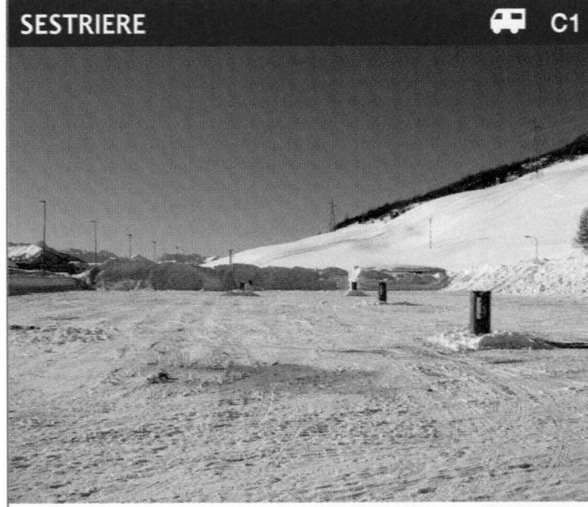

Area attrezzata autocaravan, Strada Azzurri d' Italia

Directions: Take exit 9 or 12 Oulx Circonvallazione off the A32/E70 and travel south 16.5km joining the SS24 to Cesana Torinese. Where the road splits at Cesana Torinese take the left fork, the SR23, 12km to Sestriere. Pass through the village and the Aire is past the football ground. If barrier is down, open it, park, and phone number on cabin to summon attendant. This Aire is marked on the Tourist Office map of the town.

Sanitation:

Parking:

30; €10 Elec €3

This is Italy's first purpose built resort. It looks sixties in style but started in the thirties, it is very popular with excitable Italians at weekends. The Aire is 900m from the ski lift. In town the Tourist Office has the shuttle bus timetable and internet. Walking, horse riding and rafting are popular in summer.

Activities and Facilities:

PRAGELATO

C1 | 8 | N44°59.397' E006°55.241' 1613m

Frazione Pattemouche, Via Rohrbach, 10060 Pragelato

Directions: From Sestriere follow the SR23 towards Pragelato. 2.5km before Pragelato turn right at a roundabout to the small village of Plan. The parking area is adjacent to Via Rohrbach on the left. The chairlift is 200m further on the left.

Sanitation:

Parking:

100; Day None

This day car park is just 200m from the lifts but before staying, check what lifts are/will be working the next day as this area is prone to lift closure on a whim. This area is very popular with Italian skiers on weekends so best avoided. There is a nice ski area for children. The village has bars and cafes.

Activities and Facilities:

AGIP A55/E70

C1 | 9 | N44°58.579' E007°39.477' 280m

Agip fuel station, Moncalieri

Directions: Located on A55/E70 westbound on free section of motorway, south of Turin 1km west of the SR2, Statale 20 junction, Moncalieri.

Sanitation:

Parking:

50; Not recommended Custom

This is a very useful service station with a motorhome service point. Stop, empty and replenish before you travel up to Val di Susa to resort of Sauze d'Oulx.

Activities and Facilities:

COURMAYEUR

B1 | 10 | N45°48.874' E006°57.376' 1300m

Val Veny Gondola Station, Strada Della Villette

Directions: Drive to the end of the A5/E26 toll motorway to the Val Veny Gondola Station, 1km from town. Drive past town towards the Funivie Monte Bianco. The parking is on the left. Use the last section of toll roads to avoid bad roads, hill climbs, and hairpin bends.

Sanitation:

Parking:

20 Custom

This is a top class village in the shadows of Mont Blanc. The gondola station is only 20m from the parking and a heli skiing pad and restaurant is adjacent. A ski bus runs to town and another bus goes to Chamonix. The nearby Funivie Monte Bianco is a sightseeing gondola open all year and offering great views of Mont Blanc/Monte Bianco and the Alps.

Activities and Facilities:

LA THUILE (VILLARET)  B1 | 11 | N45°42.509' E006°57.213' 1444m

Area Attrezzata Azzurra, Frazione Pierre-Carree

Directions: From Courmayeur take the SS26 south towards France for 13km to La Thuile. In La Thuile follow the main river Dora Rutor, keeping it on the right and not crossing it. This will take you straight to the Aire, which is on the right adjacent to the river in the Villaret area of the resort.

Sanitation:

Parking:

  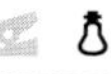  

 30; €10   Custom, Elec 6amp €4 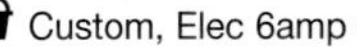

This new well-run private Aire is 100m from slopes and 50m from a Pizza bar. It is very busy at weekends but quiet mid-week. La Thuile is a quaint old mining town with lots of bars and cafés and has links to La Rosiare in France. The long tree-lined red run down to the main lift centre is highly recommended: it is steep, narrow, and twisty with occasional rocky patches. The resort is popular with mountain bikers in the summer.

Activities and Facilities:

AOSTA (PILA)  B1 | 12 | N45°44.187' E007°19.821' 580m

Via Caduti de Lavoro

Directions: Travelling west, exit the A5/E25 at the Aosta airport junction and join the SS26 and travel 3.4km toward Aosta and exit the SS26 signed to the station and Pila. Follow the road round to the left and at the Esso station take the left fork onto Via Clavalite. Drive 700m crossing the river and keeping the track on your left and the Aire is on the right adjacent to the road just before roundabout.

Sanitation:

Parking:

20; 80c p/h day. 20c p/h night (p/h = per hr)

None

Aosta is an industrial town with steel works but has Roman origins and has plenty of Roman ruins. This motorhome only parking area is suitable for a short stop when passing through. The 1km walk to the lifts in Aosta for the main Pila Gondola is not pleasant. There is big pay car park at main gondola station, which gets busy at weekends with motorhomes.

Activities and Facilities:

AYMAVILLES  B1 13 N45°42.074' E007°14.371' 600m

Frazione Moulins

Directions: Exit the A5 to Aymavilles, 2km west of Aosta. Follow the SR47 into town past the church and at the monument by the cemetery turn right off the SR47 onto Strada Comunale del Moulins. The Aire is 100m on the left.

Sanitation:

Parking:

  10; €8 1/05 - 31/10  Custom

This is an area with old castles and vineyards making this a nice summer Aire, it is also a lot nicer than the Aire at Aosta. A useful place to exchange water before heading up the Aosta valley. There is a bar and shop in the village. There is a campsite 10km to the south, it has not been inspected so please see website: www.campeggiolapineta.it

Activities and Facilities:

 COGNE  B1 14 N45°36.504' E007°21.529' 1534m

Circonvallazione Nord

Directions: From Aymavilles follow the SR47 out of the town to Cogne. At the roundabout, at the entrance to Cogne, turn left following the main route to Lillaz. Immediately before the river bridge turn right and follow the road to the far end of the car park.

Sanitation:

Parking:

 60; €8  Elec 6amp €2 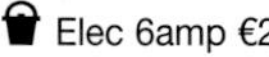

A small but very endearing alpine village that is an ideal area to spend a few days. There are pleasant walks taking in churches, rivers, and waterfalls. The Aire is large and well organised with easy access via a ski bus to the gondola. It is excellent for cross-country skiers and walkers, and has a good children's ski slope. The resort is empty during the week, a couple of restaurants open at weekends. The SPA supermarket sells local cheese and wine at reasonable prices.

Activities and Facilities:

LILLAZ B1 15 N45°35.761' E007°23.289' 1560m

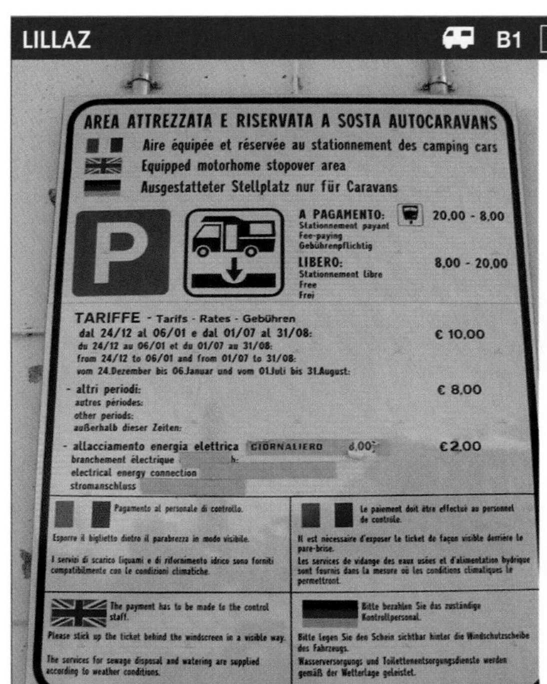

Frazione Lillaz

Directions: From Cogne, follow the main road to Lillaz. As you enter Lillaz go straight on at the road fork and the Aire is immediately in the car park on your right.

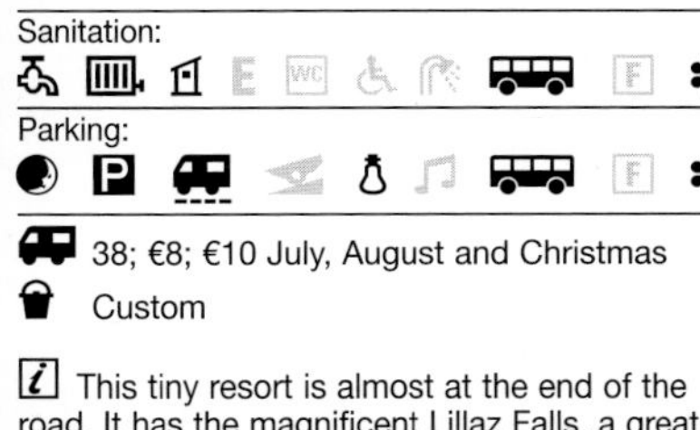

Sanitation:

Parking:

38; €8; €10 July, August and Christmas

Custom

This tiny resort is almost at the end of the road. It has the magnificent Lillaz Falls, a great attraction for tourists in summer and ice climbers in winter. As well as an Aire there are two campsites located next to each other alongside the river, both are open all year.

Activities and Facilities:

CERVINA B1 16 N45°55.554' E007°37.228' 1990m

Piazzale Funivie

Directions: From Chatillon take the SR46 up through Valtourneche to Cervina. Before entering Cervina you will pass Lac Blue then the road forks, take the left fork and the Aire is on the right before the tunnel.

Sanitation:

Parking:

50; €6 collected by warden

Custom; If water frozen try garage opp

Fantastic ski resort, huge Aire with regular and convenient ski bus, €1, see adjacent bus stop for timetable. The village is an easy 1km level walk via tunnel or a forest track; there are bars, swimming pool, and bowling. This resort is 1990m high so wait for fine weather when you can appreciate the view. It will be colder here, even in summer, but in winter temperatures of -17.5° are possible, so service your motorhome at Verres 19.

Activities and Facilities:

GRESSONEY-LA-TRINITE/STAFAL TSCHAVAL B1 17 N45°51.373' E007°48.803' 1850m

SR43/44

Directions: From the A5 turn off towards Pont-St-Martin and follow the SR44 through Gressoney St Jean (see 18) to Gressoney-La-Trinité. This is a steep, winding road up from valley and at weekends it is busy with Italians who frequently cross the central white line. Drive through Gressoney-La-Trinité to Stafal Tschaval and the Aire is on the left in a large car park before the gondola station.

Sanitation:

Parking:

20; €12 Custom; Heated; Elec 3 amp €3

This is a well-run, clean, private Aire. You pay €12 for 24hrs parking so you can arrive late and depart late. The electricity reset switch is locked in the warden's office at night, so don't blow your fuse! Day parking costs €5. The gondola and ticket office is 50m walk but check that lifts are open before deciding to stay. It is also popular to access the Tour Monte Rosa hike from here. The Glasgows recommend that you experience the adjacent Finnish bar.

Activities and Facilities:

GRESSONEY-ST-JEAN B1 18 N45°45.593' E007°50.132' 1348m

SR44

Directions: From the A5 turn off towards Pont-St-Martin and follow the SR44 towards Gressoney-St-Jean. The Aire is just before the gondola station in the large car park on the left at Bieltschocke to the south of Gressoney-St-Jean.

Sanitation:

Parking:

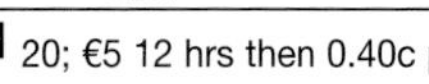

20; €5 12 hrs then 0.40c per hour

Custom; Heated; 6amp elec inc

Tschaval, entry 17, is higher with better downhill skiing, but this resort is more convenient in bad weather and heavy snow. There is good cross-country skiing and walking. The ski lifts are just 50m away across the car park and a swimming pool and a bar are onsite. The Aire is council run and while more basic than its neighbour has a better supply of electricity. This lovely valley feels very Swiss with signs in German and is dominated by Italian owned weekend chalets.

Activities and Facilities:

VERRES

B1 | 19 | N45°39.770' E007°41.623' 377m

Via Duca d'Aosta

Directions: Verres sits at the entrance of the Aosta valley. Travelling north on the SS26 which runs alongside the A5/E25, just as you enter the village take the right fork at the Agip fuel station. The Aire is 300m on the right adjacent to a Tamoil fuel station and opposite the Lavazza coffee-roasting factory and the smell makes you constantly hungry.

Sanitation:

Parking:

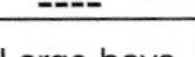
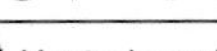
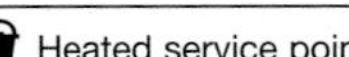

10 Large bays | Heated service point

An excellent service area with overnight parking on the southern edge of a small village. This is an ideal place to service when entering and leaving Aosta valley in summer or winter with a guaranteed unfrozen water supply from the heated service point. It is highly recommended that you call in here for services if heading to any other higher resort in case they are frozen.

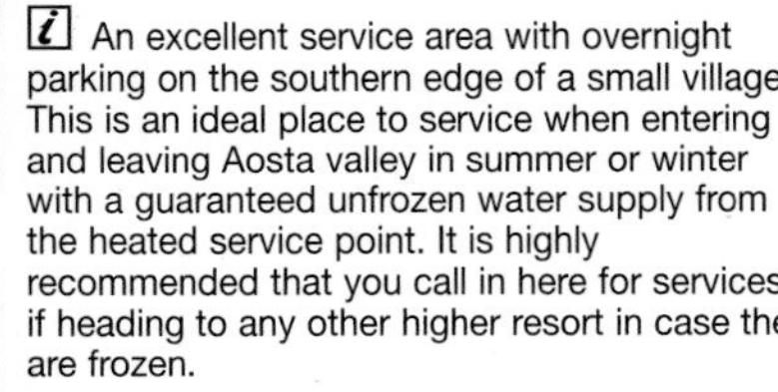

Activities and Facilities:

TIRANO

B3 | 20 | N46°12.833' E10°09.425' 430m

Via San Giuseppe

Directions: Travelling from the east side of Tirano on the SS38. After crossing the storm gully on a bridge turn left after the train station onto Via San Giuseppe and the Aire is in 650m on the left.

Sanitation:

Parking:

50; €5 | 10amp elec inc

A very convenient Aire with reliable winter service point making it an ideal stopover if heading to Bormio or using the Bernina Pass to Switzerland. There is a Lidl nearby and LPG in the valley. This large Aire is well maintained and the 10amp electric is unmetered. The Bernina Express station is 500m away, the little red Bernina train takes you to St. Moritz.

Activities and Facilities:

BORMIO

A3 | 21 | N46°27.739' E10°22.291' 1210m

Via Battaglion Morbegno

Directions: In the centre of the village turn off the SS38, onto the SS300 and into Via Don Peccedi. Go straight on and cross the river bridge into Via Funivia. At the large roundabout turn left (2nd exit) into Via Ferruccio Parri and at the end of the road turn right into Via Battaglion Morbegno. The Aire is at the end of the road adjacent to the gondola. If barrier closed when arrive open barrier and drive in, but shut it behind you otherwise cars fill Aire.

Sanitation:

Parking:

50; €8 — 50; €8 per 24hrs

This large Aire should always have space and the slopes are accessed by gondola 10m away, a ski bus runs in winter. A 5 minutes walk gets you to the ancient medieval village centre with old churches and towers, and events in the square. Visit the alpine dairy and cheese shop at Via di Simoni, it sells Alpine milk by the litre and has good value cheeses with samples on the counter. There are very nice thermal baths locally www.bormioterme.it.

Activities and Facilities:

EIRA, LIVIGNO

A3 | 22 | N46°32.326' E10°09.885' 2200m

SS301

Directions: From Bormio follow the SS301 over the high Passo di Foscagno. The Aire is located adjacent to the SS301 as you exit the tiny resort of Eira towards Livigno.

Sanitation:

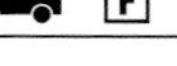

Parking:

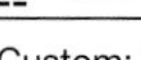

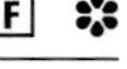

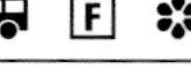

20 — Custom; May be frozen in winter

This is a very high (2200m) free Aire with stunning views and access to the Livigno ski area. The service point may be frozen and during heavy snow you may have to become a resident!

Activities and Facilities:

PALIPERT, LIVIGNO

A3 | 23 | N46°30.341' E10°07.124' 1872m

Campeggio Stellaalpina, Via Palipert 570
www.campingstellaalpina.it

Directions: Follow to SS301 past Livigno towards the Swiss border. 2km from Livigno, at Palipert, the campsite is located on the right adjacent to the road.

Sanitation:

Parking:

30; €15

Custom; Showers €1; 3 amp elec

A nice campsite with good views and the free bus that stops outside takes campers 2km to the village and ski slopes. This is one of four campsites in Livigno all charging the same price. The area has 3,200km of mountain bike trails, walks and horse riding.

Activities and Facilities:

PALIPERT, LIVIGNO

A3 | 24 | N46°30.361' E10°07.182' 1872m

Camping Palipert, Via Palipert 530

Directions: Follow to SS301 past Livigno towards the Swiss border. 2km from Livigno, at Palipert, the campsite is located on the left.

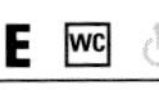

Sanitation:

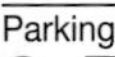

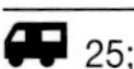

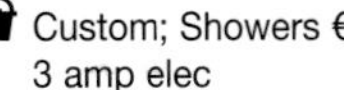

Parking:

25; €15

Custom; Showers €1; 3 amp elec

A nice campsite with good views and the free bus that stops outside takes campers 2km to the village and ski slopes. There is a bar and restaurant on site. This is one of four campsites in Livigno all charging the same price. The area has 3,200km of mountain bike trails, walks and horse riding.

Activities and Facilities:

PALIPERT, LIVIGNO

A3 | 25 | N46°30.432' E10°07.129' 1872m

Camping Aquafresco, Via Palipert 374
Tel: 0342 970418

Directions: Follow to SS301 past Livigno towards the Swiss border. 2km from Livigno, at Palipert, the campsite is located on the right adjacent to the road and is the first of three adjacent campsites.

Sanitation:

E

Parking:

P

20; €15

Custom, Shower €1, 3 amp elec

A nice campsite with good views and the free bus that stops outside takes campers 2km to the village and ski slopes. There is a bar and restaurant on site. This is one of four campsites in Livigno all charging the same price. The area has 3,200km of mountain bike trails, walks and horse riding.

Activities and Facilities:

LIVIGNO

A3 | 26 | N46°32.852' E10°08.701' 1871m

Camping Pemont, Via Pemont 11,
Tel: 0342 997536

Directions: From Bormio follow the SS301 into town and at the roundabout turn right into the main street. Go straight across the next roundabout and then turn first right crossing a bridge. Follow this road turning left when the road forks and the campsite is on the left in 200m.

Sanitation:

E

Parking:

P

30; €17

Custom; Underground WC; Showers

All four local campsites are the same quality but this is the largest and the only one within walking distance of a large après ski/bar and hotel. The campsite is popular with Germans and full-time workers from the resort. It is an easy walk into town and there is a ski bus to the gondola station.

Activities and Facilities:

ST CATERINA VALFURVA

A4 | 27 | N46°24.573' E10°30.552' 1756m

Via Forni

Directions: From Bormio take the SS300 for 10km to S. Caterina Valfurva along a valley road. When you enter the village turn left into Via Frodolfo which leads onto Via Forni following the river. The Aire is on the right 1km from the village.

Sanitation:

E

Parking:

20; €8 — Custom; Elec €2

The resort is small and popular with Italians at weekends but it is higher, colder, and has more snow than Bormio. Ski tip: Valle dell Alpe with new fast quad chairlift gets early sun, save the north facing Blachs hill until after lunch when the sun swings around.

Activities and Facilities:

PASSO DEL TONALE

A4 | 28 | N46°15.421' E10°35.011' 1883m

SS42

Directions: Adjacent to the SS42 between Trento and Sondrio at Passo del Tonale by the ski lifts.

Sanitation:

Parking:

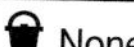

15 — None

Excellent overnight motorhome parking at the ski lifts. Other motorhome parking is signed off the main road but they charge €10. The resort is very busy with British school groups and at weekends with Italians creating a lively nightlife, but has its own strange 'End of the World' feel. The pass to the resort is windy and there are WW1 war memorials to visit en route.

Activities and Facilities:

PREDAZZO

A4 | 29 | N46°19.581' E11°35.988' 1744m

Latemar Gondola Station, SS48

Directions: Follow the SS48 2km north of Predazzo and the Aire is at the gondola station on the right.

Sanitation:

Parking:

20 None

Nice spot next to the gondola station. A Wild West style mini train runs through all day between gondola and village to encourage you into the centre. There is a nice geology museum and a swimming pool on outskirts, signed from village centre. Popular at weekends as there is good skiing via several interlinked areas all the way to Obereggen. There is a local food produce tour featuring cheese, honey and beer around the local resorts.

Activities and Facilities:

FORNO/MOENA

A4 | 30 | N46°21.137' E11°37.887' 1168m

Bar Il Giardino, Via F Facchini 12, 38035 SS48

Directions: Adjacent to the SS48 3km south of Moena as you enter Forno on the left at the Bar Il Giardino.

Sanitation:

Parking:

20; €12 inc elec 6amp Custom

Moena is larger and livelier than Predazzo. The valley is served by many ski buses that link up the various resorts. Bus timetables are found here and 3km away at Predazzo Gondola station. Bar Il Giardino is a nice friendly bar and this would make a good summer base for exploring the region.

Activities and Facilities:

SAN MARTINO DI CASTROZZA  A5 31 N46°15.189' E11°48.049' 1323m

Area Camper Tognola
www.campingsassmaor.it

Directions: From Predazzo follow the SS50 to San Martino Di Castrozza. This involves driving the 1970m Rolle Pass. Usually the pass is ok even though it's a minor road. The motorhome parking is 100m from the Tognola lift station at the southern edge of the village, well signed. The parking has a ticket issuing, automatic gate, you pay when you leave.

Sanitation:

Parking:

20; €12 Heated indoor service station; Elec €1 for 80 minutes; Service only €2.50

The Aire is 100m from the Tognola lift station taking you up to easy intermediate runs. Ski buses call at entrance to Aire, making visiting Predazzo easy. Take a trip to the top of the 2743m Mount Rosseta, on the sightseeing cable car, included with ski pass. There is a BBQ area onsite.

Activities and Facilities:

SAN MARTINO DI CASTROZZA   A5 32 N46°15.660' E11°47.821' 1350m

SASS Maor Campsite, Via Laghetto 48, 38054,
www.campingsassmaor.it

Directions: From Predazzo follow the SS50 to San Martino Di Castrozza. This involves driving the 1970m Rolle Pass. Usually the pass is ok even though it's a minor road. Follow signs to the campsite, which is at the ski lifts on west outskirts of town.

Sanitation:

Parking:

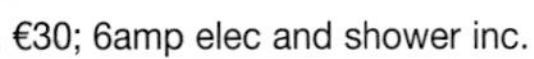

20, €30; 6amp elec and shower inc.

€5 service only

The same family who also run the excellent motorhome parking run this campsite. The slopes, 50m from the campsite, suit beginners, otherwise free ski buses take you to other areas and the nice village centre. Take a trip to the top of the 2743m Mount Rosseta on the sightseeing cable car, included with ski pass.

Activities and Facilities:

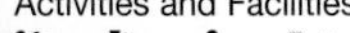
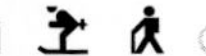

CAVALESE

A4 | 33 | N46°17.077' E11°28.184' 1300m

Main gondola car park SS232

Directions: From Ora follow the SS48 up the valley to Cavalese. At Cavalese follow the SP232 towards Predazzo. The parking is in the main gondola car park adjacent to the SP232.

Sanitation:

Parking:

50; Day None

This resort and Predazzo rely on weekend skiers so they provide large organised car parks, with motorhome areas at the base of the gondola stations. Park where directed and don't abuse situation so that motorhomes continue to be welcome. There are no facilities but overnight parking allowed/expected. You can catch a ski bus 1km to the village with plenty of life.

Activities and Facilities:

CANAZEI

A5 | 34 | N46°28.369' E11°46.548' 1436m

Camping Marmolada, Via Pareda SS64, 38032. www.campingmarmoloda.com

Directions: From the west follow the valley on the SS48 into Canazei. The campsite is in Canazei on the left before the SS48/SS641 roundabout 20m from the gondola station. Travelling this direction means there are no passes to cross.

Sanitation:

   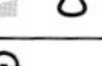  

Parking:

50; €28.50 6amp elec inc

Located in the village just 20m from the gondola station. There are hot showers and a washing machine so you might want to treat yourself. This is a good site for caravans and very popular with Dutch caravanners.

Activities and Facilities:

MALGA CIAPELA A5 35 N46°25.754' E11°55.050' 1200m

Camping Malgo Ciapela Marmolada, Loc. Malga Ciapela, 116, 32020 Rocca Pietore, www.camping.dolomiti.com/malgaciapela

Directions: Adjacent to the SS641 between Alleghe and Canazie. Easiest route is to turn off the SS203 4.4km north of Alleghe to Rocca Pietore, drive past Rocca Pietore following the SS641 to Malga Ciapela. The campsite is 50m from the gondola station.

Sanitation:

Parking:

150; €21.20 inc elec

Custom; Elec inc

This campsite is in a lovely setting under a mountain and real care has been taken to make it appealing. There is a nice restaurant and bar. This campsite would make a nice summer base for exploring excellent gorge walks and forest trails. Not that convenient for Sella Ronda skiing but right under a big gondola up the 3343m Mount Marmolada with huge red runs down. There is a ski bus to Arabba/Alleghe.

Activities and Facilities:

MALGA CIAPELA A5 36 N46°25.632' E11°54.664' 1210m

Localita Malga Ciapela, at main gondola station

Directions: Adjacent to the SS641 between Alleghe and Canazei. Easiest route is to turn off the SS203 north of Alleghe to Rocca Pietore, drive past Rocca Pietore following the SS641 to Malga Ciapela. The parking is at the gondola.

Sanitation:

Parking:

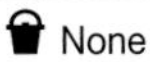

20; Day None

Large unrestricted car park directly under the gondola, many Italian motorhomes park here at weekends. The gondola goes up the 3343m Mount Marmolada with its famous long red runs. Glasgows tip: Walk the gorge footpath; it's a dramatic walk along the bottom of 20m wide gorge with river running down it. In winter check if it is skiable, but don't blame us if it all ends in tears!

Activities and Facilities:

ARABBA

A5 | 37 | N46°29.826' E11°52.675' 1600m

Area Sosta Camper Attrezzata, Via Piagn 6, 32020

Directions: Adjacent to the SS641. Can access from Canazei via Passo Pordoi or from Corvara via Passo di Campolongo. The easiest route is to turn off the SS203 north of Alleghe to Rocca Pietore, drive past Rocca Pietore following the SS641 to Arabba. The parking area is on outskirts to the left as you drive to ski lifts which lead to the Marmolada area.

Sanitation:

Parking:

18, €12 or €15 inc 16 amp elec

Custom; Showers €3

Nice private Aire run by a couple from the small bar. A floodlit ice skating rink is adjacent. This is the best base in the area for Sella Ronda route. The village centre is 200m and the gondola is a 5 minutes walk. The gondola links into Sella Ronda circuit and an easy link to Mount Marmolada ski area.

Activities and Facilities:

COLFOSCO

A5 | 38 | N46°33.014' E11°51.585' 1700m

Camping Colfosco, Str Sorega 15, Colfosco. www.campingcolfosco.org

Directions: From Corvara follow the SS243 to Colfosco. The campsite is on the left as you enter the town.

Sanitation:

 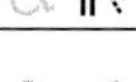 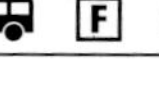

Parking:

 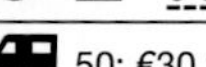 

50; €30.20

Custom, Elec 0.50c per kwh

Convenient location just 100m from the slopes, which are most suitable for beginners but there are lifts to the Sella Ronda. Colfosco village is 300m and Corvara is 1km along a forest path.

Activities and Facilities:

PASSO FALZAREGO

A5 | 39 | N46°31.186' E12°00.522' 2116m

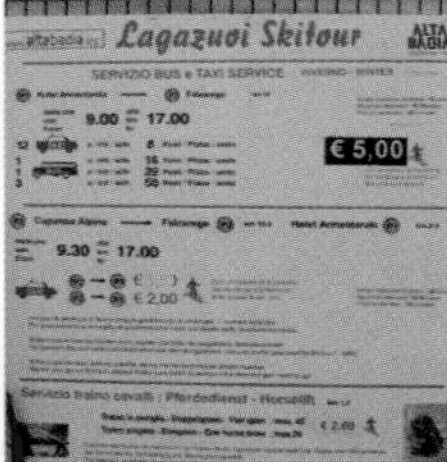

SR 48 11km from Cortina

Directions: Passo Falzarego is located on the SR48 between Cortina d'Ampezzo 14km east and Arabba 20km west. The parking is at the gondola station adjacent to the SR48 junction with the SP37 road to La Villa.

Sanitation:

Parking:

20 None

It is worth spending a night at this car park to be the first skier down the valley in the morning, almost a religious experience. This is only a car park allowing overnight motorhome parking but what a location, at base of the gondola which takes you to the top of the 2778m Mount La Gazvio. There is also an interesting WWI mountain war museum at the Aire.

Activities and Facilities:

SELVA DI VAL GARDENA

A5 | 40 | N46°31.968' E11°46.345' 1780m

Strada Plan de Gralba, SS242

Directions: From Selva Di Val Gardena travel south on the SS242 towards Canazei. 2km after the last houses of Selva, the ski station and parking for Plan de Gralba is on the right. Alternatively from Canazei follow the SS242 across the Stella Pass towards Selva di Val Gardena. The Stella Pass is high (2300m), avoid after fresh snow and cross at noon when wind driven snow has melted. Take the SS243 turning toward Selva and the Aire is on the left at the gondola station.

Sanitation:

Parking:

20; €6 day; €6 night None

The ski station is 20m away but there is no village just a collection of bars and hotels.

Activities and Facilities:

SELVA DI VAL GARDENA  A5 | 41 | N46°32.807' E11°46.061' 1594m

Strada Ciampinei Selva

Directions: From Selva Di Val Gardena travel south on the SS242 heading towards Canazei. Just before exiting the town the ski station and parking is on the right. Alternatively from Canazei follow the SS242 across the Stella Pass towards Selva di Val Gardena. The Stella Pass is high (2300m), avoid after fresh snow and cross at noon when wind driven snow has melted. Take the SS243 turning to Selva and drive to the village and the Aire is on the left at the gondola station.

Sanitation:

Parking:

 10; €12  None

This is the nicer of the two Selva motorhome aires. The ski slopes are 50m and there are a few bars across the river. It is also significantly lower than the other motorhome parking.

Activities and Facilities:

ALLEGHE  A5 | 42 | N46°24.757' E12°00.976' 1000m

SR 203

Directions: From Alleghe follow the SS203 1km north along the river valley. The large, easy access, designated motorhome parking area is on the left at the north end of the lake.

Sanitation:

Parking:

  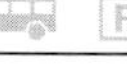 

 50   None

This area is on the northern edge of Alleghe lake. The slopes and gondola are 2km by ski bus to the lakeside village. In summer the local area is popular with climbers. Alleghe has Ice disco dancing in winter, Ski Civetta museum with skeleton, and a nail museum (the building sort)!

Activities and Facilities:

ALLEGHE

A5 | 43 | N46°23.745' E12°00.474' | 950m

SR 203 Masare-Col Badiot, Alleghe.

Directions: From Alleghe follow the SS203 south along the river valley. The campsite is 550m past the south end of the lake where the road bends.

Sanitation:

Parking:

30; €23.50 Elec 2amp

This is a nice looking campsite but couldn't find anyone to enquire further (3 hour lunch break). Although the town Aire is very good, if you want luxury, try here.

Activities and Facilities:

CORTINA D'AMPEZZO

A5 | 44 | N46°32.666' E12°07.909' | 1219m

Base of Col Druscie Gondola, Via Dello Stadio

Directions: From Arabba enter town on the SS48. After a hairpin bend follow the SS48 to a 'Z' bend. On the second bend turn left into Via Alberto Bonacossa and follow this 500m to the parking at the gondola at the base of Col Druscie, 200m from the old centre. Height barrier at car park not in use as car park is also ski bus terminal and coach park.

Sanitation:

Parking:

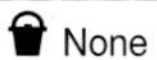

10; Day parking None

Ideal day parking and possibly tolerated night parking, readers must make their own assessments. Warning, your vehicle will get boxed in during day here until 5pm, but the traffic quiet at night until 8am in morning. The old village centre is just 200m away, and the resort is posh but the skiing is not too demanding.

Activities and Facilities:

CORTINA D'AMPEZZO

 A5 45 N46°34.337' E12°07.030' 1200m

Localita Fiames, SS51

Directions: Head out of Cortina D'Ampezzo on the SS51. Located 3km north on the left of SS51 on the opposite side of a sports stadium.

Sanitation:

Parking:

 10; poss pay  None

The park office may charge for use of Aire. Seems Cortina might be in a period of change for Aires/motorhomes as this official Aire seems to be a bit neglected. There is a river 3 minutes walk and a sports stadium across the road.

Activities and Facilities:

CORTINA D'AMPEZZO

A5 46 N46°34.341' E12°06.945' 1230m

International Camping Olympia, 32043 Cordina d'Ampezzo, www.campingolympiacortina.it

Directions: Head out of Cortina D'Ampezzo on the SS51 and in 3km when you enter the Localita Fiames, turn left sp 'camping'. If you pass a sports stadium on the SS51 you have gone too far! Follow the road across a bridge to the campsite. Don't worry about 3m height barrier as the entrance to left of the main gate can be opened.

Sanitation:

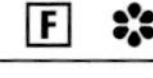

Parking:

 100; €24 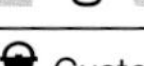 Custom, 16amp elec inc

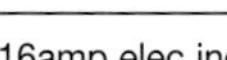

Nice picturesque campsite set in lovely valley adjacent to Olympic cross-country area. Convenient ski bus takes you 3km to downhill slopes. Snow Polo is also played in the area (bring your own pony!).

Activities and Facilities:

ST VIGILIO DE MAREBBE A5 47 N46°42.349' E11°55.808' 1250m

St Vigilio, Ritterkeller,Kronplatze, Val Badia, www.ritterkeller.it

Directions: From Brunico/Bruneck/SS49 travel 11km south towards Corvara on the S244 then come off S244 (straight ahead) onto Longega Strasse/SP43 4km to St Vigilio de Marebbe. Once you reach the village turn left onto Plan de Corones Strasse continuing on the SP43 through St Vigilio de Marebbe towards Valdaora. Turn left into gondola car park as exit St Vigilio de Marebbe.

Sanitation:

Parking:

50; €20 ticket issued on entry

Custom, Elec 4amp

This is an undiscovered Italian gem overlooking Switzerland. Very popular and deservedly so as the Aire is in an up and coming Italian resort, and the Aire is slope side. You can ski out with a 50m walk back. Be warned the wastewater point is tricky if icy. 10kg Italian gas cylinders can be exchanged for €28, and German type cylinders are on sale. The reception has a pleasant bar that sells nice pizza. The village is a pleasant 10 minutes stroll and has ice skating and a swimming pool.

Activities and Facilities:

BOLZANO A4 48 N46°28.419' E11°19.612' 340m

Via Bruno Buozzi

Directions: Exit the A22 sign posted 'Bozen Sud' and turn into Bolzano onto Torricelli strasse. At the first roundabout turn right. At the next roundabout turn right. Follow this road turning left into a car park before crossing the railway line.

Sanitation:

Parking:

Not recommended Custom

A very convenient service point near the entry/exit Brenner Pass or when skiing in Kronplatz. It is possible to park overnight but it is a busy and noisy car park. The smell of kebabs from adjacent kebab shop and noise from the railway station would keep you awake till late.

Activities and Facilities:

SAN CANDIDO

A5 | 49 | N46°44.344' E12°21.964' 1246m

Via Pusteria 1, 39038 S.Candido

Directions: From San Candido follow the SS49 towards Austria along Val Pusteria for 2km. Located between the road and a small river

Sanitation:

Parking:

30; €12

Custom; 16amp elec inc

Located 1km from Austrian border, so convenient for skiing and walking in the National Park. Possible to book ahead if arriving late, phone 0474 010039. The Aire is good value, well kept, has bar/restaurant, bike hire in summer and has a nice owner. Convenient to ski Sesto, a nice compact ski area with views of 3 towers 'Tre Cimes'. An Austrian vignette is available at the border fuel station, 2km east.

Activities and Facilities:

SESTO/SEXTEN

A5 | 50 | N46°40.018' E12°24.000' 1530m

Caravan Park Sexten, St Joseph Strasse, S4, www.patzenfeld.com

Directions: From San Candido head south on the SS52 along the Pustena Valley. The campsite is 5.5km south of Sesto, adjacent to SS52.

Sanitation:

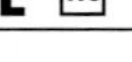

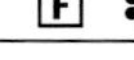

Parking:

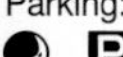

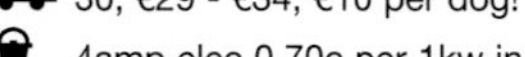

30; €29 - €34; €10 per dog!

4amp elec 0.70c per 1kw in campsite

Campsite with Aire in an adjacent car park. Both very expensive and campsite aimed at 'Wellness'. Fine views if clear, and can ski out but will have to bus back, and not linked to other resorts. The campsite/Aire is 5.5km from the village.

Activities and Facilities:

CATANIA

F4 | 51 | N37°31.969' E15°07.203' Sea level

Camping Jonio, Via Villini a Mare 2, 95126 Catania, www.campingjonio.com

Directions: Directly on seafront northeast of Catania centre and 600m north of the marina. Follow signs from SS114 dual carriageway. Ring bell to open security gates.

Sanitation:

Parking:

 30; €15 - €43 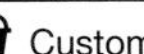 Custom

This is a pleasant campsite and an ideal place to wait for clear weather, which is needed when intending to ski on Mount Etna. WiFi €10 for 7 days.

Activities and Facilities:

NICOLOSI

F4 | 52 | N37°37.375' E15°00.52' 870m

Etna camping Nicolosi, Via Wolfgang Goethe

Directions: Follow the SP92 from Nicolosi towards Etna Sud. Turn off the SP92 onto Via W Goethe, then turn left at the stadium and the parking is before the large roundabout on the left.

Sanitation:

  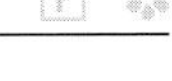

Parking:

 130; €21  Custom; 6 amp elec

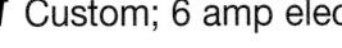

The campsite is set amidst trees with a swimming pool that is open in summer. The cable car up south side of Mount Etna is a short drive away. Town centre is 2km away.

Activities and Facilities:

ETNA SUD

F4 53 N37°41.951' E15°00.064' 1923m

Refuge Sapienza

Directions: Follow SP92 main road up to Etna sign posted 'Etna Sud'. Large car park at Etna visitor centre.

Sanitation:

Parking:

20; €5 None

This Aire is a great place to overnight, waiting for clear weather to ski, however it is bleak and windswept - you have been warned! Ski hire in adjacent car park.

Activities and Facilities:

Mount Etna lava buried house

Renteria

Espinosa de los Monteros

SPAIN

Mount Teide

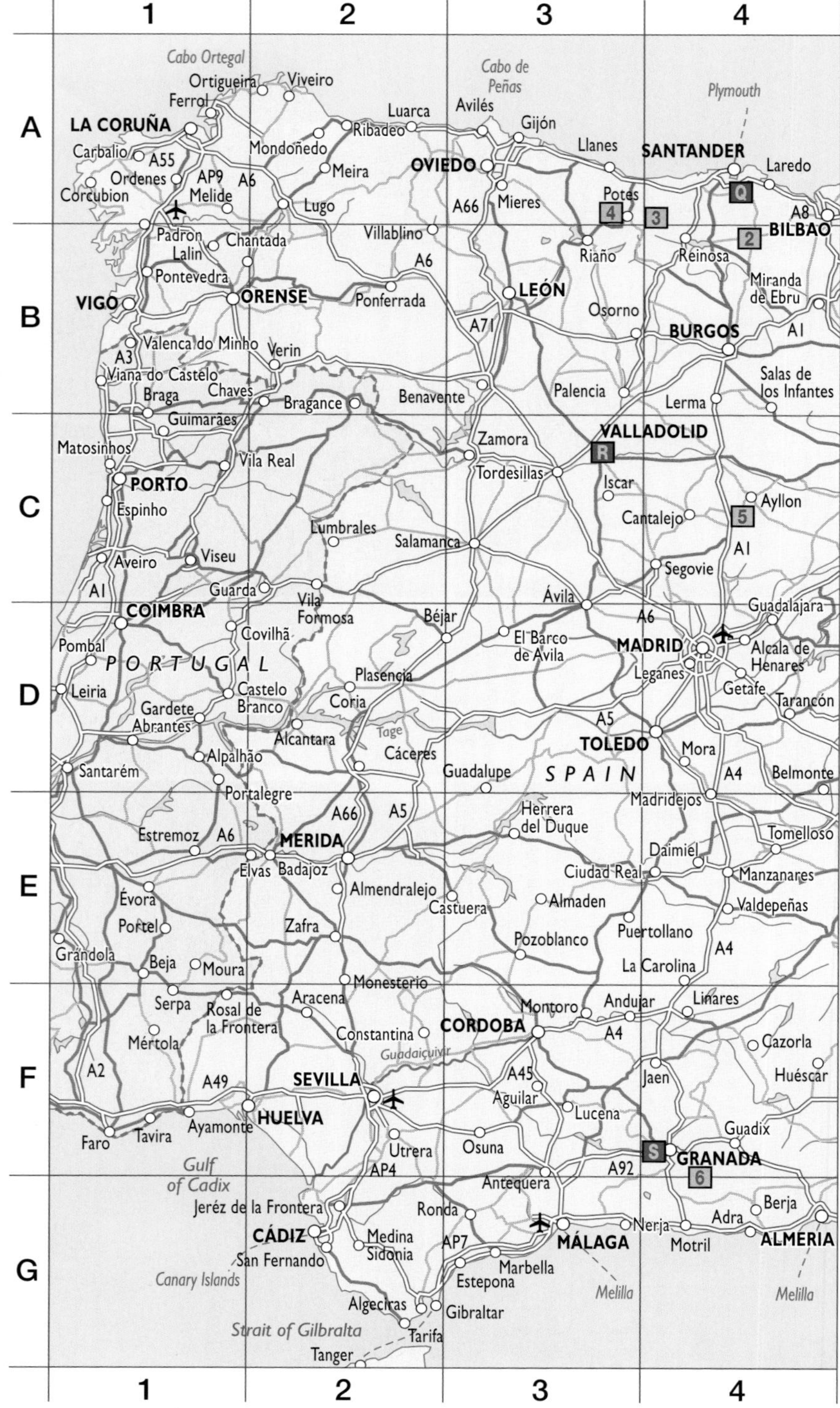
1
2
3
4
A
B
C
D
E
F
G
Cabo Ortegal
Ortigueira
Viveiro
Ferrol
LA CORUÑA
Carbalio
A55
Ordenes
AP9
A6
Corcubion
Melide
Mondoñedo
Ribadeo
Luarca
Meira
Lugo
Cabo de Peñas
Avilés
Gijón
OVIEDO
Mieres
A66
Llanes
Potes
Plymouth
SANTANDER
Laredo
A8
BILBAO
Padron
Lalin
Chantada
Villablino
Riaño
Reinosa
Pontevedra
A6
VIGO
ORENSE
Ponferrada
LEÓN
Miranda de Ebru
Osorno
A71
BURGOS
A1
Valenca do Minho
A3
Verin
Viana do Castelo
Braga
Chaves
Bragance
Benavente
Palencia
Lerma
Salas de los Infantes
Guimarães
VALLADOLID
Zamora
Matosinhos
Vila Real
Tordesillas
PORTO
Iscar
Espinho
Ayllon
Cantalejo
Lumbrales
Salamanca
Aveiro
Viseu
Segovie
Guarda
Vila Formosa
A1
Ávila
COIMBRA
Béjar
A6
Guadalajara
Covilhã
El Barco de Avila
MADRID
Pombal
PORTUGAL
Alcala de Henares
Leganes
Leiria
Plasencia
Castelo Branco
Getafe
Coria
Gardete
Abrantes
Tarancón
Alcantara
Tage
A5
TOLEDO
Alpalhão
Cáceres
Mora
Santarém
Guadalupe
SPAIN
A4
Belmonte
Portalegre
Madridejos
A66
A5
Herrera del Duque
Estremoz
A6
MERIDA
Tomelloso
Daimiel
Elvas
Badajoz
Ciudad Real
Manzanares
Évora
Almendralejo
Castuera
Almaden
Valdepeñas
Portel
Zafra
Puertollano
Pozoblanco
A4
Grândola
Beja
Moura
La Carolina
Monesterio
Serpa
Rosal de la Frontera
Aracena
Montoro
Andujar
Linares
Mértola
Constantina
CORDOBA
A4
Cazorla
Guadaiquivir
A2
A49
SEVILLA
A45
Jaen
Huéscar
Aguilar
Lucena
HUELVA
Ayamonte
Tavira
Faro
Utrera
Osuna
Guadix
Gulf of Cadix
AP4
Antequera
A92
GRANADA
Jeréz de la Frontera
Ronda
Berja
CÁDIZ
Medina Sidonia
AP7
MÁLAGA
Nerja
Motril
Adra
ALMERIA
San Fernando
Marbella
Canary Islands
Estepona
Melilla
Melilla
Algeciras
Gibraltar
Strait of Gilbralta
Tarifa
Tanger
Q
4
3
2
R
5
S
6

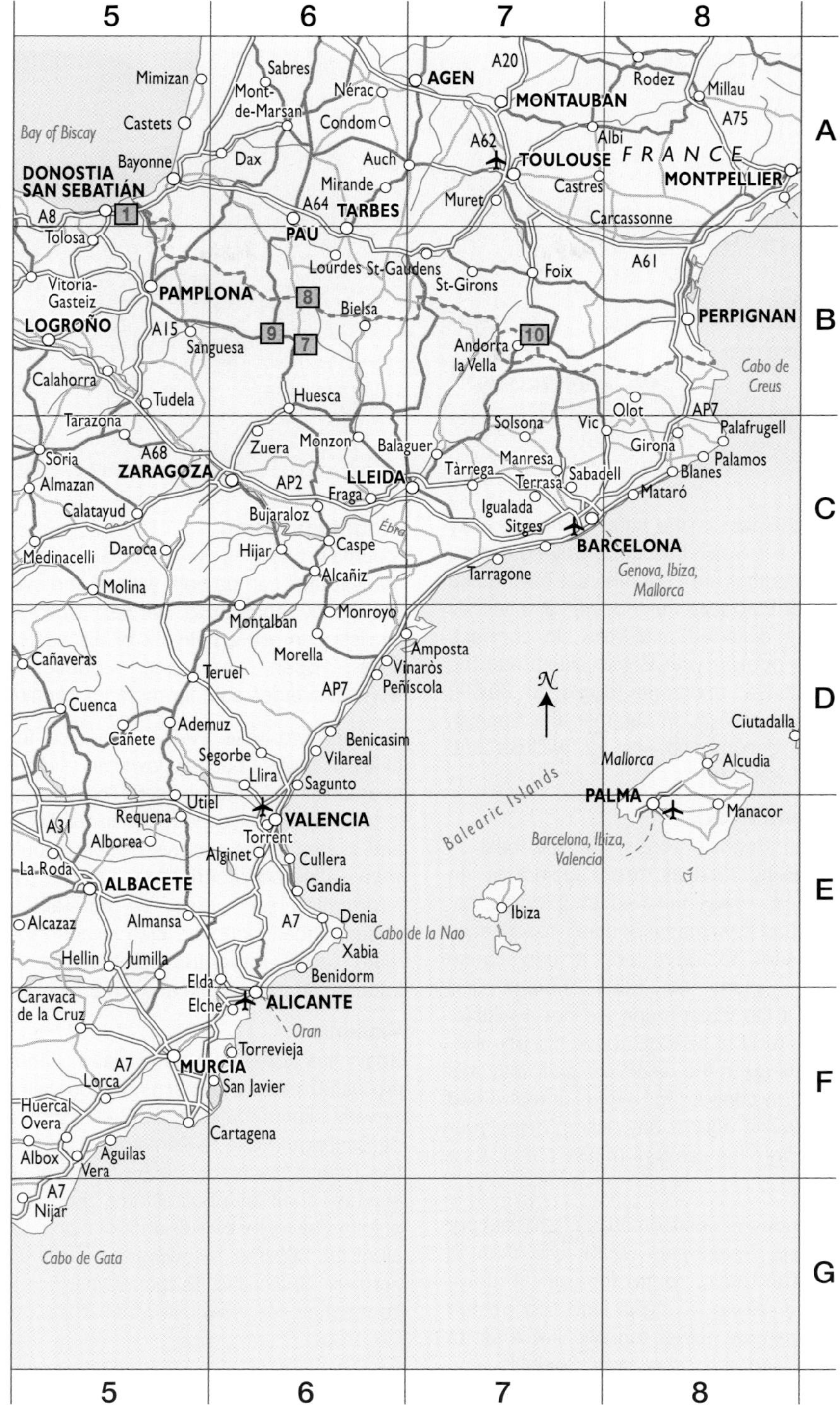
5
6
7
8
A
B
C
D
E
F
G
Mimizan
Sabres
Mont-de-Marsan
Nerac
AGEN
A20
Rodez
Millau
MONTAUBAN
A75
Castets
Bay of Biscay
Condom
A62
Albi
Bayonne
Dax
Auch
TOULOUSE
FRANCE
DONOSTIA SAN SEBATIÁN
Mirande
Castres
MONTPELLIER
A8
1
A64
TARBES
Muret
Carcassonne
Tolosa
PAU
A61
Lourdes
St-Gaudens
St-Girons
Foix
Vitoria-Gasteiz
PAMPLONA
8
Bielsa
PERPIGNAN
LOGROÑO
A15
Sanguesa
9
7
Andorra la Vella
10
Cabo de Creus
Calahorra
Tudela
Huesca
Olot
AP7
Tarazona
Solsona
Vic
Palafrugell
Soria
A68
Zuera
Monzon
Balaguer
Girona
Manresa
Palamos
ZARAGOZA
Tàrrega
Sabadell
Blanes
Almazan
AP2
LLEIDA
Terrasa
Fraga
Mataró
Calatayud
Bujaraloz
Igualada
Ebro
Sitges
Daroca
Caspe
BARCELONA
Medinacelli
Hijar
Alcañiz
Tarragone
Genova, Ibiza, Mallorca
Molina
Montalban
Monroyo
Morella
Amposta
Cañaveras
Vinaròs
Teruel
Peñiscola
AP7
N
Cuenca
Ciutadalla
Ademuz
Cañete
Benicasim
Mallorca
Alcudia
Segorbe
Vilareal
Llira
Sagunto
Balearic Islands
PALMA
Utiel
Requena
VALENCIA
Manacor
A31
Torrent
Alborea
Barcelona, Ibiza, Valencia
La Roda
Alginet
Cullera
ALBACETE
Gandia
Ibiza
Alcazaz
Almansa
A7
Denia
Cabo de la Nao
Xabia
Hellin
Jumilla
Benidorm
Elda
Caravaca de la Cruz
Elche
ALICANTE
Oran
Torrevieja
A7
MURCIA
Lorca
San Javier
Huercal Overa
Cartagena
Albox
Aguilas
Vera
A7
Nijar
Cabo de Gata

Photo: Keith and Patricia Dyer

Skiing and Spain in the same sentence may seem odd, but Spain has some well-equipped, quiet resorts that are very different from those found in its European neighbours. Spanish ski resorts are deserted mid-week. In contrast, Andorra is popular with British skiers and the tiny principality opens its doors to 80,000 visitors each season. In summer, the Spanish mountains become havens for walkers and mountain bikers.

Driving and Roads

In general, Spanish roads are the best in Europe having recently been subject to an extensive EU road improvement programme. Although this has made Spanish roads easy and pleasant to drive on, it can cause navigation issues for both humans and machines if the latest maps are not available. Ski resorts tend to be high above the tree line, so the drive up to the resort car park may feel long and exposed. To avoid unrestrained Spanish driving after a day skiing, delay your departure from the car park to give the locals a head start.

Fuel in Andorra is approximately €0.10 less per litre than in Spain and €0.20 less than in France. The main route through Andorra takes you along a tight and congested valley. Expensive tolled tunnels link Andorra to France and the drive from Spain is long and tedious.

Mountain Biking

Mountain biking is very popular in Spain and many routes can be both walked and cycled. If you fancy something gentler, walkers and cyclists can use a network of disused railway lines open to the public, visit www.viasverdes.com for more information.

The Vallnord Bike Park in Andorra features miles of cross-country, downhill, and a wood course for mountain bikers. The bike park is located at La Massana and utilises the ski lifts and slopes in the summer. Riders should visit www.vallnordbikepark.com for detailed information on routes, lift timetables and prices. Other mountain bike routes include a 'hard rated' route from Soldeu to Canillo. Information is available at www.andorra.ad.

Walking

Spain has some very good walking and there are well-marked walks in most mountain areas. Several pilgrim routes cross Spain, the Camino de Santiago (Road to Santiago) also known as the French route, is clearly marked with a scallop shell symbol. Many thousands of pilgrims travel by bike or on foot along some or all of the 800kms, following the shells through northern Spain and its mountains. For further information see www.followthecamino.com

Parque Nacional de los Picos de Europe is well organised for walkers with plenty of footpaths. A cable car transports visitors 900m providing some fine views across the park. For more information on this and other Spanish national parks visit http://reddeparquesnacionales.mma.es and www.walkingworld.com

Andorra's official website www.andorra.ad provides details of walks listed under Multi Media then click the Nature and Mountain Guide, it is available as a printable PDF but it would be worth investing in a better map. Walks range from a few hours to a few days. There are several walks from Canello starting from 1-hour return.

Skiing in Spain and Andorra

Pyrenees: **Panticoas** is a modest, sheltered ski resort, popular at weekends with families who might find nearby **Formigal** Olympic resort a little daunting. Motorhomes are welcome to use the car park at Panticoas but it's best to avoid weekends and be careful where you park as late afternoon can become a free for all with visitors pushing cars up the incline out of the car park in slippery conditions.

The **Formigal** ski area has a huge free car park that stretches along the base of the resort under the lifts and space should be available even at weekends. The resort, exposed car park and ski runs are well above tree line and the access road is prone to drifting snow and high winds! See www.formigal.com for further information also see the entries in this guide for Camping Gavin 7 15km and Camping Escarra 8 4km.

Baqueira Beret ski area is a favourite with Spanish royalty and the well heeled. www.baqueira.es There are extensive slopes at a reasonable height but the sun and ever-changing weather has adverse effects on them. The resorts huge, free car park is empty except for overnighting motorhomes that change daily and at weekends with local cars. Astun www.astun.com and Candanchu www.candanchu.com are two smaller ski areas close to the French border.

Sierra Nevada: Granada is a marvellous Arab influenced Spanish city packed full of lovely ruins but is dominated by the Sierra Nevada mountains, home to Europe's most southerly ski resort, just one day's drive from the hot sunny beaches of southern Spain, www.sierranevadaski.com A long winding road snakes up the mountain to the main resort complex of Pradollano at 2100m. This road is prone to icy patches as it swings in and out of sunshine and shade. Check weather reports and resort webcams as snowfall can be unpredictable; the Glasgows left Cabo Gato with 25°C temperatures and drove into two feet of freshly fallen snow! The dedicated motorhome parking is situated above the main reception area. Marked motorhome bays are level and have 16amp electric hook-ups. The water tap can freeze, so if you have sufficient payload, arrive with a full tank. If you arrive late and the motorhome parking is full, park nearby and sort yourself out during the morning shuffle. After heavy snow, it is possible to ski back to your motorhome. A regular shuttle bus collects from the motorhome parking and takes you down the hill to the main ticket office and ski lift area.

Northern Spain: Northern Spain has smaller undiscovered resorts waiting to be found. The **Alto Campoo** www.altocampoo.com resort in Northern Spain is ideal for beginners and intermediates. There is motorhome parking in the car park at the base of the ski lifts.

Andorra: The skiing in Andorra is high and impressive. Andorra is trying to improve its image and is burying its 'cheap and cheerful' days of the 80s under upmarket apartments and hotels. The **Canillo** resort with its stone built traditional houses and narrow alleys is surprisingly quaint for Andorra. From Canillo there is a fast gondola up to El Forn, with easy links onto runs down to Soldeu. You cannot ski back to Canillo so use the gondola to return. Visit Andorra's official website for lots of useful information www.andorra.ad

RENTERIA  A5 | 1 | N43°16.076' W001°54.071' 200m

Directions: From Astigarraga take the GI2132 to Ugaldetxo. Turn off GI2132 onto GI3671 sp 'Enrenteria', then turn right and follow road sp 'Mugarize' restaurant for 1.5km to picnic spot. Service point in parking to left. To avoid low trees exit service point the same way as entered. New roads being built will confuse the map-reader and GPS!

Sanitation:

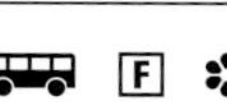
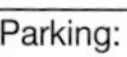

Parking:

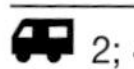

2; 48hrs; space for more 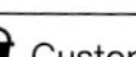 Custom

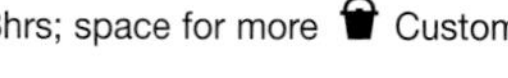

Beautiful wooded picnic spot in isolated location with popular municipal BBQs, excellent marked walks and riding stables adjacent. Two restaurants are located at the end of parking area that accommodates the service point, it is best to walk to these because of low trees and narrow road.

Activities and Facilities:

ESPINOSA DE LOS MONTEROS  B4 | 2 | N43°05.125' W003°33.462' 750m

BU570, 09560 Espinosa de los Monteros

Directions: BU570. North of town. Exit town on the BU570 towards Barcenas sp 'Instituto Conde Sancho Carcia'. Just past last house turn left onto unsurfaced road past picnic area. Service point and parking area 100m on left below snow plough machine.

Sanitation:

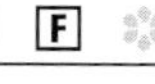

Parking:

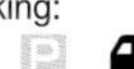

 15; 48hrs

Custom; water turned off in Nov

Near a ski resort the motorhome area is 750m above sea level. There is a picnic area with BBQs adj and town is 5 minutes.

Activities and Facilities:

ALTO CAMPOO

A4 | 3 | N43°02.248' W004°22.374' 1650m

Photo: Keith and Patricia Dyer

Barrio de la Brañavieja

Directions: CA183. Located at Alto Campoo at the ski station at the end of the CA183 . Turn off the A67 sp 'Reinosa' and 'Alto Campoo'. Follow sp 'Alto Campoo'. Service point and parking in the ski station car park, signed.

Sanitation:

Parking:

12; May be charge in season   Custom

At intermediate ski resort - www.altocampoo.com - with ski lift/shops/café in season. Alt 1650m. Downhill adult day €28. Cross-country skiing €12.50. Remote and cool in summer, but pleasant. Fuel and supermarket in Reinosa.

Activities and Facilities:

POTES

A3 | 4 | N43°09.233' W004°38.683' 400m

Camping La Viorna, Carretera de Santo Toribio 39570 Potes
www.campinglaviorna.com

Directions: From the E70/A8, take exit 272 for N621 toward Unquera/Panes/Potes. Travel 38km south on the N621 to Potes then join the CA185 in Potes following the river towards the mountains. Then turn left, near the statue of a man walking, onto the CA885 towards the monastery of Santo Toribio. The campsite is in 1km.

Sanitation:

 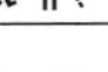

Parking:

20; €25; Apr - Oct   Custom

Built on a hillside overlooking the Picos de Europa National Reserve, this is a very well organised, clean campsite with a restaurant, bar and WiFi. The campsite is located 2km west of Potes when driving towards the National Reserve and the large monastery of Santo Toribio, a popular pilgrimage site, 2km further down the road.

Activities and Facilities:

Library image

Tenerife

For somewhere different why not head for Spain's tallest mountain, Mount Teide in Tenerife. Admittedly it is a long way away and involves several ferries, but there is a good reason as the average winter temperature is 18°C, so Tenerife could be a very pleasant destination to spend the winter, www.webtenerifeuk.co.uk. When we visited in January 2010 there were about 20 motorhomes touring the island. Walking on Mount Teide was very pleasant but unfortunately there is no skiing.

Mount Teide is in the centre of the island and is visible from almost everywhere, it is not just a mountain but also an active volcano. Once in Mount Teide National Park, park at the Roques de Garcia visitor centre, alt 2000m, N28°13.407' W16°37.698', just off the TF21. Across the road from the visitor centre there is a viewing platform looking over the interesting volcanic landscape and the start of a short 30 minute walk. There are 12 circular walks in the National Park that surrounds Mount Teide ranging from 3.5 - 15km. If you wish to walk to Mount Teide's 3700m summit, there is a walk that takes around five hours, but before you set off you have to obtain a permit from the National Park Offices in Santa Cruz de Tenerife and they require to see your passport. Alternatively you can take a cable car up to 3500m and back down the volcano for €25, www.telefericoteide.com

Although not over 1000m, there is excellent hill walking in the Anaga mountains to the north of Santa Cruz de Tenerife. Details of the walks can be obtained from the Tourist Office, purchased at www.realtenerifeislanddrives.com/Walking%20Tenerife.html and Sunflower Books publish a walking and car tour guide to Tenerife.

Getting There:

Navier Armas, www.navieraarmas.com, has ferries departing from Portimao in Portugal, via Madeira, then onto Tenerife, taking 43 hours. Acciona, www.trasmediterranea.es has ferries departing from Cadiz in Spain and the route takes 50 hours. Motorhomers and Caravanners should expect to pay over €1000 for a return ticket.

Where to stay:

MEDANO, TENERIFE  N28°02.120' W16°33.514' 20m

Camping Montana Roja, Ctra. Gral. El Médano-Los Abrigos, km 3, 38612 Médano, El, Granadilla de Abona (Tenerife) www.tenerifecampingplaya.com/Ecamping.html Tel: 0034 922179903 recepcion@camping-tenerife.com

Directions: From the port at Santa Cruz de Tenerife take the TF1 south towards Playa de les Americas. Exit at San Isidro junction 22 and turn right heading towards Médano and the sea on the TF64. Then turn right sp 'Los Abrigos' onto the TF643. The campsite is on the left in 3km.

There is a beach popular with windsurfers and kite surfers adjacent. There is a bus stop outside the campsite entrance. Mount Teide is a one hour drive. The campsite is between the sea and the airport, so expect aeroplane noise.

25; €11 Custom; Elec €3

Sanitation:

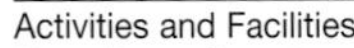

Parking:

Activities and Facilities:

RIAZA

C4 | 5 | **N41°16.191' W003°28.993' 1000m**

Library image

Camping Riaza, Ctra. de la Estación, 40500
www.camping-riaza.com

Directions: 85km north of Madrid exit the A1/E5 at exit 103/104 and travel 10km northeast on the N110 towards Riaza. After 10km turn right to Riaza onto the N110 and take right fork in 900m then in 300m turn right, first exit at the roundabout onto the SG111. In 300m at the roundabout, take the first exit onto Av Doctor García Tapiain. In 500m, turn right onto the road signed towards the railway station (FF.CC.) The entrance to the campsite is 50m on the left next to the municipal football grounds.

Sanitation:

Parking:

€15 Custom; Serviced pitches

The staff and owners are proud of the campsite's appearance. Hedges divide grass pitches. There is a restaurant, play area, swimming pool and a spa. La Pinilla ski resort, N41°12.325'W003°28.251', 9km away has reasonable free day parking by the ticket office. The resort is busy at weekends with skiers from Madrid and Seville.

Activities and Facilities:

SIERRA NEVADA

F4 | 6 | **N37°05.922' W003°23.610' 2349m**

Photo: Andy & Sue Glasgow

Urbanizacion de Solynieve, 18196, Monachil

Directions: From Granada take the A395 to Sierra Nevada. Road can be icy. Parking and service point at top of resort at car park Los Penones, well signed, adj to Juvenile Auberge. Snow chains required during ski season.

Sanitation:

   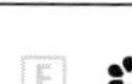

Parking:

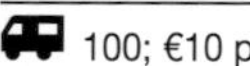  

100; €10 per 24hrs Custom; 16amp

Service point does freeze so arrive with water but without waste. Pay custodian who visits daily. Possible to ski back to parking area. Ski bus to resort bottom €1. Lift pass €40 per day high season. www.sierranevadaski.com

Activities and Facilities:

GAVIN/BIESCAS

B6 | 7 | N42°37.260' W000°18.290' 1200m

Library image

Camping Gavin, N260, Km 503. 22639 Gavin
www.campinggavin.com

Directions: From Biescas, drive 1.5km east on the N260 towards Ordesa y Monte Perdido National Park. The campsite is signposted on the right between Biescas and Gavin. The road leading down to the campsite is a bit tight for large outfits.

Sanitation:

Parking:

€25 Custom; 10amp elec

Camping Gavin is built on a terraced hillside overlooking a wooded valley and is a lovely setting with a relaxed atmosphere. The campsite is clean and the facilities and the separated pitches are well maintained. There is a restaurant onsite and the village is a short walk away. The site is normally below snow line making winter pitching easy but is 15km south of the ski areas of Panticosa/Formigal.

Activities and Facilities:

ESCARRILLA

B6 | 8 | N42°44.111' W000°18.758' 1100m

Library image

Camping Escarra, Calle de Barrio Llano, 22660, Sallent de Gállego, Aragon
www.campingescarra.com

Directions: Located on the left of the A136 main road when driving towards the French border, 14km further north. Well sign posted.

Sanitation:

Parking:

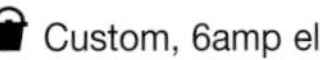

€21 Custom, 6amp elec

This busy and sometimes crowded campsite is located midway between the ski resorts of Panticosa and Formigal and is serviced by a ski bus. The campsite features a family bathroom with bath, outdoor swimming pool, large bar and restaurant. There are large lakes alongside the A136 in 2km in both directions.

Activities and Facilities:

SANTA CILIA DE JACA B6 9 N42°33.378' W000°43.519' 620m

Library images

Camping Pirineos, N240, km 300, 22791
Santa Cilia
www.pirinet.com/pirineos

Directions: Located 2km west of Santa Cilia village, 13.5km west of Jaca, adjacent to the N240 at the km300 marker.

Sanitation:

Parking:

€24 inc 6amp elec Custom

Established in 1962 this campsite has numerous facilities including a shop, tennis courts and an indoor BBQ area. Camping pitches are located under trees. The campsite is adjacent to the Santiago pilgrimage route making it ideal for a rest whether walking or after skiing at the nearby ski areas of Astun and Canduchu to the north. Jaca has a good example of a star fort also housing a miniature figures museum.

Activities and Facilities:

CANILLO, ANDORRA B7 10 N42°34.080' E001°36.238' 1500m

Library image

Camping Pla, Ctra General, Canillo
www.campingpla.cyberandorra.com

Directions: CG2. 15km from French border driving east on the CG2. Campsite adjacent to road on left as enter Canillo, 9.5km before Andorra la Vella. Not suitable for large outfits.

Sanitation:

Parking:

€20 Custom

This small campsite is only 100m from the fast gondola up to El Forn. From there it is easy to link onto runs down to Soldeu. You cannot ski back to the campsite so use the gondola to return. The campsite could be cleaner and is prone to becoming boggy after a thaw. Canillo is a quiet place with little nightlife. The huge village swimming pool complex is excellent, and the supermarket and shops are only a 400m stroll away.

Activities and Facilities:

Matterhorn

Matterhorn cable car

SWITZERLAND

Les Crosets

Sledges in Switzerland

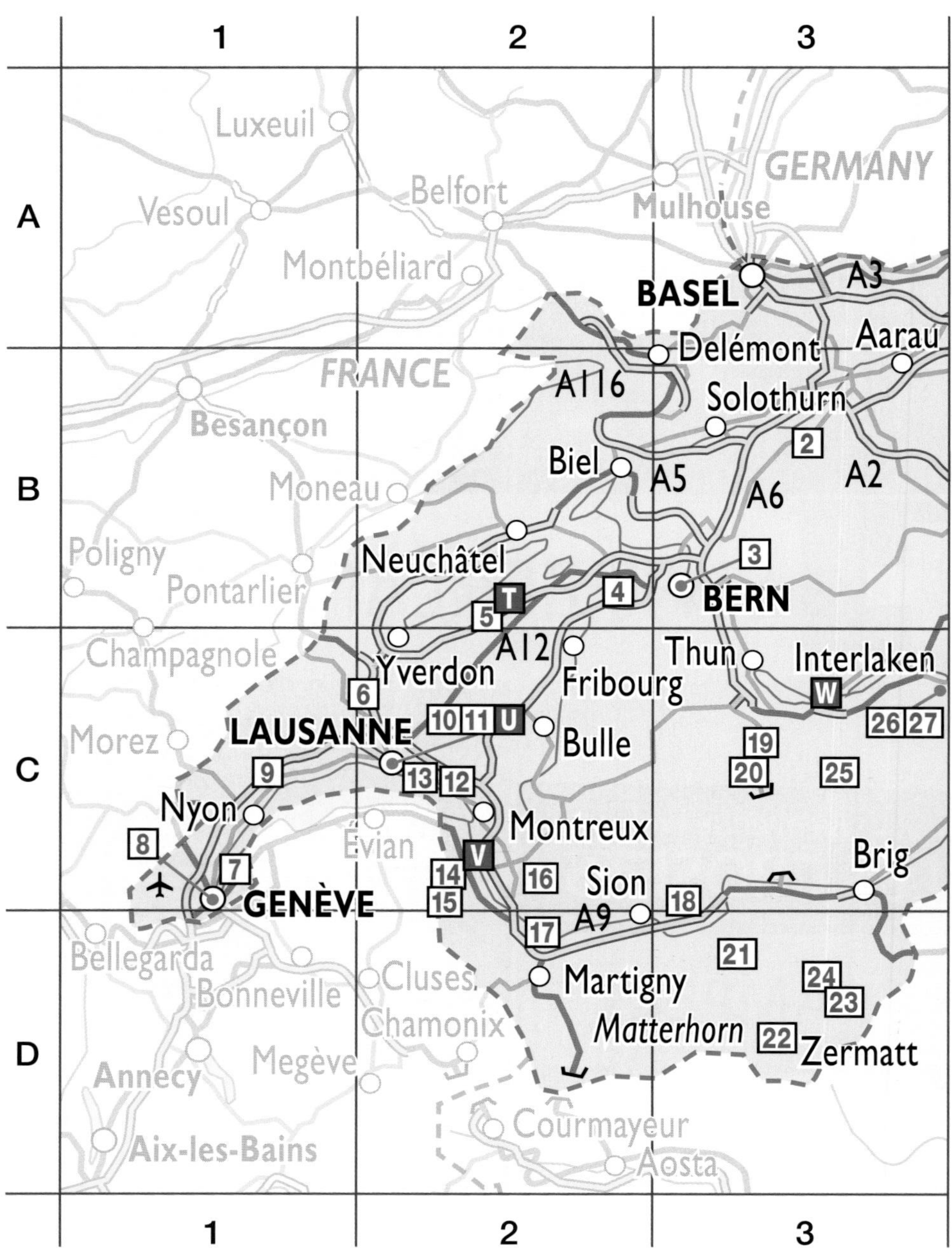
1
2
3
A
B
C
D
Luxeuil
GERMANY
Belfort
Vesoul
Mulhouse
Montbéliard
BASEL
A3
Aarau
Delémont
FRANCE
A116
Solothurn
Besançon
2
Biel
A5
A2
Moneau
A6
Poligny
Neuchâtel
3
Pontarlier
4
BERN
T
5
Champagnole
A12
Thun
Interlaken
Yverdon
Fribourg
6
W
10
11
U
26
27
LAUSANNE
Bulle
Morez
19
9
20
25
13
12
Nyon
Montreux
8
Évian
V
Brig
7
14
16
Sion
GENÈVE
15
18
A9
17
Bellegarda
21
Cluses
Martigny
24
Bonneville
23
Chamonix
Matterhorn
22
Zermatt
Megève
Annecy
Courmayeur
Aix-les-Bains
Aosta

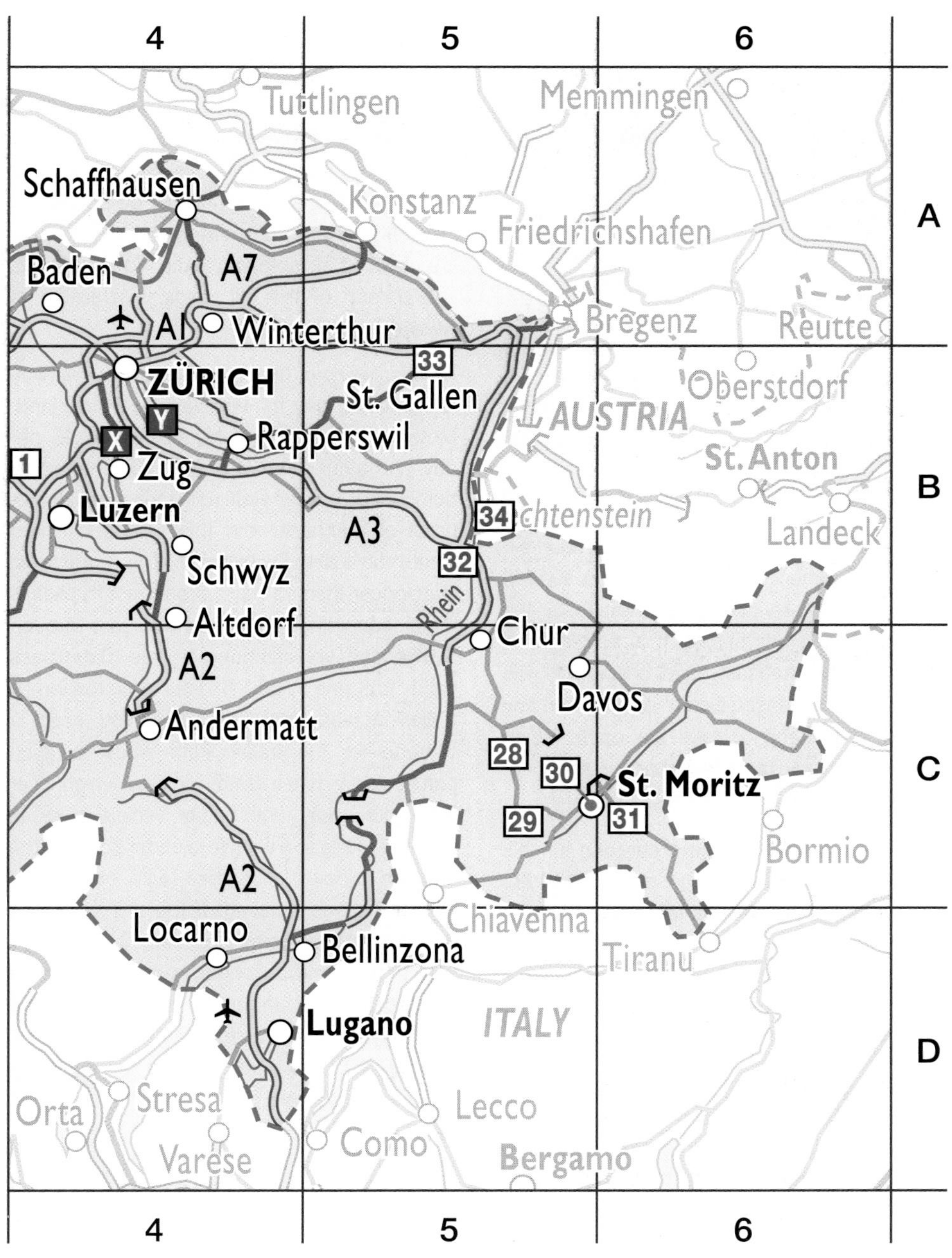
4
5
6
A
B
C
D
Tuttlingen
Memmingen
Schaffhausen
Konstanz
Friedrichshafen
Baden
A7
A1
Winterthur
Bregenz
Reutte
33
ZÜRICH
Y
St. Gallen
Oberstdorf
AUSTRIA
X
Rapperswil
1
Zug
St. Anton
Luzern
34
Liechtenstein
A3
Landeck
32
Schwyz
Rhein
Altdorf
Chur
A2
Davos
Andermatt
28
30
St. Moritz
29
31
Bormio
A2
Chiavenna
Locarno
Bellinzona
Tiranu
Lugano
ITALY
Orta
Stresa
Lecco
Como
Varese
Bergamo

Switzerland is not high up on the destinations list for most campers but there is more to Switzerland than clocks, chocolate and cheese. There are well-known, excellent ski resorts, which in summer make ideal destinations for outdoor enthusiasts and 20,000km of non-motorised routes for walking, cycling and canoeing are accessible. www.switzerlandmobility.ch

Switzerland's western border adjoins Lichtenstein and this 24km long country shares many links with Switzerland, including its currency, the Swiss Franc (SF). Lichtenstein is independent, with its own monarchy and parliament but it does not have an army.

Driving and Roads

The Alps dominate the bottom third of Switzerland and many routes have mountain passes. In winter, spring and autumn sudden snow showers are common, so abide by the law and carry snow chains. It is advisable to check weather forecasts and check with the local police or Tourist Office to confirm that any passes you intend to take are open. When travelling on any mountain road give way to yellow PostBuses, it's the law!

Some mountain passes have car-train tunnels (a similar system to the channel tunnel) where you turn up, pay a fee, and drive onto the train that transports you through the tunnel. This can save considerable time, but take care when driving on and off the train.

Swiss motorways are excellent and you really need to use them to get around. All vehicles weighing less than 3.5t are charged to use Swiss motorways. Proof of payment comes in the form of a sticker called a vignette, which you attach to the windscreen. Take care when removing the sticker from its backing as the sticker is cut into circular strips to make it impossible to remove from the windscreen intact, you do not want to invalidate it before you have used it! Vehicles under 3.5t are charged SF40/€30 for 14 months from 1st December. If you are towing a trailer/caravan under 3.5t, you need two vignettes, one for the tow vehicle and one for the trailer. Vignettes can be purchased in advance at www.myswitzerland.com or can be purchased in Euros or Swiss Francs at the border. Stickers are checked at motorway exits. Further details and a map of the toll roads is available at www.vignette.ch

All vehicles over 3.5t have to pay heavy vehicle tax for every day the vehicle is in Switzerland. Motorhome and heavy car tax is SF3.25 per day, and a minimum of SF25/7 days has to be purchased. Border staff will issue a receipt as proof of purchase, and this will be checked when you leave Switzerland. If you intend to stay longer than 18 days, a one-month pass is more economical. If you intend to pass through Switzerland, you can buy a flexible 10 day pass valid for one year. If you are towing a trailer/caravan less than 3.5t, you need a vignette for the trailer. Fifth wheel caravan combination: when both vehicles weigh over 3.5t each, only one heavy vehicle pass is required. If the tow vehicle is under 3.5t and the caravan is over 3.5t then only one heavy vehicle pass is required. If the tow vehicle is over 3.5t and the caravan is under 3.5t, a heavy vehicle pass and a vignette is required. If both vehicles are under 3.5t each then two vignettes are required. Further details and a map of the toll roads is available at www.vignette.ch, email: enquiries ozd.zentrale@ezv.admin.ch

Many Swiss service stations have dedicated motorhome parking, service points, and free 16amp electric. It appears that motorhomes are permitted to park at service stations from four to 15hrs, always check the sign. These parking areas range from huge motorway service areas to small mountain service stations with fantastic views. It is not uncommon to see 4 - 5 Swiss motorhomes park overnight and be connected to the power. Swiss crime rates are low but Vicarious Books does not recommend stopping overnight on motorways because we receive a few reports each year of vehicle burglary. That said we have never had a report of or heard a rumour of a burglary on a Swiss motorway. If you do stop at a motorway service station or lay-by, be cautious and vigilant; lock your vehicle, lock away valuables and set alarms.

Mountain Biking and Cycling

Switzerland is keen to promote cycling and mountain biking. Listed on www.veloland.ch there are detailed cycle routes including; 9 national, 52 regional and 30 local. They provide route marker information, things to look out for, length, difficulty, topography, maps, and public transport options.

Walking

Switzerland is keen to promote walking and hiking and has set up Switzerland Mobility. Listed on www.wanderland.ch there are detailed routes including; 6 national, 57 regional and 143 local. They provide route marker information, things to look out for, length, difficulty, topography, maps, and public transport options. Walks in Switzerland are not necessarily circular but make use of public transport to return you to your departure point, details of public transport are provided with the walk information. There are several themed walks in Switzerland. The Swiss Path, created to celebrate 700 years of the Confederation, is a 35km walk from the Rütli Meadow to Brunnen. From Brunnen catch the boat across the lake to Rütli and then walk back to Brunnen following the trail around the lake. If you fancy a longer walk then the 600km Cultural Walk across Switzerland should do. The entire walk takes 30 days and crosses 15 passes.

Spas and Thermal Water

There are plenty of spa and wellness facilities in Switzerland, look under wellness on www.myswitzerland.com for an extensive list. For something a little different the Säntispark, www.saentispark.ch, in Abtwil is a combination of wellness and water park. There are salty Jacuzzi pools, water chutes and an outdoor wild water course.

Skiing

The Rhone Valley: Just south of Lac Leman (Lake Geneva) along the French border there are several ski resorts overlooking the river Rhone. From this ski area there are road and ski lift links to the French Alps. **Champéry** and its neighbour **Les Crosets** are part of the Ports du Soleil ski area so you can ski in Switzerland and France on the same day. Champéry provides nightlife and off slope activities but Les Crosets has the slopes on its doorstep. This resort is ideal for intermediate downhill skiers. On the other side of the valley Villars ski resort links to Les Diablerets and Glacier 3000. **Gryon** links into this area via a cable car. There are plenty of blue runs so this resort will suit beginners.

Interlaken: Cross-country skiers and tobogganers should head to **Kandersteg**, this resort and the local resort of **Frutigen** also provide limited downhill skiing. **Lauterbrunnen** is an ideal base to visit the resorts of Mürren, Wengen and Grindelwald. Mürren held the first ever downhill ski race in 1922. From Lauterbrunnen, Wengen and Grindelwald are reachable via a cog railway. All three ski areas are known for their scenery. **Meiringen** is slightly further away from Interlaken but is good for beginner skiers.

Zermatt area: The resorts in this area offer some of the highest and most snow prone slopes in the Alps, making them ideal for some late season, fair weather skiing. **Zermatt,** with its famous Matterhorn Mountain, is a popular resort offering excellent skiing for intermediate and advanced skiers though the ski passes are expensive. **Saas-Fee**, and its neighbour **Saas-Grund**, are located across the mountains east of Zermatt. Saas Fee is the highest resort in the Alps, a ski bus links it with its neighbour, and both resorts have limited intermediate ski areas but are quieter and cheaper than Zermatt. Across the mountains to the west of Zermatt, is the unspoilt Val d'Anniviers. There are several different ski areas along the Val d'Anniviers including St Luc, Vercorin, Zinal and **Grimentz**, which is known for its off-piste skiing.

St Moritz area: Trendy skiers will really appreciate **St Moritz;** it is Switzerland's fashionable resort. There is a good nightlife and expensive boutiques. Numerous activities are organised throughout the winter season. The skiing is best suited to intermediates and cross-country skiers. Snow boarders are welcomed and there are good facilities including a terrain park. If the glitz of St Moritz scares you to bits, then head north to the tiny resort of **Bivio** or the mid-sized resort of **Savognin**.

Grimentz

LUZERN

B4 | 1 | N47°06.725' E008°13.986' 500m

A2/E35, 6023 Rothenburg

Directions: Services on both carriageways of E35/A2, north of Luzern at junction 22.

Sanitation:

Parking:

50; €10/SF15 per night 7pm - 5am; be vigilant

None

There is designated overnight parking at this new service station. It is pricey with no facilities and noisy but with lake views. There is free overnight parking on both carriageways to the west on the A2/E35.

Activities and Facilities:

LANGENTHAL

B3 | 2 | N47°13.497' E007°46.795' 500m

Lexa Wohnmobile (Motorhomes), Bern-Zurich-Strasse 49B, 4900 Langenthal
www.lexa.ch

Directions: Route 1. Directly adjacent to 1, main route past Langenthal, follow sp 'Zurich' and 'Industrie Nord Langenthal'. At Lexa Wohnmobile, 20m from roundabout with Avica petrol station.

Sanitation:

Parking:

5

Custom

You can use the stellplatze at any time at this reputable and large motorhome dealer. They sell LPG during business hours, have a good selection of parts, and offer useful advice. Monday closed. Tuesday- Friday 8.00-12.00 and 13.30-16.00, Saturday 9.00 - 16.00.
+41 (0) 62 923 46 64

Activities and Facilities:

BERN - CENTRE

B3 | 3 | N46°57.147' E007°26.479' 540m

Schützenmattstrasse 11

Directions: Exit A1/E25 at junction 35 and follow sp 'Zentrum' 'Bahnhof'. Follow this road right through the centre of Bern, it bends left after a strange silver cover at the tram stops then winds past Hotel Schweizerhof. Take the left hand lane and turn left before the river bridge sp 'P Bahnhof'. The parking is on the left directly behind the old city train station on Speichergasse. The easier route is from the 12/6/1 following sp 'Zentrum' and turn left just under a railway bridge into the non-height barriered parking. Take it slowly on approach as you pass under the tramlines and complicated lane markings.

Sanitation:

Parking:

100; Sunday only None

This is the only non-height restricted parking in the centre of Bern, it is 200 yards from the Kunst museum and old city. Only attempt to reach this car park on Sunday before 9am, because at any other time it would be too much grief and full when you arrive. Bern has beer gardens, a nice cathedral, Einstein's house, and excellent art galleries. www.bern.ch

Activities and Facilities:

BOSINGEN

B2 | 4 | N46°52.158' E007°13.281' 600m

E27/A12, 3185 Schmitten

Directions: Motorway rest area on both sides of carriageway of E27/A12 between junction 9 and 10. Exit sp 'P'.

Sanitation:

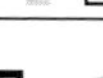

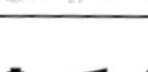

Parking:

20; 15 hours; be vigilant Toilet only

This is the only good, clean unrestricted motorhome parking on a motorway within a convenient distance of the capital Bern. Although we do not recommend stopping at motorway service areas, this is a good place for a rest before/after visiting Bern. The motorhome designated parking allows stops of 15 hours. Motorhome and lorry parking separated from toilets and car parking. There is no restaurant on site.

Activities and Facilities:

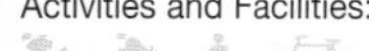

PAYERNE

  B2 | 5 | N46°49.195' E006°56.272' 500m

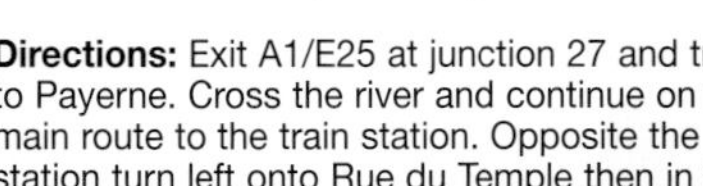

Rue de la Concorde, 1530 Payerne

Directions: Exit A1/E25 at junction 27 and travel to Payerne. Cross the river and continue on the main route to the train station. Opposite the station turn left onto Rue du Temple then in 80m turn second left into Rue de la Concorde. The parking space is directly under village church, the service point is to the right of wine dealer in a busy car park.

Sanitation:

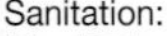 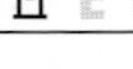  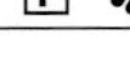

Parking:

1 Raclet

One parking space provided directly under the largest Romanesque church in Switzerland, and its bells - best of luck for quiet undisturbed sleep! The church is open to the public. This is a wine producing area and wine tasting is available at various cellars. More info about the local wine is available at www.advb.ch and the local tourist office www.estavayer-payerne.ch

Activities and Facilities:

A1 / BAVOIS

   C2 | 6 | N46°40.478' E006°34.231' 500m

A1 motorway, 1372 Bavois

Directions: There are parking areas on both sides of carriageway on A1 between junction 21 and 22 but the service point is located on the side with the restaurant (a road bridge links both sides). Follow restaurant signs and once the Autogrill is in front of you follow the road to the left through the truck parking. The service point is at the end of the truck parking and may be blocked by trucks.

Sanitation:

Parking:

 None  Euro Relais Maxi

Camper service - no overnight parking.

Activities and Facilities:

LAKE GENEVA

  C1 | 7 | N46°13.699' E006°11.170' 400m

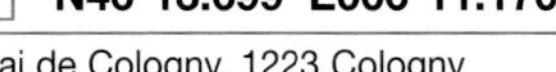

Quai de Cologny, 1223 Cologny

Directions: Located 4km northeast from Geneva alongside the south shore of the lake. Head towards Geneva on the D1005 driving from France. The parking is directly alongside the lake 500m after the road travels alongside the lake. If coming from Lausanne take major road sp 'LAC'. Don't aim for Geneva centre!

Sanitation:

Parking:

50; 2 hours | None

If you really must drive to Geneva for a lake fountain view, this is the best place for motorhomes to park - unrestricted, easy access and usually quiet. Driving through Geneva can be a nightmare especially at rush hour and at any time of day expect delays and constant sets of traffic lights. Beware of 3-section 'Bendy Buses' at junctions and corners! www.geneva-tourism.ch

Activities and Facilities:

GENEVA

C1 | 8 | N46°12.057' E006°03.961' 400m

Camping du Bois de Bay, Route Bois de bay, 1242 Satigny

Directions: Turn off the A1/E25 sp 'Vernier'. Follow sp to 'Vernier'. Drive through Vernier to a right hand bend and a school then turn left at a traffic lighted junction sp 'Peney'. Follow this road, Route de Peney for 2km, turning left once you reach an industrial area (by the Prelco building), signed with camping symbols. The campsite is on the left.

Sanitation:

 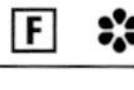

Parking:

None | Euro Relais Maxi

Free camper service outside a campsite that is also open in winter. The campsite, located just west of Geneva, is adjacent to a large river but is also near a quarry that creates a lot of dust so we could not recommend the campsite. www.geneva-tourism.ch

Activities and Facilities:

A1 LA COTE

  C1 9 N46°26.745' E006°17.824' 400m

A1/E25/E62, 1183 Bursins

Directions: On A1/E25/E62 motorway between junctions 12 and 13 at service station La Côte. There are service points on both sides of the road.

Sanitation:

Parking:

 20; Be vigilant  Euro Relais Maxi

Service point available on both north and south carriageways but north is a little quieter. There is a Co-op supermarket onsite and showers and toilets at the entrance.

Activities and Facilities:

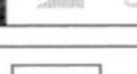  

LAUSANNE

  C2 10 N46°31.041' E006°35.873' 400m

Chemin du Camping, 1007 Lausanne

Directions: Follow the A1a/E23 toward Lausanne and at the large roundabout drive almost all the way around and turn off sp 'Geneva', camping symbols and signed. In 350m at the traffic lighted junction, turn left sp 'camping symbols'. Pass under the motorway bridge and go straight across the roundabout. The campsite is in front of you. The stellplatze is on left just before campsite entrance.

Sanitation:

Parking:

15; SF10 day/SF23 overnight inc service.

Euro Relais Maxi; €3; Pay at reception

This open all year stellplatze is outside a more expensive campsite 50m from the grassy banks of Lake Geneva. The service point is accessible without paying for parking which is charged day and night and includes use of campsite facilities. Swiss power adaptors are available at reception. www.lausanne.ch

Activities and Facilities:

LAUSANNE

   C2 | 11 | N46°31.041' E006°35.873' 400m

Camping de Vidy, Chemin du Camping, 1007 Lausanne www.clv.ch

Directions: Follow the A1a/E23 toward Lausanne and at the large roundabout drive almost all the way around and turn off sp 'Geneva', camping symbols and signed. In 350m at the traffic lighted junction, turn left sp 'camping symbols'. Pass under the motorway bridge and go straight across the roundabout. The campsite is in front of you. The stellplatze is on left just before campsite entrance.

Sanitation:

Parking:

200; SF33.10

Euro Relais Maxi; €3; Pay at reception.

This campsite is located on the shore at the northern most point of Lake Geneva with nice grassy banks. There is a park one side of the campsite and a sports ground the other. There are good hot showers but the site shop is only open in the summer. Swiss power adaptor available at reception. www.lausanne.ch

Activities and Facilities:

MONTREUX-CLARENS

 C2 | 12 | N46°26.390' E006°53.397' 400m

Rue du Torrent, 1815 Montreux

Directions: Located at the eastern end of the lake. From Montreux take the 9, Rue du Lac, 2km towards Clarens. Turn left at the traffic lights, signed, opposite the Tamoil fuel station (under flats). The service point is at the end of the road before the lake.

Sanitation:

Parking:

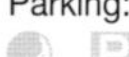  

Day Euro Relais Maxi

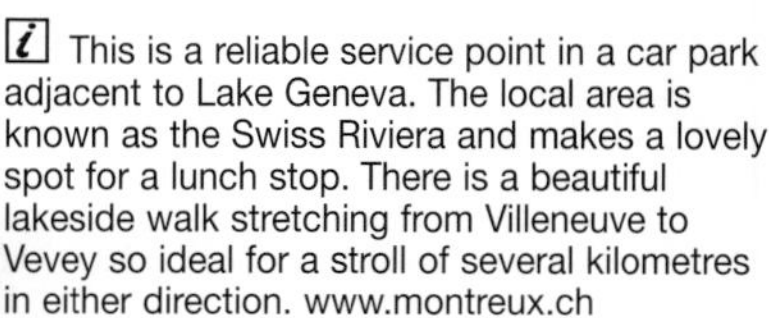

This is a reliable service point in a car park adjacent to Lake Geneva. The local area is known as the Swiss Riviera and makes a lovely spot for a lunch stop. There is a beautiful lakeside walk stretching from Villeneuve to Vevey so ideal for a stroll of several kilometres in either direction. www.montreux.ch

Activities and Facilities:

VILLETTE A9

C2 | 13 | N46°30.341' E006°42.608' 600m

A9/E62, 1091 Villette

Directions: Lavaux motorway services, located on both sides of the motorway between junction 12 and 13 of A9/E62. Service point located adjacent to the truck parking.

Sanitation:

Parking:

20+; 15 hrs max; Be vigilant

Euro Relais Maxi

A reliable service point at a well-kept motorway service station with a small restaurant.

Activities and Facilities:

LES CROSETS

C2 | 14 | N46°11.052' E006°50.097' 1600m

Route des Crosets, 1873 Les Crosets

Directions: From Monthey follow the road to Champery. At Val d'Illiez just past the church, turn right at the roundabout sp 'Les Crosets Champoussin'. Follow the narrow and winding road to Les Crosets. The car park is adjacent to main chairlift station.

Sanitation:

Parking:

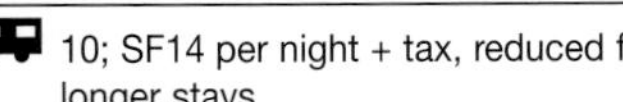

10; SF14 per night + tax, reduced for longer stays

Toilets; Elec SF5 per night

The cable car company seem to be 'trialling' overnight motorhome parking, so keep the area clean and tidy (especially toilets!). There is no service point so use Champery before assent. Adjacent ski lift provides good access to fantastic skiing and the Port du Soleil ski area and Avoriaz is one chairlift ride away. The ski area converts into a mountain bike park in summer with chairlift access and plenty of well-marked cycle and walking trails. Fresh bread and milk available from chairlift shop. http://lescrosets.ch

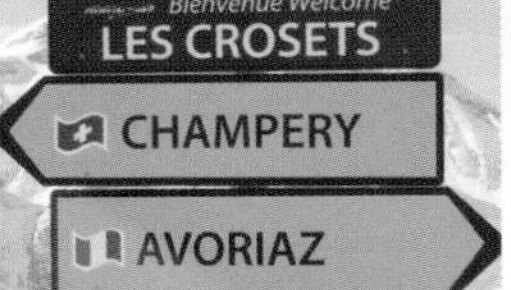

Activities and Facilities:

CHAMPERY

  C2 | 15 | N46°10.532' E006°52.234' 1000m

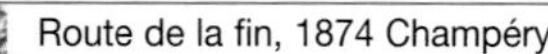

Route de la fin, 1874 Champéry

Directions: From Monthey follow the road to Champery. In Champery stay on the road and follow sp 'Planachaux Grand Paradis' and the cable car symbol. The service point and parking is on the left opposite and just before the Tourist Office, below road level.

Sanitation:

Parking:

 6; SF18 per night inc all services; Pay at supermarket

Euro Relais Maxi

This is a very convenient, but usually full, stellplatze. It is very popular with young all season skiers and boarders. There is a good service point which is accessible without stopping at the stellplatze and free when we visited. Champery has good intermediate skiing but lifts are required up and down to access the slopes/village. The resort is part of the Portes du Soleil ski area with links to France. www.champery.ch

Activities and Facilities:

GRYON

C2 | 16 | N46°16.948' E007°04.222' 1200m

Route de Villars, 1882 Gryon

Directions: Turn off the A9 sp 'Villars', 'Ollon' and 'Col de la Croix'. From Ollon follow the road to Villars-s-Ollon turning right at Villars towards Gryon up narrow winding and steep roads. The parking is on the right as you approach Gryon.

Sanitation:

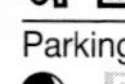 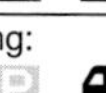   

Parking:

 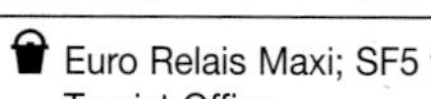

10 — Euro Relais Maxi; SF5 to Tourist Office.

The attractive village has wooden houses and is central for winter skiing and summer walking. The good reliable service point is located in a small and crowded car park sometimes used overnight by skiers. The ski lifts are 5 minutes walk from the car park and they provide access to several mountains and a glacier. www.villars.ch

Activities and Facilities:

MARTIGNY

D2 | 17 | N46°07.678 E007°03.654' 460m

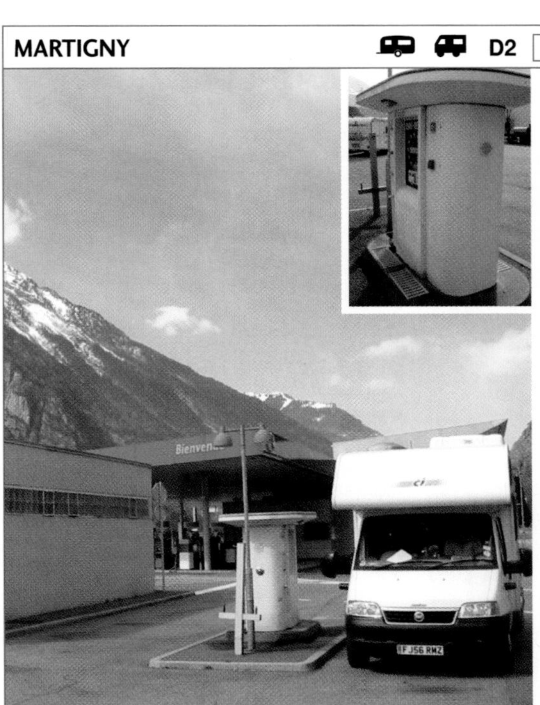

A9/E62, 1920 Martigny

Directions: Located between junctions 21 and 20 on the A9/E62. Turn off sp 'Relais du Grand St Bernard' motorway service, access from both carriageways. The service point is located behind the white building near the fuel station.

Sanitation:

Parking:

Be vigilant   Euro Relais Maxi

This is a large motorway service area with unrestricted, designated motorhome parking and free service point. This is a noisy night halt but very useful camper service before or after crossing Italy! Nice green area and lake walk behind restaurant. As with all motorway services, be vigilant.

Activities and Facilities:

ST LEONARD

C3 | 18 | N46°15.336' E007°25.566' 500m

Parking du Lac Souterrain, Rue des Rocailles, 1958 Saint-Léonard

Directions: Travelling southwest from Sierre heading towards Sion take the A9 to St Leonard. After entering St Leonard take the first right turn beside a small Mitsubishi dealership, sp 'Lac Souterrain'. The large parking area is in the midst of housing area in 150m, the stellplatze is in a separate green area located behind flags.

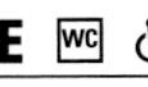

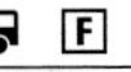

Sanitation:

Parking:

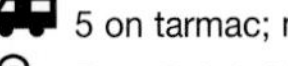
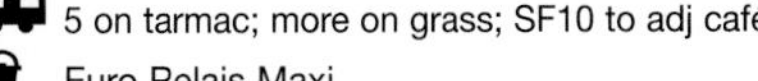

5 on tarmac; more on grass; SF10 to adj café.

Euro Relais Maxi

This is a pleasant rural stellplatze with toilets and an adjacent picnic area. It is conveniently located for an overnight halt if in transit along the valley, a good wine producing area. Parking is possible in winter but service point is closed. Visit the famous underground lake, the largest in Europe, and take a half hour boat ride! www.lac-souterrain.com

Activities and Facilities:

FRUTIGEN

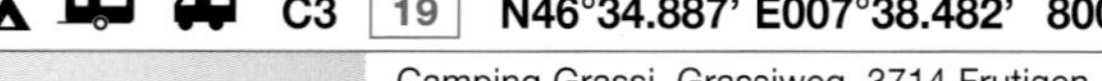

C3 | 19 | N46°34.887' E007°38.482' 800m

Camping Grassi, Grassiweg, 3714 Frutigen
www.camping-grassi.ch

Directions: From the village centre travel southeast and cross the river bridge, in 100m turn right and follow the campsite sign off the main village road. After 100m veer right along a narrow road, pass the large modern wooden church on the right and then onto the campsite.

Sanitation:

Parking:

20; €22 Custom

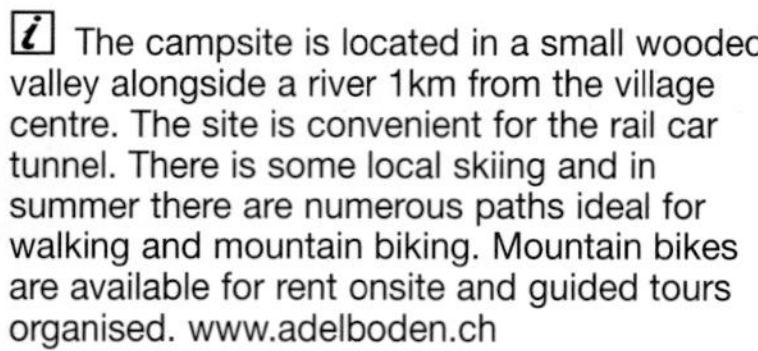

The campsite is located in a small wooded valley alongside a river 1km from the village centre. The site is convenient for the rail car tunnel. There is some local skiing and in summer there are numerous paths ideal for walking and mountain biking. Mountain bikes are available for rent onsite and guided tours organised. www.adelboden.ch

Activities and Facilities:

KANDERSTEG

C3 | 20 | N46°29.829' E007°40.922' 1200m

Camping Rendezvous, Sesselbahnstrasse, 3718 Kandersteg
www.camping-kandersteg.ch

Directions: Turn off the main route, Hauptstrasse, through the village following the campsite signs onto Oschistrasse. This road is alongside the river (on right), and goes uphill to the campsite which is signposted on the right just before bottom gondola station. You may need to fit snow chains for last 100m if fresh snow on road.

Sanitation:

Parking:

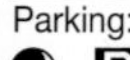

10; SF43 + metered elec. Custom

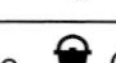

An understated campsite situated adjacent to the bottom ski lift. In winter the lift transports skiers and tobogganers, whilst in summer it transports walkers and mountain bikers. The area is very popular with cross-country skiers and there is excellent summer walking. Heated swimming pool 500m. www.kandersteg.ch

Activities and Facilities:

GRIMENTZ D3 21 N46°10.422' E007°34.287' 1600m

Aire Camping l'Ilot Bosquet, Route de Moiry, 3961 Anniviers

Directions: From Sierre head south along Val d'Anniviers to Vissoie. At Vissoie follow the long, steep and scenic road up the valley through St Jean to Grimentz. The stellplatze is signposted with a caravan sign as you drive through the village and pass the ski lift on right.

Sanitation:

Parking:

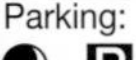

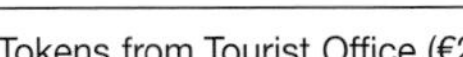

20 Raclet; Tokens from Tourist Office (€2)

The narrow, winding and steep road through this scenic valley may not be to everyone's liking. The chocolate box village is popular at weekends. In winter there is skiing and in summer excellent walking and mountain biking. Until now, this resort was undiscovered but with new hotels, spas and ski runs under construction it will not be for long, so visit soon. www.grimentz.ch

Activities and Facilities:

ZERMATT-RANDA D3 22 N46°05.120' E007°46.829' 1400m

Camping Attermenzen, 3928 Randa
www.camping-randa.ch

Directions: Turn south off the 9 in Visp at the roundabout sp 'Saas Fee' and follow the valley 9.2km to and through Stalden then turn right towards Zermatt. Travel 19.5km up the valley and the campsite is on the left just past Randa, behind the "Hole in One" restaurant, clearly sp 'camping'. Do not try to enter Randa, but use by-pass.

Sanitation:

Parking:

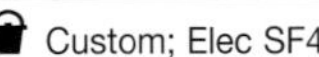

30; SF24 Custom; Elec SF4

This small, rustic campsite in the foothills of the Matterhorn is one of the best in Switzerland because the 6A electric is unmetered, and in 2010 they accepted the ACSI Camping Card (€13 in 2010). A taxi ski shuttle (SF6, pp, each way) calls at campsite at 9am and ferries you to the outskirts of Zermatt. Then it is an easy 10 minutes walk to the main square or you can catch a ski bus. Arrange shuttle taxi for evening/afternoon collection time. Choose a clear, wind-free day to ski the 3900m Klein Matterhorn glacier. In summer you can scare yourself at the Forest Fun Park where you step, swing and climb from tree to tree. www.zermatt-fun.ch. www.zermatt.ch

Activities and Facilities:

SAAS-FEE

D3 | 23 | N46°06.727' E007°56.055' 1800m

Kapellenweg, 3906 Saas-Fee

Directions: Turn south off the 9 at the roundabout in Visp sp 'Saas-Fee' and follow the valley road for 26km to and through Saas-Grund up to Saas-Fee. The parking is on the left behind the multi-storey car park beside a large round building. The parking is well signed, and you take ticket on entry.

Sanitation:

Parking:

50; SF25 without guest card, SF17 with guest card

Custom; 13amp, only 8 sockets!

Take parking ticket to Tourist Office (opposite the Post Office, 100m) for SF1.20 per person per day they issue guest cards, and programme your parking ticket for reduced rate. For elec (13amp unmetered SF1-2), get key (SF20 deposit) and an adaptor (SF7 deposit) from the office just past car entry point into multi-storey car park. Drinking water and toilets can be frozen. The transport hub (50m) has buses to Saas-Grund ski lift (SF13 return) and free shuttle buses to Saas-Fee lifts. Highly recommended is the gondola up Hannig Mountain, only transporting walkers and sledgers (rent sledge at bottom station). www.saas-fee.ch

 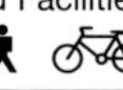  

Activities and Facilities:

SAAS-GRUND

D3 | 24 | N46°07.634' E007°56.153' 1600m

Camping Bergheimat, 3910 Saas-Grund

Directions: Turn south off the 9 at the roundabout in Visp sp 'Saas-Fee' and follow the valley road for 25.5km to Saas-Grund. In Saas-Grund turn right off the main road towards the river sp "camping Bergheimat".

Sanitation:

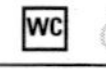 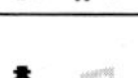 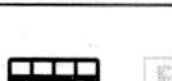

Parking:

30; €22 Custom; SF6 for 6amp elec

This is a conveniently located winter campsite adjacent to the main ski lift station in Saas-Grund and the ski bus up to Saas-Fee (10 minutes) stops directly outside the campsite. Catch the bus here as most tourers get on at next stop and it is often full! The village has none of the glamour of Saas-Fee but it is cheaper and the campsite has nice clean showers and toilets and the novelty of huge llamas in an adjacent field! www.saas-grund.ch

Activities and Facilities:

 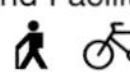    

LAUTERBRUNNEN

C3 | 25 | N46°35.385' E007°54.473' 800m

Camping Jungfrau, Weid 406, 3822 Lauterbrunnen www.camping-jungfrau.ch

Directions: Drive through the village on the main valley road. Just before parking "kirche" and a Z-bend, turn right down a narrow lane following Camping Jungfrau signs, the site is in 200m. If you cross the river in the village, you have gone too far. Grindlewald campsite has only four spaces for tourers, all full! So do not even waste diesel driving up to check.

Sanitation:

Parking:

40; SF51, Elec extra metered Euro Relais Maxi; Inc

This is a luxury campsite with high prices but what a location; 1000m high rock walls on both sides, the views are awesome! 15 minutes level stroll or a free shuttle bus to village and ski lift. Lauterbrunnen is the local hub for a cog and pinion mountain railway system up to the ski resorts of Murren and Wenger and the famous train via a mountain tunnel to Jungfraujoch, the highest railway station in Europe at 3454m. The ski slopes of Grindelwald are mostly between the Eiger train station (7612 feet) and the gondola station of Mannlichen. The 4.5km sledge run "Eiger Northface Run" is stunning, directly under the north face of the Eiger! Also marked as a footpath, and is an easy and safe downhill walk to Grindelwald. www.lauterbrunnen.ch

Activities and Facilities:

MEIRINGEN

C3 | 26 | N46°43.536' E008°10.247' 600m

Ski camp Balmweid, 3860 Balmweidstrasse www.camping-meiringen.ch

Directions: Approach Meiringen on the 6/11 from Brienz. The campsite is 100m from the roundabout on the 6/11 as you approach Meiringen. Turn right at the roundabout and then left and the campsite is on the right. Follow sp 'camping Balmweid'.

Sanitation:

   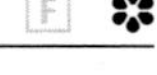

Parking:

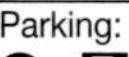    

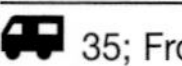 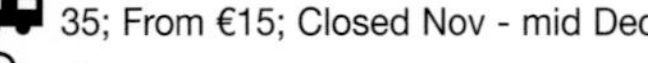

35; From €15; Closed Nov - mid Dec

Custom

Situated in a stunning location under steep valley walls with waterfalls, mountain views and adjacent to Reichenbach falls where Sherlock Holmes met his end. The campsite is in the sun all day, has 10A unmetered elec, good hot unlimited showers, clean facilities and free WiFi in the campsite café making it the best site around. The ski bus calls by the campsite to carry passengers to the bottom of main lift up to surrounding ski fields. www.meiringen.ch

Activities and Facilities:

MEIRINGEN

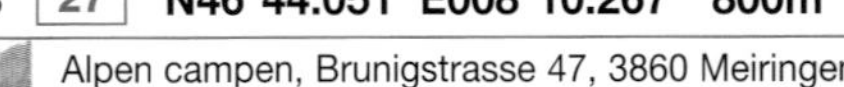

C3 | 27 | N46°44.051' E008°10.267' 800m

Alpen campen, Brunigstrasse 47, 3860 Meiringen
www.alpencamping.ch

Directions: Approach Meiringen on the 6/11 from Brienz. At the roundabout turn left and cross the river. Cross two railway tracks and turn left on a right hand bend onto the 4 to Lungern. The campsite is on the left in 700m. The campsite is sp as "Alpencamp".

Sanitation:

Parking:

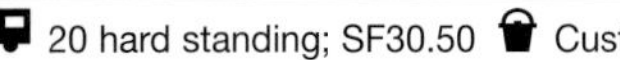

20 hard standing; SF30.50 Custom

This is a new campsite with a dedicated stellplatze area in the outskirts of Meiringen. There are open views of valley meadows. The free ski bus stops outside the campsite and delivers you to good skiing. In Meiringen there is a Sherlock Holmes Museum at Conan Doyle Place and it is possible to visit Reichenbach Falls, the place where Sherlock Holmes met his death, which is about a 30 minutes walk from the train station. www.meiringen.ch

Activities and Facilities:

SAVOGNIN

C5 | 28 | N46°35.825' E009°35.532' 1180m

Via Sandeilas 14, 7460 Savognin

Directions: From Tiefencastel head south on the 3 to Savognin. In the village centre turn right and drive to the bottom of the resort chairlift station. Then drive to Cube hotel barrier, pressing button to gain entry into the small parking area behind the motel.

Sanitation:

Parking:

10 Custom

This is a small stellplatze attached to a motel (max 8m vans) and at weekends it gets very busy and possibly full. The village has bars, banks and supermarkets. There is extensive skiing and sledging above the village in winter and 240km of signed mountain biking trails in the area in summer. Various routes for walking, snow shoeing and mountain biking are available on the Tourist Office website; www.savognin.ch

Activities and Facilities:

BIVIO

  C5 | 29 | N46°27.804' E009°39.373' 1800m

Route 3, 7457 Bivio

Directions: The stellplatze is located between the village and the Julier pass. From Savognin travel up on the 3 through village to ski lift TVA. The stellplatze is clearly visible on left. It is small so you may have to be content with a place in adjacent car park until place with electric becomes available.

Sanitation:

Parking:

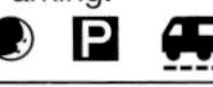   

 11; €10 van; €1.40 tax per person; €3 elec.

Euro Relais; Free for stellplatze users.

This small stellplatze and car park is directly adjacent to TVA chairlift. There is good summer walking and winter skiing but it is high so keep a 'weather eye' open as heavy snow blocks roads until cleared. The slopes are wide, sunny easy reds and blues with superb views.They are busy at weekends and holidays but other times quiet. The T-bars are long but there are no queues mid-week. In summer, there are plenty of day walks including a circular walk to the set of the Heidi film. www.savognin.ch

Activities and Facilities:

ST MORITZ

  C5 | 30 | N46°28.903' E009°49.846' 1800m

27 via San Gian, 7500 St Moritz

Directions: From St Moritz head south on the 27 towards Silvaplane. The parking is at the bottom of the Corviglia Gondola which is adjacent to the 27 at far end of car park amongst buses.

Sanitation:

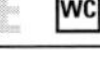  

Parking:

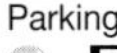   

 100; SF5; Until 5pm. 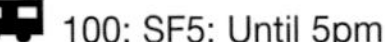 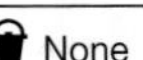 None

This is the only car park accepting motorhomes in St Moritz but it is located directly under the best skiing area. Car park staff will direct you to the far end to park amongst buses. Only SF5 during the day but stay overnight and it rises to SF50! Take the hint and overnight outside St Moritz and return before 9am. There are fantastic south facing slopes high above the tree line with miles of perfectly groomed blues and reds with expansive views. Take packed lunches as café prices will break the bank! www.stmoritz.ch

Activities and Facilities:

    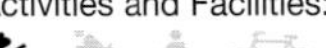  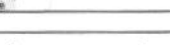

ST MORITZ / PUNT MURAGL C6 31 N46°30.593' E009°52.821' 1778m

Camping Punt Huragl, 29 Punt Muragl, 7503 Samedan www.reisen-tcs.ch

Directions: From St Moritz exit the town to the north on the 27. At the roundabout take the 29 towards Pontresina. The campsite is adjacent to the 29 and on the other side of R29 to gondola station 'Punt Muragl'.

Sanitation:

Parking:

30; Winter - SF40; CCI discount.

Custom; elec metered.

This is a nice campsite in summer and winter, run by TCS (Swiss touring club). It has good facilities and scenic woodland pitches. This campsite is central for St Moritz for winter sports and the ski bus calls am/pm. The gondola opposite is only for summer walkers and winter sledging, at 2500m high! www.graubuenden.ch

Activities and Facilities:

BAD RAGAZ B5 32 N47°00.711' E009°30.789' 500m

A13/E43, 7304 Maienfeld

Directions: Between junction 12 and 13 of A13/E43. Accessible from both sides of road, follow signs for motorhome parking.

Sanitation:

Parking:

10; Be vigilant. None

Designated unrestricted motorhome parking at a Shell and BP motorway service station. It is noisy but useful especially since the only stellplatze in Lichtenstein, to the north, closed and the Kressern stellplatze on the A13 has gone.

Activities and Facilities:

ST GALLEN

B5 | 33 | N47°26.016' E009°24.288' 660m

Grütlistrasse 24, 9000 St Gallen

Directions: Heading south from Bodensee enter St Gallen on the 7. Turn off this road sp 'Paul Gruninger Stadium', and follow the road uphill and stelleplatze is on the left.

Sanitation:

Parking:

2; SF16; 24 hrs

Holiday Clean; Water €1, Elec €0.50 per kwh, accepts € and SF

A useful service point just off the main A1 motorway. The service takes SF and Euros. The parking and service point is at a sports centre and the small bays may be full of cars.

Activities and Facilities:

LIECHTENSTEIN

B5 | 34 | N47°08.367' E009°31.238' 500m

Badwegli 3, 9490 Vaduz

Directions: Directly opposite 'Kunstmuseum' in town centre under Prince's castle in Vaduz. Exit the A13 in Switzerland at junction 9 and cross the river into Liechtenstein. At the first roundabout turn right. At the second roundabout turn left onto the 28. Go straight over the next roundabout staying on the 28. Go right around and back on yourself at the fourth roundabout and the parking in on the right in a large car park.

Sanitation:

Parking:

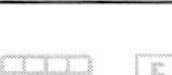

30; SF1 3hrs, Sat and Sun free; 3 hrs None

This car park has no barrier but has parking for 6 - 8m motorhomes; the first hour is free then SF1 for 3 hours. Blink and you will miss Liechtenstein as you hurtle down the motorway on your way to St Moritz. Town centre is a pleasant place for a wander and novelty souvenir shopping! NOTE: The stellplatze at Rheinpark is now closed and being refurbished into a barrier controlled pay and display car park for the adjacent football stadium.

Activities and Facilities:

Aigle

Brixen

LPG

Fernpass

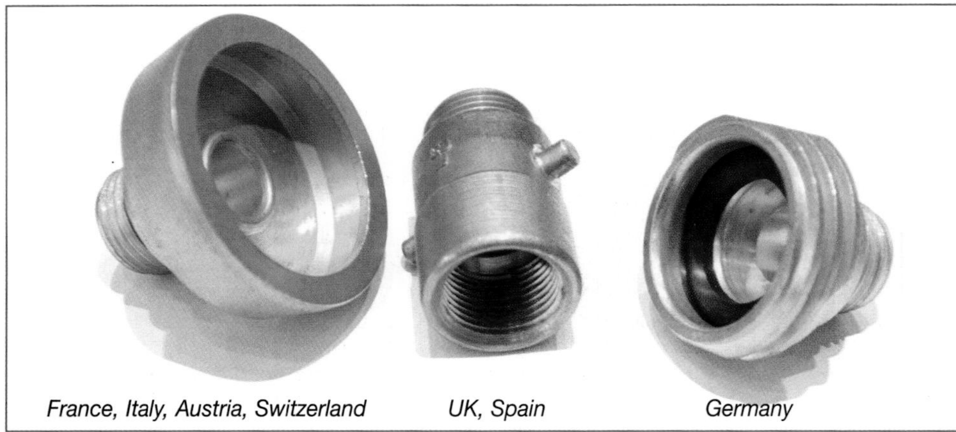

France, Italy, Austria, Switzerland *UK, Spain* *Germany*

The availability of LPG Autogas and bottled gas varies from country to country, and the following chapter provides details of some conveniently located LPG outlets.

Austria has its own methane gas, called Erdgas, which is produced near Vienna; do not fill up your LPG tanks with this gas. LPG is rare and a list of 15 LPG stations can be viewed at www.fluessiggas.net/autogas/tankstellen and www.bp.com

France has truly adopted LPG and it is widely available at many supermarket fuel stations. Bottled gas is also sold at supermarket fuel stations. See http://stations.gpl.online.fr for LPG stations.

LPG is widely available in Germany, see www.autogastanken.de/de/tanken. Gas bottles are widely available in Germany and you might find it convenient to buy an 11kg bottle (bottle €35, filling €17). The DIY chain OBI is a good place to buy/fill German gas cylinders as they have good parking, stock and many stores throughout Germany. Keep your receipt and reclaim your money when you return the unwanted bottle. German law now requires a red plastic cover be fitted onto unused cylinder valves during transport. A cap should always come with a new cylinder.

LPG is available throughout Italy, see www.autofficinalfa.it/distribution.htm. Gas cylinders are not as widely available as in France. A rubber washer should come with each new exchange, check before accepting. Exchange cost €25 - 30 for Italian gas cylinder available in standard 10kg size with a 20mm left hand thread connection. Usually only propane is available but ask dealers near German border to exchange German cylinders.

There are 25 LPG refilling points in Spain. Always refill when you can. Typically the Dutch/UK Bayonet fitting is used, which is the same fitting you use in the UK. All the Aires Spain and Portugal have full details on 15 GPL outlets. www.spainautogas.com/repostar.htm

LPG is available from only 18 outlets in Switzerland. In winter be aware Agip gas has a very high percentage of Butane. The PanGas outlets are good, staff operated, and the LPG is a 60%/40% Propane Butane mix in winter which should get you through those -20°C nights. Swiss gas cylinders are different from other neighbouring countries. Adaptors are available (and pigtails) from PanGas outlets. www.pangas.ch Pick up a catalogue; it makes interesting reading for gadget-minded campers.

www.jaquet-ge.ch/gaz/stations_gpl.php
www.autogas-suisse.com/LPG-Tankstellen-Schweiz.pdf

TOWN	Map Ref	Letter	GPS	DIRECTIONS
AUSTRIA			See page 26 for map.	
INNSBRUCK	B2	A	N47°15.780' E11°27.213'	E60/E45/A12. Service Station located between junction 70 and 73, southeast outskirts of Innsbruck. The BP Ampass service area is only accessible to motorists travelling west. It would be a 10km round trip to visit this area if travelling the other direction.
FERNPASS	A2	B	N47°21.772' E10°49.929'	Tank Stop Dolle on R179 at top of pass, 8km north of Nassereith.
KIRCHDORF IN TIROL	A3	C	N47°32.286' E12°26.464'	168 adjacent to the 168 on the left heading to Kirchdorf in Tirol from St Johann in Tirol.
FRANCE			See page 52 for Alps map and pages 54/55 for Pyrenees map.	
LOURDES (Pyranees)	G2	D	N43°06.620' W000°02.310'	N.21. Located at the E.Leclerc Supermarket, adjacent to the N21 in the northern outskirts of Lourdes.
EMBRUN (Alps)	D2	E	N44°32.757' E006°28.917'	N94. Located at the Intermarche Supermarket, adjacent to the N94 in the southern outskirts of Embrun, just past the D40 roundabout when travelling towards Crots.
AIGUEBLANCHE (Alps)	B2	F	N45°30.169' E006°30.068'	Rue du Canal. Exit N90 at junction 38. Travel southwest into Aigueblanche and turn right at the junction with the D990. Travel 200m and turn left off the D990 onto the D94 sp 'St Oyen Doucy' and drive 750m to the Super U Supermarket.
GERMANY			See page 102 for map.	
SCHARNITZ	C2	G	N47°23.958' E11°15.972'	Insbrukke Strasse B177/E533. Adjacent to B177/E533 500m north of Scharnitz (Austria) immediately after the Austrian border.
TRAUSTEIN	B3	H	N47°52.144' E12°40.117	B304. From Traustein travel 1km east on the B304 and the LPG is on the left.
ITALY			See page 132 for map.	
DIMARO	A4	I	N46°20.272' E10°53.743'	SS42. Adjacent to the SS42 between Trento and Sondrio, 2km east of Dimaro. This is the last chance to get LPG before heading into Adamello ski area
SONDRIO	B3	J	N46°09.777' E09°47.429'	Via Andevenno, SS38. 5km west of Sondrio, just off the SS38 at the Andevenno suburb. LPG station convenient for Bormio/Livigno and there is a Lidl 3km from Sondrio at N46°09.721' E009°49.147'
SALORNO	A4	K	N46°14.766' E11°12.780'	Adjacent to SS12 at Tamoil fuel station 500m north of Salorno.
PREDAZZO	A4	L	N46°18.295' E11°35.712'	Via Paolo Oss Mazzurona. Travelling north on the SS48 take the right fork at the roundabout onto Via Fiamme Gialle as you enter Predazzo. The LPG is at the Agip fuel station on the left in 600m.
BRONZOLO	A4	M	N46°23.530' E11°18.928'	SS12. 600m south of Bronzolo at the Agip fuel station. Conveniently located LPG on way to and from Brenner Pass (Austria) and when skiing in the Kronplatz area (St Viglio).
(BRESSANONE)	A4	N	N46°41.238' E11°37.874'	SS12. 3km south of Brixen. This is the last LPG station before heading east along Val Puster towards Kronplatz ski resort.
CHIENES/ KIENS	A5	O	N46°48.186' E11°50.589'	Frazione La Serra. SS49/E66 in fuel station forecourt. No LPG, this is a bottled gas shop. Bottled gas is harder to find in this area. There is a second station selling bottled gas but it is harder to find; Lahner Franz Srl, I-39030 San Lorenzo, Zona Artigianale Aue, 28. Open weekdays 08:00 - 12:00 and 14:00 - 18:00.
RUGGERI CAMPER SHOP, TRENTO	B4	P	N46°07.105' E11°05.934'	Motorhome dealer/ Repair shop. Exit the E45 at the northern side of Trento sp 'Trento Nord Interporto Doganale'. At the roundabout, turn right onto Localita Spini di Gardolo. Follow this road for 1km and the camper dealer is on the left. Open Monday - Saturday This is the only place with van spares and workshop in this area. Can supply and fit Italian hose and adaptor for your own regulator if needed. www.ruggericampers.it

TOWN	Map Ref	Letter	GPS	DIRECTIONS
SPAIN			See pages 164/165 for map.	
HOZNAYO	A4	Q	N43°23.402' W003°42.210'	N634. Located just off the A8 at Hoznayo, accessible from both directions on the A8. Exit A8 at Junction 197, drive under A8 if necessary, the Repsol service station just off the roundabout. The GLP is at the Repsol fuel station behind the shop and truck parking.
VALLADOLID	C3	R	N41°36.936' W004°44.179'	Calla Bronce. Located in the south of the town, 200m off the CL610 ring road. Turn off the CL610 ring road at the Indal building onto road Calle Arca Real. Then turn right at the Mimo Sofa building. The GLP is at the Repsol fuel station 150m on left next to the bus depot. Difficult to find without GPS.
GRANADA - BOBADILLA	F4	S	N37°11.447' W003°38.179'	Ctra de Malaga. Located north west of Granada in Bobadilla. Exit A92 junction 230 to Granada on the A92G. Exit A29G to 'Bobadilla' opposite Coca Cola depot with large sign. Drive through Bobadilla and GPL is at the Repsol fuel station on left, signed.
SWITZERLAND			See pages 176/177 for map.	
PAYERNE	B2	T	N46°48.701' E006°55.750'	Rue de Châtelard 11. Follow signs for 'Zone Industrial Boverie'. The Pan Gas fuel station is on its own surrounded by fields. Open Mon - Fri 07:30 - 12:00, 13:30 - 17:30, not open on weekends.
LAUSANNE - ECUBLENSU	C2	U	N46°32.059' E006°34.073'	Pan Gas, Route du Bois 14. Follow the 1a into Laussanne and at the large roundabout go almost right around and turn off sp 'Geneve', camping symbols and signed. Now follow this road following sp 'Ecublens' going straight across all junctions. In Ecublens turn right at the roundabout sp 'Centre Commercial' 'Zone Industrielle'. At the next roundabout, turn right into the Pan Gas opposite Co-op Centre Commecial. LPG refilling requires a German adaptor - good parts and adaptors and Swiss 30mb regulators. Open Mon - Fri 07.15 - 12:00, 13:15 - 17.30 (Fri 17.00) Sat 09:00 - 12:00.
AIGLE	C2	V	N46°18.745' E006°56.507'	Pan Gas, Route Industrielle 18. From E27/9 exit at Junction 17 sp 'Aigle Ollon'. Follow the white sp 'Z.I. Aigle service autos'. At the roundabout turn left sp 'Z.I. Aigle service autos'. Follow this road through the industrial park crossing a further 2 roundabouts then look for flags. Open: Mon - Fri 07:15 - 12:00, 13:15 - 17:30, Sat 09:00 - 12:00. Cash sale - not self-service. Shop has some supplies including German/Swiss bottle adaptors.
INTERLAKEN	C3	W	N46°40.754' E007°51.026'	Fabrikstrasse 8. The road layout has recently changed so first set your GPS machine for: N46°41.032' E007°51.073' this should take you to the train station then reset GPS with final destination co-ordinates. Exit A8 at Junction 24 and follow sp to 'Interlaken West' eventually turning left sp 'Interlaken West' and 'Zentrum'. Go straight across the first roundabout and at the second roundabout, next to the train station, turn left sp 'Spital'. Cross the railway track and then turn immediately left sp 'IBI' alongside railway track. Follow this road until you reach the IBI fuel station. LPG (propane) and bottled gas, LPG gas pump to the left of bottled gas. Open Mon - Fri 09:00 - 12:00 and 14:00 - 17:00.
ZUG	B4	X	N47°11.116' E008°29.326'	Exit Zug on the 25/4 travelling northwest around lake. After crossing the river turn right in 500m into 'Steinhauserstrasse' exactly when the road runs parallel to the railway track. Follow this road for 900m and at the roundabout turn left and the LPG station is 350m. If you are following GPS, there has been a lot of new building so it may take a while for GPS to find it. LPG cash sale, also bottled gas for sale.
HORGEN	B4	Y	N47°14.286' E008°36.669'	At side of A3, at junction 35, 18km south of Zurich. Exit A3 at junction 35 sp 'Horgen'. Then follow sp 'Hirzel' LPG station, adjacent to a Mercedes Benz outlet. Pay cash at pump. Open for cash sales Mon - Sun, 05:00 - 11:00.

INDEX

INDEX

SUBMISSION FORM

Please use this form to update the area information in this guide. We particularly need good photographs that represent the area. Nominations for new areas are very welcome. If area is already listed, complete only sections where changes apply. Please fill in answers in capital letters and circle appropriate symbols.

Town/Village: Country:

Road name/number: Date Visited:

Units accepted:

Tent | Touring Caravan | Motorhome
Day parking

Please circle 1 or more symbols as appropriate

Page Number: Postcode – if known:

Number of Spaces: Time limit: Cost:

Parking symbols:

Overnight parking possible | Hard surface | Large motorhomes
Designated motorhome parking | Sloping | Free of charge
Illuminated | Open all year
Noisy

Please circle 1 or more symbols as appropriate

Service Point type: Cost:

Payment/Token type:

Sanitation symbols:

Water | Electric hook up | Showers
Grey water disposal | Toilets | Free of charge
Toilet disposal | Disabled toilet | Open all year
Services accessible by large motorhomes

Please circle 1 or more symbols as appropriate

Activities and Facilities Symbols:

Downhill skiing | Walking - path or trail | Ski storage / drying room
Cross country skiing | Dishwashing facilities | Swimming pool
Marked cycle route | Laundry | Ski bus

Please circle 1 or more symbols as appropriate

Please turn over

SUBMISSION FORM

Directions - Brief, specific directions to Aire:

GPS Coordinates:

Information - Brief description of location and amenities:

Photo(s) included ☐ None ☐ Emailed ☐ Picture posted with form

email pictures to: aires@vicariousbooks.co.uk

Name and email or address - so information can be credited:

Submit entries online at: www.alltheaires.co.uk/submissions.htm

Please use a separate form for each Aire/LPG. Forms can be printed off and can be found at www.alltheaires.co.uk/submission.htm

Send completed forms to:

Vicarious books, 62 Tontine Street, Folkestone, Kent, CT20 1JP

aires@vicariousbooks.co.uk

Thank you very much for your time.